More
of my Life

C000090963

by the same author

LANGUAGE, TRUTH AND LOGIC
THE FOUNDATIONS OF EMPIRICAL KNOWLEDGE
PHILOSOPHICAL ESSAYS
THE PROBLEM OF KNOWLEDGE
THE CONCEPT OF A PERSON
THE ORIGINS OF PRAGMATISM
METAPHYSICS AND COMMON SENSE
RUSSELL AND MOORE: THE ANALYTICAL HERITAGE
PROBABILITY AND EVIDENCE
BERTRAND RUSSELL
THE CENTRAL QUESTIONS OF PHILOSOPHY
PART OF MY LIFE
HUME
PHILOSOPHY IN THE TWENTIETH CENTURY
FREEDOM AND MORALITY AND OTHER ESSAYS

More
of my Life

A. J. AYER

OXFORD UNIVERSITY PRESS
1985

Oxford University Press, Walton Street, Oxford OX2 6DP

London New York Toronto
Delhi Bombay Calcutta Madras Karachi
Kuala Lumpur Singapore Hong Kong Tokyo
Nairobi Dar es Salaam Cape Town
Melbourne Auckland

and associated companies in
Beirut Berlin Ibadan Mexico City Nicosia

Oxford is a trade mark of Oxford University Press

© A. J. Ayer 1984

First published 1984 by William Collins Sons & Co. Ltd.
First issued as an Oxford University Press paperback 1985

All rights reserved. No part of this publication may be reproduced,
stored in a retrieval system, or transmitted, in any form or by any means,
electronic, mechanical, photocopying, recording, or otherwise, without
the prior permission of Oxford University Press

This book is sold subject to the condition that it shall not, by way
of trade or otherwise, be lent, re-sold, hired out or otherwise circulated
without the publisher's prior consent in any form of binding or cover
other than that in which it is published and without a similar condition
including this condition being imposed on the subsequent purchaser

British Library Cataloguing in Publication Data
Ayer, A. J.
More of my life.— (Oxford paperbacks)
1. Ayer, A. J.   2. Philosophers—England—Biography
I. Title
192   B1618.A94
ISBN 0–19–281878–3

Printed in Great Britain by
Richard Clay (The Chaucer Press) Ltd.
Bungay, Suffolk

To Nicholas

Contents

Illustrations

Preface

This book is a sequel to *Part of My Life* which was published by Collins also in hardback in 1977, and by the Oxford University Press in paperback in 1978. It covers the period from October 1946 when, at the age of thirty-five, I resigned my fellowship at Wadham College, Oxford, in order to become Grote Professor of the Philosophy of Mind and Logic at University College, London, to the birth of my second son Nicholas on 2 April 1963. It describes my social life during those years including my marriage to Dee Wells in 1960, my employment as a broadcaster, my involvement in politics, my activities as a lecturer, which extended literally from China to Peru, my return to Oxford in 1959 as Wykeham Professor of Logic and Fellow of New College, the works which I wrote and edited, my relations with other philosophers both in England and abroad, and my own philosophical development.

As in the previous volume, I have relied chiefly on my memory but in this case I have had the benefit of rather more documentary evidence. I have drawn upon the records of the *Institut International de Philosophie* and *Fédération Internationale des Sociétés de Philosophie* and I owe a special debt of gratitude to Miss Challis Reed for allowing me to extract from the BBC's archives a list of my radio and television broadcasts, including my contributions to the Lunar Society of the Air and the television Brains Trust. I have reason also to be grateful to the staff of the Marylebone Public Library for the references which they helped me to verify, to Dr. J. L. Watling for his recollections of the growth of the department of philosophy at University College, London, to Professor Ted Honderich for information about my editorship of the Pelican Philosophy Series and Routledge and

Kegan Paul's International Library of Philosophy and Scientific Method, and especially to my wife Vanessa for her assistance and advice.

Finally my thanks are again due to Mrs Guida Crowley for typing my manuscript and helping me to see the book through the press.

A. J. AYER
51 York Street
London W1
14 November 1983

1 *Philosophy in London and Paris*

The Grote Professorship of the Philosophy of Mind and Logic at the University of London, to which, at the age of thirty-five, I was elected in 1946, had not had a particularly distinguished history. The Chair was attached to University College, in Gower Street, which was the oldest of the London colleges. The college had been founded in 1828, mainly for the benefit of those who were debarred on religious grounds from entry to Oxford or Cambridge. One of its guiding principles, therefore, was that it was in no way sectarian. The ancient historian, George Grote, for whom the Professorship of the Philosophy of Mind and Logic was named, was a member of the council of the college. So, among others, were Lord Brougham and James Mill, himself a historian and philosopher of some consequence, though better known as a disciple of Jeremy Bentham and the father of John Stuart Mill.

When the Grote Chair was advertised in 1828, a dissenting minister called Hoppus was considered to be the best of a poor set of candidates. His appointment was, however, prevented by Grote, with the assistance of Brougham and Mill, not primarily on the ground of his professional incompetence but rather because it seemed to them inconsistent with the character intended for the college that its first professor of philosophy should be a clergyman, however tame. Accordingly, no election was made until the following year when Brougham and Mill relented and their defection left the way clear for Hoppus, even though George Grote maintained his opposition, to the point of resigning from the council.

So the Reverend Hoppus acquired a position which he held for thirty-seven years, without contributing to his subject anything of the slightest importance. When the Chair became vacant in 1866, there was a suggestion that it be offered to James Martineau who had acquired some reputation as a moral philosopher. But Martineau was yet another clergyman, which was more than George Grote could bear. On this occasion his protests carried the day and the appointment went to George Croom Robertson, a young man of twenty-four, who was a lecturer in Greek at Aberdeen. He had been born and educated at Aberdeen but had also taken a course in English Literature at University College, London and studied philosophy at Berlin and Göttingen in Germany. What was perhaps more to the point was that he was a protégé of Alexander Bain, the Professor of Logic at Aberdeen, who followed closely in the footsteps of the Mills.

Croom Robertson, who held the Chair from 1866 until his death in 1892, was more gifted than his predecessor. For instance, he wrote a short book on Thomas Hobbes, which not only contains a standard biography but is still treated with respect by exponents of Hobbes's views. Nevertheless he is now chiefly remembered as the first editor of *Mind*, which for more than a hundred years has held pride of place in the English-speaking world as a quarterly journal of philosophy. *Mind* was actually founded in 1876, on Bain's initiative and with his financial support, and at the outset it was concerned as much with psychology as with philosophy: indeed it was sub-titled a quarterly review of psychology and philosophy. This accorded with Bain's and Croom Robertson's view that philosophy was founded on psychology. It was Croom Robertson's achievement that he secured contributions both from psychologists and from the best philosophers of every current school of thought. G. F. Stout, who succeeded him in the editorship was also a psychologist as well as a philosopher and it was not until G. E. Moore became editor in 1920 that *Mind* was turned into an almost purely philosophical journal.

The Grote Chair underwent a similar vicissitude. Professor Sully who succeeded Croom Robertson in 1892 and Professor Carveth Read who succeeded Sully in 1904, at the unusually advanced age of fifty-six, were both oriented towards psychology. Carveth Read did indeed publish books on logic, metaphysics, morals and the origin of man, but in his contribution to the first series of *Contemporary British Philosophy*, published in 1924, after his retirement, he lists psychology and anthropology as his principal interests. It may be for this reason that a Chair of Moral Philosophy was instituted at University College in 1904. The man appointed to it, G. Dawes Hicks, harked back to Hoppus in that he had spent a period as a minister at a Unity Church, but he was of a higher philosophical standing. He was chiefly known for his realistic theory of perception which earned him a mention in Professor C. D. Broad's *Scientific Thought*. He figures also in a story which concisely illustrates the difference between the Oxford and Cambridge approach to philosophy between the wars. Dr A. C. Ewing was imported into Cambridge in 1931 to teach the history of philosophy. In one of his early lectures he was discussing the problem of perception and, in the Oxford manner, was working his way through the theories that different philosophers had advanced. He was roughly interrupted by a voice from the audience 'We don't want to know what Dawes Hicks said. We want the truth.'

I got to know Dr Ewing quite well in later years, mainly through our common assiduity in attending international congresses of philosophy. He was not well treated at Cambridge which did eventually make him a Reader but kept him as a lecturer for many years before any college offered him a fellowship. He was an able philosopher, a good scholar and a prolific writer, but he never caught the idiom which was largely foisted on Cambridge in the 1930s by Ludwig Wittgenstein. A most unworldly man, he lived very simply with two maiden cousins to keep house for him. He was also religious. I teased him once by asking him what he most looked forward to in the next world. He replied without hesitation 'God will tell me whether there are synthetic *a priori* propositions.' It says something not only about Ewing's character but also about the nature of the subject that this answer should be endearingly absurd.

Dawes Hicks also held a lectureship at Cambridge, concurrently with his professorship in London, though, since he was born in 1862, he can hardly have overlapped with Ewing. In 1911 the title of his Chair at University College was changed simply to that of Philosophy without qualification. I think the reason may have been that, with the retirement of Carveth Read, the Grote Chair passed into the hands of a pure psychologist, Professor C. A. Spearman. Professor Spearman was a fervent practitioner of factor analysis and is famous, or notorious, for the introduction of the symbol g, which was intended to stand for general intelligence, measured by intelligence tests. The question whether 'intelligence tests measure the value of g' comes to anything more than the tautology 'intelligence tests measure what they measure' is still disputed by psychologists. The party of the intelligence testers has lately undergone a setback through the discovery that Sir Cyril Burt, who succeeded Spearman, was given, at least in his later years, to falsifying his experimental evidence. His adherents have rightly pointed out that this still leaves it open for his conclusions to be supported on other grounds, but it should also be noted that there are many to whom the very concept of g, as a unitary factor, has always been suspect in itself.

Sir Cyril Burt was a member of the selection board which interviewed me for my appointment at London University, and we were colleagues at University College for several years. He was personally civil to me but, though there existed a joint school of philosophy and psychology, we never made any attempt to collaborate professionally. He was then officially the holder of a Chair of Psychology, as I think Spearman's had already become. The reversion of the Grote Chair to philosophy probably took place in the late 1920s when John Macmurray was appointed to it.

Macmurray had been a Fellow of Balliol and he brought to London a full measure of the missionary spirit which that college has distilled for more than the century since Jowett was its Master. Macmurray's main interests were in ethics and politics and he liked to preach his doctrines outside academic circles. Unfortunately he did not display the same enthusiasm for invigorating his department, which became further depressed when he accepted the more congenial offer of a Chair at Edinburgh, not long before the war, and nobody was appointed to replace him. The department was left in the charge of a senior lecturer, Dr S. V. Keeling, a product of Cambridge and an admirer of the metaphysician J. E. McTaggart. He was also the author of a good book on Descartes. I have described him in a previous volume as a stage Frenchman and indeed he was so firmly convinced that 'they order this matter better in France' that he made no effort to acquire either assistants or pupils. Macmurray's former secretary, a Greek lady, had somehow contrived to emerge as a temporary lecturer on ethics and when I first visited the department, after being notified of my appointment, I found that it contained about six undergraduates and had the use of two small rooms, nothing more.

The rooms were in 15 Gordon Square, outside the college, and I managed to extend their number to four. I also took advantage of the fact that the appointment of the Greek lady was only temporary to advertise for an authentic lecturer. I was lucky enough to secure the services of Stuart Hampshire, who remained in the department till 1954, when he returned to All Souls as Bursar, subsequently succeeding me in London and then emigrating to a professorship at Princeton.

I should have liked to increase my staff but first I had to acquire more undergraduates, and if possible graduates also, in order to obtain a defensible ratio, and the money had to be forthcoming from the college. Unfortunately our Provost, an amiable engineer called Pye, was not assertive and University College fell behind in the scramble for government funds in which academic institutions engaged after the war. Moreover, the college had suffered badly from enemy bombardment and such money as could be spared from making good the damage was snaffled by the powerful heads of the scientific departments.

So for two years the entire staff of the philosophical department consisted of Keeling, Hampshire and myself. In 1949, however, Sir Stafford Cripps decided that greater research in sociology would be of benefit to the nation and declared himself willing to provide money for this purpose. University College had no department of sociology or anything that could pass for one. Though it did have a modest department of economics, which had once employed Hugh Gaitskell, it had no serious intention of competing with the London School. This did not deter its scientific barons. All at once new subjects sprang into existence: physical sociology, chemical sociology, pharmaceutical sociology, and demands were made for lectures to teach them. I spoke up at the professorial board, saying that I was sorry to be a spoil-sport, but if an appointment was to be made which had something more than a merely nominal relation to the field of sociology, the addition to my own department of a political philosopher appeared to come nearer the mark than any of the suggestions that had so far been made. Knowing that the history department, under the strong leadership of Sir John Neale, was firmly wedded to Elizabethan studies, I felt that I ran little risk in adding that I should have no objection to its also calling upon the services of such a lecturer.

By these means I recruited Richard Wollheim, who remained in the department for well over thirty years and still retains some connection with it, though the attractions of a post at Columbia in New York have led him to renounce the Chair, in which he succeeded me, with Stuart

Hampshire reigning briefly and aloofly in between. He had been trained at Balliol, chiefly under Marcus Dick, his undergraduate career being interrupted by the war, in which he served as an infantry officer, was captured and escaped. I had met him not long before at a party in Oxford, had learned from him that he was looking for a job, and promised to bear his claims in mind if I was ever in a position to make an appointment for which he was fitted. At that time I had no reason to think that I ever should be, but in the event fortune favoured us both.

Not only was I able to acquire Richard Wollheim, but I further strengthened the department by the appointment of two research assistants, soon promoted to lectureships, who were both local products. James Thomson was one of the few undergraduates who were already enrolled in the department before I arrived. During the war he had served in the Air Force as a rear-gunner and had had his interest in philosophy aroused by reading my *Language, Truth and Logic* during the idle periods of his bombing missions. He had become very depressed by the stagnant atmosphere of his first year at University College and was, I think, disappointed by my failure instantaneously to effect a magical transformation. After a short time, however, he came to appreciate my method of teaching and emerged as one of the best pupils that I have ever had. In 1953 I lost him to Cambridge, and not long after that he became a Fellow of Corpus Christi College, Oxford. Some years later he emigrated to America and when I last saw him in 1970 he was Chairman of the department of philosophy at the Massachusetts Institute of Technology. Unfortunately some lack of self-confidence has inhibited his writing and the three or four papers that he has published, good though they are, give no adequate impression of his philosophical ability.

John Watling was enrolled in the psychology department and took his doctorate as a psychologist, but his interest lay in the area where psychology borders on philosophy and he regularly attended the all-purpose seminar that I held every week. I appointed him a research assistant at the same time as James Thomson. I was soon after to promote them both to lectureships, and Johnny, who advanced to a readership, after I had left the department, remains there to this day and is now its Chairman. He too has published less than one could have hoped, only a short, if shrewd, account of the early philosophy of Bertrand Russell, and a few perceptive articles. He was at his best in philosophical debate and contributed greatly to the success of the weekly seminars, which were attended by the whole department, including members of the staff.

These seminars which were held every week on Mondays in the late afternoon were a great stimulus to the growth of the department. They attracted visitors not only from other departments of the college, but also from other colleges that belonged to the loose federation which constituted the University, and they were sometimes frequented by philosophers on leave from universities abroad. I remember the Australians John Passmore and David Armstrong, both of whom have acquired a deservedly high professional standing, as regularly contributing to our discussions in the early days. The proceedings were informal, though I usually asked someone to prepare a short paper as a means of getting the discussion under way and several successive meetings might be devoted to the same topic. After the meetings, which lasted as a rule for a couple of hours, a number of us would walk together to 'The Rising Sun' in Tottenham Court Road for one or two rounds of drinks. It was a pleasant, unpretentious pub, not yet saddled with the garish modernity which now disfigures it.

The numbers of applicants to the department increased, with its growing reputation, but I made sure that they never exceeded our capacity to tutor them individually. I interviewed all the applicants personally, sometimes but by no means always with a colleague present to advise me, and my decision, however capricious, was final. The college authorities never tried to interfere. Especially in the early days, we formed a close-knit group, taking some professional interest in the work of the psychologists, but not otherwise having much to do with the college, which its size, its physical dispersion and the poverty of its catering anyhow prevented from functioning effectively as a corporate institution. This may seem regrettable but we did not find it so.

I still have a clear and affectionate memory of my first London set of pupils. Two of the ablest were Martin Shearn, who graduated as a psychologist and then wrote an uncommonly subtle thesis on the problem of other minds, and Peter Newnham, who was an uncompromising empiricist. Like Johnny Watling, Peter had been a conscientious objector in the war, but his temperament was bellicose. His reluctance to do any of the necessary spadework resulted in his taking a poor degree, so that I could not recruit him to my staff, but he retained his interest in philosophy and continued to frequent the department for a number of years. When I last heard of him he had emigrated to Australia and obtained a post in a department of education there.

His robustness contrasted with the timidity of Michael Hearn, who also failed to do himself justice in his final Schools. His father, a district commissioner in Africa, regarded the study of philosophy as a waste of his son's time and was correspondingly vexed when he listened to some talk that I gave on the wireless and heard me quote the verdict of a nineteenth-century Balliol undergraduate that philosophy was 'organized piffle'. He thought that I was expressing my own opinion. I felt some responsibility for Michael Hearn's future and persuaded Henry Yorke, better known by the pseudonym Henry Green, under which he wrote his remarkable series of novels, to employ him as an accountant in the firm of Pontifex Limited, makers of wash basins, which Henry Yorke ran in an improbable partnership with Goronwy Rees. The experiment failed, not because Michael Hearn was unequal to the work, which he easily mastered, but because his brooding on philosophy disturbed the other clerks. He rejoined his family in what was then Nyasaland and I do not know what next became of him.

There were very few women in the department, then or later, though one, Veronica Benton, published a lively novel under her married name of Veronica Hull and another, Brenda Almond, subsequently Brenda Cohen, took a first class degree and is still enjoying a successful academic career. One who was there when I arrived was a handsome girl called Pamela Haddy, who emerged into prominence at an annual congress of the Labour Party, then newly in power, at which she delivered a rousing speech. It was through her that I first met Denis Healey who was then, I think, not yet in Parliament but working at Transport House. I became quite a close friend of his, as I did of most of the Labour leaders in the next three decades. It is only in fairly recent years that I have tended to lose touch with them.

One of my very first pupils whom I have good cause to remember was Harry Spencely, who helped me in the revival of the University College Philosophical Society which Carveth Read had founded in 1907. The neglect into which the Society had fallen is shown by the fact that no meeting is recorded in the minute-book between the ninety-fifth general meeting which took place with Professor Macmurray in the Chair on 4 May 1932 and the nintety-sixth meeting over which Spencely presided on 4 September 1947. By the time that I left the college in 1959 the number of meetings had more than doubled as the result of my instituting the policy of holding three meetings a term. The meetings were usually scheduled for 8 pm, which allowed me to give dinner to the speaker beforehand. I had joined the Travellers' Club in July 1947 and I usually entertained the speaker there, together with one or two of my colleagues. Almost invariably, the speaker was a philosopher from Oxford or Cambridge. Except on very rare occasions, as when seventy-five members and guests assembled to hear Professor Gilbert Ryle read a paper on 'Thought and Perception', the audiences were small, perhaps averaging no more than twenty, but their powers of discussion were acute and more than one Oxford philosopher of the time has confessed to me that he found it an ordeal to submit to their criticism.

My principal reason for remembering Raymond Winch is that he collaborated with me in the production of a book called *British Empirical Philosophers*. The idea, which originated with Routledge and Kegan Paul, the publishers, was that a combination of extracts from the work of the classical British empiricists into one large volume, with a brief but enlightening introduction, would make a serviceable text-book. In the event the book, which ran to 560 pages, consisted of an abridgement into a mere 130 pages of John Locke's *Essay Concerning Human Understanding*, followed by the whole of Bishop Berkeley's *Principles of Human Knowledge*, and of the first of his *Three Dialogues between Hylas and Philonous*, together with passages from the second and third, very nearly the whole of the first book of David Hume's *Treatise of Human Nature* as well as a few passages from his *Enquiry Concerning Human Understanding*, and brief excerpts from Thomas Reid's *Essay on the Intellectual Powers of Man* and John Stuart Mill's *Examination of Sir William Hamilton's Philosophy*. The surgery was carried out by Raymond Winch, under my loose supervision. It consisted not merely in omitting chapters and paragraphs but in cutting out sentences within paragraphs and stitching the remains together so as to produce a continuous text. This bore especially hard upon Locke and though it was a skilful performance I had and still have some doubts of its propriety.

My introduction was correspondingly concise. In twenty-eight pages, I examined the character and status of the empiricist principle, which is shared in their different fashions by Locke, Berkeley, Hume and Mill, that all our knowledge of what Hume called matters of fact is based on sense-impressions; I remarked that this assumption was contested by Reid but suggested that it could yield a tenable theory of perception, if Berkeley's approach were stripped of its theism and developed on lines suggested by Hume and Mill; I supported Berkeley in his dispute with Locke over the nature of abstract ideas; I expounded and endorsed Hume's theory of causation and ended with the admission that neither he nor Mill had arrived at a satisfactory theory of personal identity.

Partly because of the labour involved in shaping the text, the book was not published until 1952. It was not notably successful and perhaps did not deserve to be, the philosophers with which it dealt being too important and too well known to warrant their being handled in quite so summary a fashion. It was left to the American publishers, Simon and Schuster, to bring out a paperback edition in 1968. I do not know how the book prospered in this format, but I have not heard that a second printing has been called for. The title page reminds me that Winch was John Stuart Mill scholar in the Philosophy of Mind and Logic at University College, but he did not proceed to a university post. Instead, he became a schoolmaster and I have been told that he avails himself of the limited opportunity to teach philosophy to his pupils that is open to him at that level.

It is appropriate that the rooms which the philosophers then occupied in Gordon Square should now form part of the London office of Ghana University, since one of the very first graduate pupils to come to me in London was Kwame Nkrumah. He had been enrolled at the London School of Economics, but had become dissatisfied with the teaching of Harold Laski and so obtained a transfer to University College, substituting the study of philosophy for that of politics. His philosophical outlook was vaguely Marxist and he was known in the department as 'The Hegelian'. He was, however, quite ready to embrace the principles of logical positivism. I remember his coming to me in some distress with a copy of the *Daily Worker* in which I was unfavourably mentioned and my reassuring him that in the actual instance no important point of doctrine was at issue. He was a man of great personal charm but I did not detect in him the force of character or the political acumen which he was soon to display in securing the independence of Ghana and installing himself in power there. Indeed, when he vanished from the department, it took me some time to realize what had become of him. I took the Kwame

Nkrumah who was winning favour in Ghana to be another man of the same name. I was subsequently to learn from his autobiography that he had a pleasant recollection of the short time that he spent at University College, but I do not think that it had any important influence on his career. Many years later, he did publish a work on philosophy, strangely enough in collaboration with a man, called Willie Abrahams, who had also been my pupil, for a very brief period at Oxford, but I could not discover that it owed anything to my teaching.

Early in 1947 I delivered my inaugural lecture at University College under the title of 'Thinking and Meaning'. In view of the long interregnum, I felt myself absolved from the usual courtesy of bestowing even a perfunctory encomium on my predecessor Professor Macmurray, of whose published work I knew next to nothing, and instead dedicated the lecture to my old tutor, Gilbert Ryle, who by that time had succeeded Robin Collingwood in the Chair of Metaphysics at Oxford. Re-reading the lecture now, I discover that my dedication was more than the pious gesture that I most probably thought it at the time. Ryle's famous book *The Concept of Mind* was not published until 1949, but he had already sent me an unpublished essay with the Miltonic title of 'The Mind is its own Place', in which some of the main ideas of the book were foreshadowed, and it seems to me now that much of my lecture bears the imprint of this essay by which I was perhaps more strongly convinced than I eventually was by the book. Thus, I deny the existence of the mind 'as something distinct from and as it were underlying mental events' and I make the Rylean points that 'in many cases what is regarded as a mental state involves at least a physical component' and that intelligence can be manifested simply in speech and action. On the other hand I do not deny the possibility of there being what I call specifically mental occurrences, like images or feelings, which may be private to the person who experiences them, and are not located in physical space. My main concern, however, was not to demarcate the mental from the physical but to clarify the concept of the 'object of thought', and here I was not very successful. I managed to show that what was required was an account of the functioning of symbols, but the account which I provided was not satisfactory. This is, indeed, a stubborn problem, and for all the work that has been done upon it, especially in recent years, it is still not clear wherein the solution to it lies.

The friends whom I had made in Paris after the liberation included philosophers, most notably Maurice Merleau-Ponty, to whom I have paid tribute in an earlier volume but, as I there remarked, our friendship did not comprise any philosophical sympathy. One reason for this was the very wide difference in our philosophical backgrounds. If there was one proposition on which the vast majority of French philosophers agreed it was that the British empirical tradition had foundered in bankruptcy. Conversely, the main body of British philosophers took no serious interest in any French philosopher later than Descartes, who died in 1650, and indeed, once Hegel had fallen into disfavour, in any German philosopher later than Kant whose principal work *The Critique of Pure Reason* appeared in 1781.

I did not wholly share this insularity. Such understanding as I had of the philosophy of science had been chiefly derived from two books of popular exposition, *Science et Méthode* and *La Science et l'hypothèse*, both published in the first decade of this century by the mathematician Henri Poincaré. I greatly admired the two essays of Jean Nicod, which were published in 1930 in an English translation under the title *Foundations of Geometry and Induction*, and while I was hostile to Henri Bergson's concept of creative evolution and to his theory of time, I was impressed by the acuity of the analyses of states of consciousness which are to be found in his early works, and by the force of the distinction between social and heroic morality which he developed in the last of his books, *Les deux sources de la morale et de la réligion*. Unfortunately, none of these French philosophers was much honoured in his own country. Bergson, who lived until 1941, had been a fashionable figure; his writings are said to have influenced Proust and may also have been responsible, however unfairly, for Bernard Shaw's conception of the 'life-force'. On the other hand, it did not appear to me that he had any substantial following in the official world of French philosophy, that is to say, among those who held academic posts. Henri Poincaré was venerated, but only as a mathematician and physicist. The uncompromising division in the French curriculum between *sciences* and *lettres* and the consigning of philosophy to *lettres* stood in the way of his recognition as a philosopher. As for Jean Nicod, who had died in 1924 at the early age of thirty-one, there were very few French philosophers who had even heard of him. This was less surprising, as he had done much of his work in Cambridge under the tutelage of Bertrand Russell and had taken Maynard Keynes's *A Treatise on Probability* as the chief springboard for the development of his arguments about induction. Two young French philosophers, Salomon and Cavaillés, had taken a fruitful interest before the war in mathematical logic but both had met their death in the Resistance, and seemed not to have left any disciples to carry on their work.

It would be untrue to say that the French philosophers of the twentieth century were entirely without honour in their own country. Bachelard, Meyerson and Léon Brunschvicq were thought to have furthered the philosophy of science. Lavelle and Le Senne had a following as moral philosophers, at least among their academic colleagues; Gueroult was rightly respected as a historian of philosophy, especially for his study of Descartes. Nevertheless the prevailing winds in French philosophy after the war were German. One reason for this was that whereas in England comparatively few philosophers took any great interest in politics and those few, like Bertrand Russell, who did, kept their philosophical and political theories in separate compartments, it was common for French philosophers not only to involve themselves in continuous political discussion but to attempt to provide their political judgements with a philosophical basis. The strength of the French Communist party, still benefiting, at a time when Stalin's tyranny had not yet been fully unmasked, from its contribution to the French Resistance, sustained an interest in the doctrines of Karl Marx from which it officially drew its inspiration. Communist apologists like Henri Lefèbre drew special attention to Marx's early writings, and it was in them that Marx most clearly displayed the influence of Hegel.

It would, however, be a mistake to suppose either that the reflowering of Hegel in France was solely, or even mainly due, to his fathering of Marx, or that Hegel and Marx exhausted or even dominated the French concern with German philosophy. The lectures of Alexandre Kojève, delivered in Paris before the war, had re-awakened an interest in the philosophy of Hegel for its own sake and the effect of their publication in 1947 was reinforced by the efforts of Jean Hyppolite, who both produced fresh translations of Hegel's works and commented on them in detail. In later years, when I had occasion to listen to Jean Hyppolite, I found his style of lecturing uncomfortably oratorical but I never had cause to question his scholarship. Like Kojève, he did something to weaken the fidelity of French philosophers to the authority of Descartes by assigning a part to reason in the play of history for which Descartes had made no provision.

An even stronger influence than that of Hegel at this period both in France and in Germany itself was that of Edmund Husserl, the founder of the movement known as phenomenology. Husserl, who lived from 1859–1938, had studied in Vienna under Franz Brentano who had advanced the theory, now very much in fashion, that the distinctive feature of all mental states is their 'intentionality', that is to say, their being directed upon some object which may or may not actually exist. Husserl, in a series of books which fitted increasingly into the tradition of German idealism, developed a method of singling out for precise inspection the objects of whatever character which consciousness was said to 'constitute'. This method was described as the intuition of essences. The most distinguished English philosopher to take it seriously was Gilbert Ryle, who thought highly of Husserl's *Logical Investigations*, first published at the turn of the century, but became critical of his later work, so much so that he did not think it worth recommending to me when I became his pupil in 1929. Otherwise Husserl's name was hardly known in England, except perhaps as one whose fairly youthful book on the philosophy of arithmetic had been demolished by Frege. On the continent, he was regarded as a major philosopher and phenomenology commanded a large and devoted following.

In Husserl's own case and in that of some of his more gifted followers such as Maurice Merleau-Ponty the practice of the method could lead to fruitful results. This was not always so. I remember an occasion on which an official of the British Council asked me to lunch with a German professor, said to be a leading phenomenologist, whom the Council had invited on a tour of British universities. Neither the professor's English nor my colloquial German was very fluent; our host was self-effacing and conversation languished. There seemed nothing for it but to resort to talking shop. 'What are you working on now?' I asked the professor. 'It is complicated,' he replied, 'but I will give an example of the kind of problem I am trying to solve. What is the essence of a glass?' On the whole I counted myself an opponent of the type of linguistic philosophy that was coming into fashion at Oxford, but here it seemed to me to meet the case. 'Surely,' I said, 'there is nothing very perplexing about the way in which the word "glass" and its counterparts in other languages are ordinarily used.' He looked at me with contempt. 'I will give you the answer,' he said. 'The essence of a glass is to be empty.' I made a sign to our host who filled our glasses. This did not please the professor who remarked rather irritably that the essence of a glass with wine was not the same as the essence of a glass without wine. 'But,' he went on, 'I will put to you a deeper question. What is the essence of emptiness? (*Was ist das Wesen von der Leere?*)' 'Ah,' I said, 'that really is deep,' and I went on to talk about the universities that he had visited.

My discussions with French philosophers were more serious, though there were very few points on which we managed to agree. It was then, and no doubt still is, the practice for members of French-speaking philosophical societies to hold an annual congress in some university town, whether in France, Belgium or Switzerland. They were said to be meetings of the *Association des sociétés philosophiques de langue française*. There was no such society in England in the late 1940s, though a philosopher called Axel Stern, who worked under me for a time in London, did later bring one into being, but I was invited to three of these congresses as an individual French-speaking philosopher, one held at Bordeaux, the second at Strasbourg and the third, of which I have only a dim memory, at Grenoble.

No doubt the reason why I remember the first two congresses more vividly is mainly due to their setting. Bordeaux is one of the great gastronomic centres of France and while we had a number of keen debates, in which I took an active, indeed almost an aggressive part, a large proportion of our time was spent in absorbing the solid meals supplied to us at one or other of the famous local restaurants and sampling the vintage wines of a series of neighbouring châteaux. I have an especially clear memory of a day's excursion to the small town of Bergerac, where the philosopher Maine de Biran had held the office of *sous-préfet* early in the nineteenth century. We had a banquet lasting four hours at which *lièvre à la royale*, hare royally cooked, was the principal dish. The mayor made us a speech of welcome. The local archivist read a long and learned address adapted to the occasion. There were numerous toasts. Afterwards we all visited the local cemetery and paid homage to Maine de Biran at his grave. It occurred to me that they really do order such matters better in France. In what small town in England would the municipal authorities even be aware of a comparable opportunity for such a display of local pride?

The Strasbourg congress gave me less enjoyment, partly because Alsatian cooking tends to be too heavy for my taste, partly because I was less interested in the discussions, no longer caring or thinking it suitable simply to play the part of an *enfant terrible*. I was rewarded with the friendship of another malcontent, the Marxist Lucien Goldmann. We happened to walk out of a meeting together and began by discovering a common interest in the pre-war cinema. Later we found that we could discuss philosophy without much doctrinal sympathy but with personal goodwill and at times a shared iconoclasm. Goldmann, who was two or three years younger than I, was a Roumanian who had spent the war in Switzerland working with the famous child-psychologist Jean Piaget. At the time I met him he had a position in Paris at the *Centre National de Recherche Scientifique*. A large shaggy man with hunched shoulders, he imposed himself not only by his appearance but also by his volubility. I call him a Marxist because he so called himself and because he was a professed disciple of the Hungarian György Lukács, one of the very few philosophers in this century to have made a fresh contribution to Marxist theory, but Goldmann was not a Communist and his socialist sympathies did not take him into politics. What he chiefly owed to Lukács, and so indirectly to Marx, was the idea of using the concept of class as a tool for explaining all cultural phenomena. So in his best book, *Le Dieu Caché*, published in 1955, he relates the predicament of the intellectual circle of Racine and Pascal, who were reduced to 'betting' on the existence of a God who had forsaken the world, to the falling fortunes of the seventeenth-century *noblesse de robe*, who were losing their influence over the monarchy. The argument of the book may appear farfetched but this does not unduly diminish the light that it throws on the work of Pascal and still more on that of Racine. Goldmann lived until 1970, and I maintained my friendship with him though I was sometimes a little irritated by his behaving as a sage. But this was less a posture that he assumed than one that his disciples thrust upon him.

One thing that surprised me at these congresses was the rarity of existentialists. Owing to the prestige of Martin Heidegger, which survived his membership of the Nazi party in the 1930s, his consequent treachery to his master Edmund Husserl, whom he contrived to have expelled from the University of Freiburg, himself remaining there as Rector, and his encomia of Hitler, a number of German universities had professors of philosophy who revered him as their master: whether they understood him, whether, indeed, there was anything there to understand, is a question that I shall not pursue here. If anyone is interested in my estimate of Heidegger's philosophy, I can only refer him to the *Reflections on Existentialism* which appeared in 1969 in my book of essays *Metaphysics and Common Sense*. The conclusions which I drew, mainly on the basis of his influential pamphlet *Was ist Metaphysik?* is that while his work raises some points of psychological interest, its pretensions to philosophical profundity are altogether hollow. In France the popularity of Sartre's *L'Être et le néant*, which is in parts almost a transcription of Heidegger's *Sein und Zeit*, made existentialism a fashionable subject among the young, but it was still academically suspect and Sartre himself was not an attender of congresses. Neither was Jean Wahl who took his existentialism from its origin in the work of Søren Kierkegaard, the Danish philosopher who had lived from 1813 to 1855 and unlike his twentieth-century successors, Heidegger and Sartre, combined existentialism with Christianity. The messages which Jean Wahl found in Kierkegaard were too rhapsodic for me to decipher, but our philosophical differences did not prevent us from being on friendly terms. He took the Chair for me at one of the first of a number of lectures that I have given at the Sorbonne in Paris since the war, on this occasion a lecture on 'Truth' addressed to the *Collège de Philosophie*. My orthodox treatment of the problem, dressing up the correspondence theory in the semantic clothes made fashionable at least among analytical philosophers by Alfred Tarski, held the interest of my audience less as a source of enlightenment than as a theatrical display. An English friend who had insinuated herself among them told me afterwards that it was mainly appreciated by her neighbours as a notable exhibition of *l'humour anglais*.

Louis Rougier, the only notable French apostle of the Vienna Circle before the war, had put himself out of court by acting as an emissary of the Vichy Government to the United States, and apart from the journalist Olivier Todd who had read philosophy at Cambridge and held no academic post in France, I cannot think of any French philosophers who in the years immediately following the war displayed even curiosity about the development of philosophy in English-speaking countries. Not much more attention was paid to the history of British philosophers, though here there were some exceptions. My friend Raymond Polin, at that time a professor at the University of Lille – which did not prevent him from continuing to live in Paris, a decision rewarded by his subsequent promotion to the Sorbonne – had made a thorough-going study of the philosophy of

Hobbes and while Locke appeared to have stayed becalmed in the approbation of Voltaire, an attempt made by Professor Gueroult to subordinate Berkeley to Malebranche had been valiantly frustrated by Doctor André-Louis Leroy, who was also responsible for a scholarly appreciation of the philosophy of David Hume.

While Polin was still a professor at Lille I gave a lecture there under his auspices. I remember nothing of the lecture except that it was politely received but I do vividly remember paying a visit to the municipal gallery which owned an exceptionally fine collection of pictures, including a magnificent Picasso of the blue period. I suppose that I was the more surprised and pleased to come across it, as Lille otherwise seemed to me an unattractive industrial city.

I met André Leroy, a small man then looking to be in his fifties, with grey hair and a lively manner and an endearing habit of referring to *mon* Berkeley and *mon* Hume, when he most unexpectedly appeared at one of the annual Joint Sessions of the Mind Association and the Aristotelian Society. He was accompanied by his friend, Philippe Devaux, a Belgian historian of philosophy who took a special interest in the work of Bertrand Russell. In general the Belgians were much less blinkered in their philosophical outlook than the French. The leading philosophers at the University of Brussels, Professors Barzin and Perelman, were both well versed in logic to the point where they set up a Centre for Logical Studies which flourishes to this day, issuing a journal of international repute under the title of *Logique et Analyse*. Devaux himself was one of the editors of a less specialized journal, which equally justified its title *Renue Internationale de Philosophie*. Though he lived in Brussels, he occupied the Chair of Philosophy at Liège. His assistant and successor, Paul Gochet, a man of exquisite politeness, worked for a year or two in London under my supervision and is now an authority on the latest writings of the leading American philosopher W. V. Quine. The University of Louvain, not yet bisected by the linguistic dispute between Flemings and Walloons, was a stronghold both of formal logic and phenomenology. Thanks to Father Van Breda, who went on a special mission to rescue them from Germany, it possessed what seemed the inexhaustible collection of Husserl's archives. At least one of its professors had taken the further step into existentialism. By contrast, the University of Ghent was later, under the young Professor Apostel, to provide a home for linguistic philosophy.

In the course of years I lectured very frequently in Brussels, usually under the auspices of the Centre of Logic, and once or twice both in Liège and Louvain. Knowing no Flemish I had to speak at Louvain in French. I made friends with the Perelmans who were both refugees from Poland and lived in concealment throughout the war. Chaim Perelman's philosophical self-confidence was matched by the warmth of his and his wife's hospitality. I have watched with particular pleasure the growth of their fine collection of modern pictures. My friendship with Philippe Devaux and his family, until his death a few years ago, was even closer. A quiet man, who had an excellent war record first as an officer in the Belgian army and then in their Resistance, he was excessively modest about his width of learning; but there was no mistaking his integrity or his strength of character.

I lectured at Liège for the first time in 1951 and was astonished when, at the conclusion of the proceedings, Philippe Devaux presented me with a commemorative medal, which I still cherish. Eleven years later the University of Brussels awarded me my first honorary degree. What I did not know was that, although the ceremony took place in the daytime, one was expected to appear in full evening dress. I did not even have a dinner jacket with me: nothing more showy than my Oxford MA gown and hood. My friend Peter Medawar, for whom such occasions were not a novelty, made no such mistake. Fortunately, our company included a Russian professor who, either acting on principle or sharing my ignorance, also restricted himself to wearing a lounge suit; and he kept me in countenance.

2 *Settling Down*

For some time after my acceptance of the London professorship had deprived me of my fellowship at Wadham, I had no settled place in which to live. I still frequently came down to Oxford, knowing that a guest room at Wadham would be at my disposal. In London I borrowed or rented flats from friends who were themselves away on business or on holiday. I remember living for a time in Highgate, a salubrious district but one that I found inconveniently remote since I did not own, or even know how to drive, a car. I lived more contentedly in Sloane Street with a very pretty girl of whom my most vivid memory at a distance of some thirty-six years is the length of time which she devoted to making herself up. I used to watch the process with something of the same fascination as the Prince Regent is said to have watched Beau Brummell's striving to obtain the perfect fit of a cravat. The girl vanished from my life as unobtrusively as she had entered it. I suppose that she was in her middle twenties, about twelve years younger than myself.

My problem of finding a place to live in London was solved for me by Ernest Stahl, the Professor of German at Oxford and friend and collaborator of Louis MacNeice. He told me, at some college dinner, that he and his wife had been thinking of taking a flat in Mayfair as a *pied-à-terre* for their visits to London but had decided against it. From his description of the place I judged that it would suit me, and lost no time in taking it as soon as I discovered that it was still available. It was at No. 2 Whitehorse Street, a short and narrow street which runs between Piccadilly and Shepherd Market. I was pleased to think of it as the venue of the old White Horse Cellar, the coaching terminus at which Esther Summerson is met by Mr Guppy in Dickens' *Bleak*

House. No. 2 was almost at the corner of the street by Shepherd Market. My flat was on the top two floors of a narrow house of which the first floor was conveniently occupied by a tailor, not too grand to do pressing and even minor repairs, and the ground floor by a shoemaker. It consisted of four rooms, all square and rather small, of which the two on the lower floor served me as a sitting room and a work room with a very narrow kitchen in between them and the two on the upper floor, separated by a correspondingly narrow bathroom, were respectively my bedroom and a spare room where I could put up a friend. I took it on a twenty-one year lease, without having to pay any premium, at a rent of £3 a week. Though the place was rather dilapidated, so that I had to spend a fair amount of money on redecoration, it was even for those days an extraordinary bargain.

In furnishing the flat I relied almost wholly upon Renée's advice. Though we had been divorced since 1941 we still saw a great deal of one another, partly but by no means altogether because of the children, and I contributed substantially towards their support. With the little money that she also had of her own, she had no need and made no attempt to earn her living, though she occasionally did some voluntary social work, such as teaching handicapped children. She had a proprietary attitude towards me, as she did towards the two other men whom she might at that time have married. From a wordly point of view one of these marriages would have been extremely advantageous and I think that what kept her from it, apart from the belief, which turned out to be false, that the opportunity would remain indefinitely open, was the fear that it would deprive her of her influence over the second man and over myself. In my case at least, sex did not enter into it, though I still thought her attractive and nearly always took pleasure in her company. Neither do I think that the jealousy which she freely displayed when I seemed to be forming a serious attachment to some other woman was straightforwardly sexual, though it may have contained a sexual element. It was rather that the power which she had acquired, ever since the start of our relations almost twenty years before, of taking practical decisions for us both was one that she still regarded as her prerogative.

What is more puzzling is my acquiescence. I do not think that it should simply be put down to her having the stronger personality, even though this may well have been the case. Part of the reason was my dislike of having to bother with practical details, so that I was glad to have her take them off my hands. It is possible that I unconsciously welcomed the limitation which her influence imposed upon my relations with other women, so that the love affairs in which I frequently engaged during the nineteen years in which I remained unmarried were furnished with a safety-net, protecting what I took to be my freedom. It is also true that I was curiously unconcerned with the part that my fellow dependants played in her life and unaware of the depth of their importance to her; so that when the one that she would have done best to marry eventually broke free from her, her inability to conceal from me the extent to which this mattered to her had the effect of bringing about my own liberation.

Renée's taste in decoration was formed in the 1930s, when there was a fashion for white walls, off-white furniture and a scarcity of ornamentation. In fact the white walls suited my small rooms, and although I had only one picture of any interest, the portrait of myself by e. e. cummings, and little or no bric-à-brac, I had comfortable chairs and a sufficient stock of books with which to furnish both my sitting room and my work room. I was therefore quite satisfied with my ambience. That others might view it differently was brought home to me one evening when I had been entertaining a number of my London pupils to drinks. They all left together at a fairly late hour and as I was closing the door of my flat I heard a voice which I identified as Peter Newnham's reaching me from the stairs. 'Poor old bugger,' he was saying, 'all alone *thinking* in those cold, cold rooms.'

The idea that I was only waiting for my guests to leave in order to resume my philosophical meditations was flattering to me, especially coming from one of my more critical pupils, but on most occasions would have been a mistaken one. I did a respectable amount of work during my early years in London, for which I did need some time to myself, but I did not lead a solitary life. My flat in Whitehorse Street was kept in order by an excellent daily woman, who came in some time before ten o'clock every weekday and made my breakfast. At the weekends, if I had no one staying with me or had not gone to Oxford or to stay with friends in the country, I breakfasted in a café in Shepherd Market. Except for the Monday seminars and meetings of our philosophical society I kept short office hours. There was a college cafeteria but I seldom used it, preferring, if I had no private engagement, to lunch with two or three members of my department in a local pub. In the evenings I went to parties or took a friend out to a restaurant, usually L'Etoile or The White Tower or the Jardin des Gourmets in Soho. I was able to afford this rather luxurious way of life not because my professional salary amounted to very much, but because I spent so little on housing and did not run a car. Neither was I a heavy drinker and being a heavy smoker was not then so costly as it has since become. On the rare occasions on which I had no engagement for the evening, I would go to the Travellers' and sometimes found a friend there but more often dined alone with a book that I had picked out from its library. The Travellers' differed from the Garrick, for which I eventually forsook it, in that one was not required to be convivial.

The only other club that I belonged to at that time was a dining club organized by Nigel Nicolson and George Weidenfeld, who may then have been in the process of setting up their publishing firm. The dinner was supposed to be preceded by a serious discussion. I remember only one meeting at which Philip Toynbee read a paper on religion and the company included Richard Crossman, Pastor Niemöller and Evelyn Waugh who came as someone's guest. He remarked on arrival 'A lot of Jews here. Which of them is Freddie Ayer?' but then relapsed into silence, intervening only once in the discussion to score a point off Richard Crossman. He did not subsequently stay to dine with us. There is an account of this meeting in his published volume of letters, wherein he says, quite truly, that a lot of nonsense was talked and refers to me as a young Yid who kept groaning throughout the proceedings. The explanation he claims to have been given for my groaning was that I was in love with Daisy Fellowes's daughter. In fact I was not particularly young, not very much younger than himself, but I may have looked young for my age. So far from being in love with Daisy Fellowes's daughter I did not even know that such a person existed. I may well have groaned but for a reason which excited part of Evelyn Waugh's own venom, the puerility of the discussion.

Whatever Evelyn Waugh may have thought or written about me, he was never directly rude to me though he had quite a number of opportunities in the ensuing years. Perhaps my friendship with Father d'Arcy restrained him, though d'Arcy's reputed description of me as a dangerous man might rather have provoked him. Most probably he did not think it worth his while. Very often when I met him he was performing an old buffer's act with his old friend John

Sutro, in a loud check suit and equipped with an ear-trumpet. They were occasionally funny without any great expenditure of effort. None of this detracted from my great admiration for Evelyn Waugh as a writer. I never made this known to him, partly because I had no reason to suppose that it would have been of any interest to him.

At the dinner which followed the reading and discussion of Philip Toynbee's paper, I made friends with Shirley Morgan, the present Lady Anglesey. I took her out to dinner a couple of times and in return she asked me to dine at home with her parents, Charles Morgan the novelist and drama critic of *The Times* and his wife Hilda Vaughan, also a novelist. There were no other guests. Hilda Vaughan received me civilly but for some reason Charles Morgan took an instant dislike to me. The first remark he made to me was 'I suppose you are the sort of young man who thinks Picasso a better painter than Landseer.' Since I was not inclined, or indeed very well equipped, to embark on a discussion of aesthetics I simply said 'Yes'. After that the conversation languished. Eventually Charles Morgan and I found a common interest in cricket, but the evening remains in my memory as one in which I most signally failed to please.

The dining club was not a success, but it was replaced a year or two later by a luncheon club with much the same membership, though the founders in this instance were Ben Nicolson, Nigel's elder brother, and Philip Toynbee. The club, which admitted only men, met once a fortnight, except for a break in summer and at Christmas, on Wednesdays at Bertorelli's Restaurant in Charlotte Street. Once a year there was a party for dinner and dancing, organized elsewhere, to which members could bring women guests. Philip Toynbee came rarely after he ceased living in London but Ben Nicolson, a learned art historian, deceptively taciturn, missing little of what went on around him, continued to run the club despotically, imposing on the company his taste in Italian food. There was a brief rebellion which took us away from Bertorelli's for a spell but we soon returned. The club still flourishes, though both its founders are dead. The novelist Peter Vansittart, another of the original members, first decided to keep it going and the work of organization is now mainly performed by Ted Honderich, a philosopher from University College. The gradual increase in membership which has taken place over the course of more than thirty years has been offset by defections as well as deaths, but a remarkable level of continuity has been preserved.

In these years immediately following the war Renée was living with the two children in an attractive house in Hampstead. Valerie, who had been born in 1936, and Julian who was three years younger were successively sent to a progressive school, of which I seem to remember that Yehudi Menuhin was a patron. Anyhow his photograph was prominently displayed on the premises, along with my own and that of some other parent. They would undoubtedly have been joined by that of Elizabeth Taylor, who was or had also been a pupil, but the school expired before her rise to fame. Neither of our children remained there very long, especially not Julian, who mistook the encouragement to express himself as a licence to damage the school's material equipment. In about 1947 Valerie went to Wychwood, a well-known girls' boarding school in Oxford with a legendary headmistress called Miss Lee but effectively run by a Miss Snodgrass, and two or three years later Julian was sent to a boarding school called Hawtry's in Wiltshire. It was a preparatory school of the traditional type. I do not know whether the headmaster, Mr Goodeve-Docker, enjoyed beating small boys, but if he conceived it to be his duty, it was not a duty that he shirked. We considered taking Julian away but he expressed a preference for overcoming the ordeal and in the end, thanks mainly to his prowess at games which made him a privileged figure as he got older, he came to speak quite favourably of the school.

One advantage which this school had, so far as I was concerned, was that it was within easy distance of a country house to which I was frequently asked for the weekend. The house which was called Stokke Farm and actually functioned as a farm, at least to some extent, belonged at the time to Mary and Robin Campbell whom I had met in Paris in 1945 when they came to visit Barley Alison. Robin had taken part in the famous commando raid on Rommel's headquarters, in which he had been so severely wounded as to lose a leg. He had been repatriated by the Germans and was starting a career as a painter. Mary was the sister of Hamish Erskine, with whom I had been at school. She had previously been married to Philip Dunn, a very rich man who derived his money, if I remember rightly, from his Canadian father. He was known at Stokke as 'the tycoon'. He lived nearby and quite often came to visit his daughters Serena, who married Jacob Rothschild, and Nell, who has made a name for herself as a playwright. I got on well with both children, but not so well with their father who believed or affected to believe that I was a Communist.

Many years later after her marriage with Robin had broken up and she had made an unfortunate venture into marriage with an American sports writer, Mary rejoined Philip Dunn and lived happily with him until his death.

I very much enjoyed my visits to Stokke. There was nearly always at least one other guest, most commonly Ben Nicolson. V. S. Pritchett, whom I had long admired as a critic and writer of short stories, lived with his wife Dorothy in a neighbouring cottage. Sometimes Henry Bath and his wife would come over from Longleat. He exemplified my image of a Regency Buck. We paid visits to Ralph and Frances Partridge at Ham Spray. It was only many years later that I learned to associate the house with the drama of Lytton Strachey and Carrington. So far as possible I avoided country walks, though I played croquet to win and sometimes made an unsuccessful attempt to defeat Ralph Partridge at badminton. If I were engaged on a piece of writing, I might bring it with me but mostly I talked and read whatever came to hand.

The only other country house at which I was at all a frequent guest at that time belonged to Maud Russell, to whom Richard Wollheim had introduced me. The house was in the neighbourhood of Winchester and better appointed than Stokke. Its parties also were more formal. Their chief attraction for me was the presence of Raymond Mortimer and Clive Bell. I was impressed by the range of Raymond Mortimer's knowledge and by the pains which he took over his reviews. The research which they demanded kept him occupied for most of the weekend. I admired his writing, though less than that of his master Lytton Strachey. Clive Bell had been a hero to me ever since my schooldays when I read his books *Art* and *Since Cézanne*. The zest for life which had caused Keynes in his *Two Memoirs* to describe him as a 'gay dog' was still very much in evidence. I was flattered by the attention which he paid me and delighted in his company.

With the children away at boarding school, Renée sold her house in Hampstead and took a flat in Dolphin Square, a solid block of flats facing the river but, apart from its sheer size, laying no claim to any architectural distinction. When I was in London at weekends during the school holidays I used to go to lunch there on Sundays. Often I would take Valerie to the cinema. During her school term I made a point of keeping many Sundays free so that I could take her out. I stayed in Wadham and used to read Jane Austen to her under the trees in the Wadham garden. John Bamborough, now Principal of Linacre College but then a Fellow of Wadham in English, and his wife Anna were very hospitable to us and so were my old friends Bill and Pussy Deakin, both when he was a Fellow of Wadham in History and when he became Warden of St Antony's. Twice in the summer holidays I took Valerie to St Jean de Luz to stay with Denyse de Bourran, a friend whom I had made at the end of the war, when I was employed by SOE in that part of France. On the second occasion we went on to stay with Hans and Aline Halban, now Lady Berlin, and her son Michel Strauss at Biarritz. The Deakins were there too and so was the financier Charles Clore and his wife Francine, soon to leave him. Charles Clore had never found time to learn to swim and was taking lessons, dangling on the end of a pole, in the shallow end of a swimming pool alongside a crowd of small children. I did not find him likable but I admired his moral courage. The Halbans drove Valerie and me home to England, passing through the north of Spain to Andorra and then going up the west coast of France. It was the only time that I was false to my resolution never to visit Spain while Franco remained in power.

In 1948 I received an invitation to spend the autumn semester at New York University. I might not have accepted, so soon after my introduction into the London Chair, had it not been for the fact that Valerie had been stricken with tuberculosis in the spring and that the Godleys, her war-time foster parents, had asked us both to spend the summer with them at their house at Morris in New York State, where the climate would favour Valerie's convalescence. I had been wrongly informed that in order to earn money in the United States I had to pretend to be an immigrant and my insincere application for American citizenship wasted much of my time and cost me some of my dignity in having to submit to medical examinations, queue for audiences and fill up forms. Since I never completed the formalities once I got to America, my application must long ago have lapsed, but I obtained a Social Security card which I kept for thirty years or so until it fell, with the rest of the contents of my wallet, into the hands of a Lancashire pickpocket at a football match at Tottenham.

The summer holiday at Morris completed Valerie's cure but proved less fortunate for me. For some years I had been receiving treatment for piles and now I suffered so bad an attack that I had to undergo an operation with a local anaesthetic at a hospital in Cooperstown, a place with which the game of baseball has some intimate association. The aftermath of the operation was extremely painful, and though I fairly soon recovered from it physically, it left me dispirited. Perhaps for this reason I did not much enjoy my semester at NYU. It is the only one of my numerous forays into the United States to lecture on which I do not look back with pleasure.

Not that I got on badly either with my colleagues or with my pupils. The head of the philosophy department was Sidney Hook, a former pupil of John Dewey, but originally less of a pragmatist than a Marxist. He had written a very good book called *From Hegel to Marx*. I do not know whether he had ever been a member of the Communist party, but by 1948 his hostility to Stalinism took almost total possession of him. It even led him in the years that followed to incur the suspicion of witch-hunting. Personally I rather liked him and I sympathized with his pragmatic background, but his political obsession, applied to the local scene and involving a firmer discrimination than I was willing or competent to make among the entourage of the *Partisan Review*, prevented us from making any common progress in philosophy. Of my pupils I best remember Nigel Dennis, the author of the novel *Cards of Identity*, who had, if I remember rightly, no special connection with NYU but nevertheless came fairly regularly to my graduate seminar. He took an active part in the discussions, and I like to think that they may have given him some ideas for his work.

Soon after I started teaching at NYU I was dismayed to find myself the victim of a spiteful piece in *Time* magazine. This came about in a rather curious fashion. Philip Toynbee, though earning his living as a literary critic for the *Observer*, had gone with his wife Anne and their two small daughters to live in a village on the Isle of Wight and had become captain of the local cricket team. A few weeks before I left for America I was invited to join a team which Ben Nicolson was taking across to play them. This team, which was called The Town Tigers, was easily beaten by the village team and to the best of my knowledge never played again. It included V. S. Pritchett, accompanied by Dorothy, J. B. Priestley, who seemed rather put out by our poor showing especially when he had to field to my bowling, Martyn Beckett, whom I had not seen since we were fellow officers at the Welsh Guards training battalion at Sandown Park in 1940, Evelyn Shuckburgh of the Foreign Office, who was the only one of us to make any runs, and Giles Romilly, whom I already knew slightly as a friend of Philip Toynbee's. Giles, who had been captured as a journalist in Norway early in the war and subsequently, as a nephew of Winston Churchill's, confined by the Germans in a special prison which they kept for particularly important persons, was now writing a column for the *New Statesman*. Being short of copy he wrote about a recent visit which he had paid to Oxford, where he claimed to have unearthed among the undergraduates a group of neo-Fascists, and still having space to fill and having in mind his recent meeting with me, he added that they were inspired by the ethical chapter of my *Language, Truth and Logic*. I do not think that he was being malicious or even wholly irresponsible. I think it possible that one or two of the young men whom he talked to had glanced at *Language, Truth and Logic* though I very much doubt if it affected their political views. There may even have been some neo-Fascists among the undergraduates though they can have formed only an insignificant group.

The story would have ended there but for my London colleague C. E. M. Joad, the Reader in Philosophy and head of the department at Birkbeck College, who had just been successfully prosecuted for travelling on the railway without a ticket and had consequently been deprived of his lucrative work for the BBC. Seeing an opportunity of rehabilitating himself by blackguarding me, he wrote an article for the *New Statesman* in which he condemned my moral philosophy as being indeed a springboard for Fascism, and exalted his own as allowing for moral objectivity. A correspondence ensued in which I took no part. Unfortunately it seemed of sufficient interest to a representative of *Time* in London for him to suggest to the New York office that there was material in it for a story. I consented to be interviewed in New York and was delivered into the hands of a young man who was out to score at my expense. Very foolishly, instead of just saying that talk of logical positivism leading to Fascism was rubbish, that the Vienna Circle had been politically left-wing, and that I myself had been a supporter of the Labour Party since some years before the war, I tried to give him a philosophical tutorial which he took in bad part. Having shown myself not averse from publicity, I was invited to *Time*'s offices to be photographed. There were two or three men present and as I faced the camera one standing on my left called my name out sharply. I turned to him with my mouth agape and that was the photograph that was printed. The text contrived to make me appear both sinister and foolish, implying that I was myself sympathetic to

Fascism and even hinting that it was my unpopularity in England that had brought me to New York. I heard many years later from Jean Campbell, Beaverbrook's granddaughter, that the fraud had been good enough to convince Oswald Mosley himself. They had gone together to visit me in Whitehorse Street but naturally had not found me there. I thought of bringing a libel action against *Time*, which I might well have won in an English court, but decided that I did not want to incur any further publicity over the affair, apart from the fact that the action would be one that I could not financially afford to lose.

Sidney Hook brushed the whole thing aside with the remark that any publicity was better than none, but I was worried about the effect on my American friends, especially the Godleys, whom the article did distress, and on the Cummings to whom I wrote explaining what had happened. His reply, written from his farmhouse at Silver Lake, New Hampshire, was most characteristic: '. . . one mild winter morning 45 years ago, some friends & I made ourselves a fine snow-fort (with plenty of iced snowballs) in the frontyard of the house where I was born. This house stood (& stands) at the corner of Irving & Scott streets, Cambridge. All around lived nothing but Harvard professors – Taussig (economics) on my left; & behind him Lanman; W. James on my right – yet (more than oddly enough) the very tough town of Somerville began only a little way up Scott Street – Presently a smallish mob of muckers (as we always called the youth of Somer-ville) materialized, & their führer-commissar suggested a friendly snowfight. I & my friends enthusiastically accepted the suggestion; war broke out. Suddenly the boy fighting beside me dropped as if hit by lightning. In less than a minute our army was annihilated. The muckers swarmed, horribly howling in total triumph – Why? Very simple! Whereas our side had merely iced its snowballs, our enemies – & not (as we'd naïvely supposed) our opponents – had put stones in theirs. More briefly; Cambridge's idea of a fight was not Somerville's. However could you dream that Marion & I would love you less because some (any) mob of muckers (& once Cantabridgian USA is about 90 pc Somerville just now) gave you the stoney snowball? Sois pas si bête.'

New York University did not pay me a very large salary and to supplement it I accepted an invitation, engineered by Sidney Hook, to lecture once a week at Bard, a small liberal arts college situated near

Rhinecliff at Annandale on the Hudson in very pleasant scenery, an easy journey by railway. I took the safe course of running through the history of modern philosophy in an orderly fashion, and maintained the numbers of my audience, securing their polite attention if nothing more. The head of the philosophy department rightly did not see me as posing any threat to his own position, and my relations with him and his wife were altogether cordial.

At the end of the summer Valerie was cured and returned to her school in Oxford. I had to find somewhere to live in New York, preferably downtown, since the branch of NYU in which I was to lecture was located in Washington Square, and I appealed for assistance in my search to my old friend Tony Bower. I had in fact already seen Tony since the war when I went to stay with him at a villa which he had taken near Florence. I stopped at Monte Carlo on the way. On my previous visit to Monte Carlo I had been too young to be allowed into the gaming rooms, but this time I paid them a brief visit. The atmosphere seemed to be dismal and the gamblers, a surprising number of whom were female and elderly, looked like zombies. If I gamble at all, which I do very seldom, it is in a frivolous spirit and for small stakes; there such an approach would have been clearly out of place.

In later years I have come to feel the charm of Florence but on this, my first, visit I was a little disappointed, comparing it unfavourably with Venice by which I had been captivated on a brief visit with Renée before the war. Perhaps I was less appreciative of Florentine art than I have since become; what I remember feeling is that the city had too much the air of a museum. One of the highlights of my visit was a call which I paid with Tony on the venerable Bernard Berenson at his famous villa I Tatti. I did not much care for the acolytes who made it their business to protect the sage, but when they allowed me to converse with him privately I enjoyed his company. He told me amusing stories about the eccentricities of Frank Russell, the second Earl and Bertie's elder brother. After a while he said 'I am at the end of my tether' – an unmistakable note of dismissal. After dutifully inspecting the library and the pictures, many of them primitives by artists whom Berenson had himself identified, Tony and I took our leave.

In New York Tony solved my housing problem by finding an apartment for us to share in Houston Street, Greenwich Village, a few minutes walk from my lecture room in Washington Square. He himself worked on an art magazine further uptown. We did not live luxuriously but we possessed a wireless set and I can still remember the enormous pleasure with which, as I listened through the night, I noted the growth of the evidence which forced the bewildered commentators to admit that Harry Truman was defeating Thomas Dewey in the election for the Presidency. The result, which Harry Truman had forecast with almost complete accuracy, state by state, was so unexpected that the *Chicago Tribune* actually put an early issue on the streets acclaiming Dewey's victory. I had no personal reason for sympathizing so strongly with Harry Truman, though I rather liked his saying that he would sooner play the piano in a whorehouse than attend an Embassy dinner, but ever since my schooldays when I started to take an interest in American politics I had supported the Democrats, first because they were then the underdogs, later, in the Roosevelt era, because I could draw a rough analogy between them and the British Labour Party and a stronger analogy between the Republicans and the detestable Conservatives.

Our apartment was large enough for us not to get in each other's way, and it may have made things easier that we had disparate sexual tastes, especially as Tony was not one of those homosexuals who were hostile to women as such. On the contrary when Jane Douglas, a friend to whom I had written despondently, came out from England to join me, the three of us got on very well together. When Jane returned to England I started an affair with Angelica Weldon, a very beautiful woman whom I had briefly met years before while she was still living with her husband. She had left him for a woman and I offered her a way of escape from a suffocating lesbian circle. Tony and she were wary of each other but never showed any open hostility, perhaps because they had many friends in common.

Both of them enjoyed motoring and after my term ended they organized an expedition which would increase their own as well as my knowledge of the United States. They took it in turns to drive and we stayed in a series of more or less comfortable hotels as we went at a steady pace from New York to Washington and then on south through Virginia, North and South Carolina, Georgia, Alabama and Louisiana as far as New Orleans. The southern states were not so prosperous as they have since become and I was depressed by the ramshackle houses in which many of the negroes seemed to live and frightened by the aura of sultry violence which pervaded so many of the small and dusty towns through which we passed. New Orleans, however, was a delight, not least because of the food and drink which it provided. It had the air of being always in readiness for a carnival. I was happy to drink Pernod in its bars but slightly embarrassed by the scantily clad girls who stood bumping and grinding on the counter a few feet away. It seemed equally impolite to stare at them or studiously avert one's gaze.

After spending a few days in New Orleans I left Angelica and Tony to go their own ways and myself took an aeroplane to Houston, Texas, to spend Christmas with my old pupil Michael Judd and his wife Jean, who was Tony's half-sister. Michael, about whom I have already written as having had a remarkable war record as an English fighter pilot, had not become at all Americanized, but he seemed to be contented with his life in Houston and becoming financially prosperous. Houston was then only starting on the course which has led to its vying with Oklahoma City for the title of the fastest growing city in the United States. It already made a show of luxury with its imitations of French châteaux, colonial mansions and English country houses, all huddled together as though they still needed mutual protection in case of an Indian attack. The men whom I met seemed to have delegated the supervision of their oil wells to others, so leaving themselves ample time for drinking. They introduced me to sazerac, a very happy mixture of Bourbon whiskey, Pernod, syrup, bitters and lemon. Their womenfolk were more interested in the arts. The Monte Carlo ballet company was in town and I had the pleasure of meeting Danilova, though I do not remember that we found anything of interest to say to one another, and perhaps because of my addiction to sazerac I missed the opportunity of seeing the company perform.

On my way back from Houston I stopped at Charlottesville, the site of the University of Virginia, where the eastern division of the American Philosophical Society was holding its annual meeting. There was nothing remarkable about the conference except for its being so congested that I had to share a bed with Sidney Hook, but I was enormously impressed by the beauty of the buildings which Thomas Jefferson had bequeathed to Charlottesville. After the congress I motored north with Nelson Goodman, then a professor at the University of Pennsylvania, and one of his colleagues who because he was black had been made to feel unwelcome at Charlottesville, something which I hope could no longer happen, and I stayed a few days with Nelson Goodman and his artist wife at their house on the outskirts of Philadelphia. I had already met Goodman on an occasion when I addressed a philosophical society with its headquarters in New York, whose members included my old friends Ernest Nagel and Meyer Schapiro. Having nothing new to offer I re-read my inaugural lecture 'Thinking and Meaning' which I had delivered in London the year before. I was considerably disconcerted to observe a man in the front row of my audience perusing a printed copy of my text. He did not, however, contribute to the discussion. Nelson Goodman did, raising an objection which I tried to parry and then producing a riposte to which I acknowledged that I had no answer. It bore on my lack of a tenable theory of reference, a deficiency which I am sorry to say that I have still to make good.

My high opinion of Nelson Goodman's philosophical gifts was confirmed by the publication in 1951 of his book *The Structure of Appearance* which was an elaboration of a doctoral thesis which he had submitted to Harvard eleven years before. I myself had renounced phenomenalism, the theory that all empirical statements are reducible to statements about sense-data, in a lecture which I delivered under that title to the Aristotelian Society in London and had published in its proceedings for 1947–8, and I still think that my reasoning was sound. The most that can be achieved, as I have subsequently argued, is to show how our conception of the physical world can be developed as a theory on the basis of sense-experience. This did not, however, bring me into conflict with Goodman, except in so far as I did and he did not attach a sense to the question of priority in the theory of knowledge. His aim, which he pursued in part through criticism of Carnap's *Logical Structure of the World*, exhibiting an even greater logical ingenuity, was to develop a language of appearance with the greatest possible economy. He left it an open question to what further use the language could be put.

The main article which I published in 1948 was one called 'The Principle of Utility' which I contributed to a collection organized by the law department of University College and entitled *Jeremy Bentham and the Law*. Its principal point, which I still believe to be valid, was that Bentham was concerned with systems of legislation rather than with individual morality, and that when he equated right actions with those that produced the greatest happiness of the greatest number he was engaged in what my fellow emotivist Charles Stevenson had called persuasive definition. My views on moral philosophy had undergone no fundamental change since I first published *Language, Truth and Logic*, though I did devote more care to their development in an article entitled 'On the Analysis of Moral Judgements' which I published in *Horizon* in 1949, after previously delivering it as a lecture to a Cambridge undergraduate society. One of the distinctions which I drew was that between meta-ethics (the theory of the status of moral judgements) and ethics proper and I argued that disagreement in the sphere of meta-ethics made very little difference to people's moral conduct. When the mild Dr Ewing, the only senior philosopher in my audience, contested this assertion, I basely resorted to an *argumentum ad hominem*. 'Surely, Dr Ewing,' I said, 'if I were to persuade you of the truth of my contention that ethical judgements are not cognitive, you would not engage in Babylonian orgies.' 'Yes I would,' he replied without hesitation, bringing the house down to my discomfiture.

I had left New York early in the new year and returned to live in Whitehorse Street. A few weeks later Angelica, who had kept in touch with me by transatlantic telephone, came over to join me. She was a sister-in-law of Jack McDougall, who had taught me in the sixth form at Eton during the short time that he was content to be a schoolmaster, and she took me to stay with his family at their house in the country. There were three small daughters who were astonished by my inability to draw anything that even remotely suggested a domestic animal or indeed anything else. Angelica was also a friend of the Hofmannsthals and of Liz's eldest sister Caroline Paget and she got us invited to the Paget stronghold of Plas Newydd in Anglesey, where I admired the Rex Whistler murals. Henry Anglesey was still very young and newly married to Shirley Morgan. We played combative games of tennis and I thought that we got on well together though Angelica reported that he found me inhuman. His researches into the family archives were to lead eventually to his writing an excellent book on the first Marquis, who as Lord Uxbridge commanded the British cavalry at Waterloo and engaged in the famous dialogue with the Duke of Wellington. Uxbridge: 'By God, sir, I've lost my leg.' Wellington: 'By God, sir, so you have.'

In spite of our mutual attraction, Angelica and I could not adjust to living together, and it was not very long before she found a flat of her own. Some time later, after she had been with him on holiday, she told me that she had fallen in love with a young married man.

Perversely I felt a stab of jealousy, though I did not want her back in Whitehorse Street. I soon overcame it and we remained good friends. Her love affair prospered for a while but she was subject to fits of despair and in one of them she killed herself, provoking, not long after, the suicide of her lover. She rang me on the night of her death, without giving me any hint of her intention, which may not yet have been formed. I do not think that I could have done anything to save her.

3 *The Metalogical and Other Societies*

One of my first acts on returning to London in 1949 was to found the Metalogical Society. My choice of title was intended to be suggestive of the Metaphysical Society of the nineteenth century which recruited eminent men of the most varied disciplines, but my net was cast less widely. It mainly served to bring together philosophers and experts in the physical and biological sciences and quite a high proportion of the members had a connection with University College. Except during the summer holidays the Society met once a month in my flat in Whitehorse Street over a period of four to five years, with an average attendance of about fifteen people. The meetings took place in the evenings after dinner; a paper was read and discussion followed. Bertrand Russell came regularly and the other philosophers included Karl Popper, recently installed at the London School of Economics, Stuart Hampshire, Richard Wollheim, James Thomson and Johnny Watling from University College, and John Wisdom who occasionally made the journey from Cambridge. We were particularly strong on the biological side, University College supplying us with the geneticist Lionel Penrose, brother of my friend the painter and art-collector Roland Penrose, as well as with J. Z. Young, Peter Medawar, who had previously held a Chair at Birmingham in zoology, J. H. Woodger, a logician as well as a biologist, and the bio-chemist F. G. Young. Ernest Hutten, who lectured at Royal Holloway College was our philosopher of physics, and Robin Skynner worked on the borderline between philosophy and psychiatry. The editorial board of *Polemic* supplied us with two amateur philosophers in the persons of Humphrey Slater and Rupert

49

Crawshay-Williams, soon to be a neighbour of Russell's in Wales, who came regularly to the meetings and wrote about them in his fascinating book *Russell Remembered*. Apart from philosophy, the humanities were represented by the Dutch historian G. J. Renier, again a professor at University College and the author of the best-seller *The English are they Human?* We sometimes admitted guests, as for example the famous logician Alfred Tarski when he came from California to deliver the Shearman Lectures. These lectures, which took place biennially, were also given during my time at University College by E. Schrödinger, who disappointed us by talking about Greek philosophy rather than physics, by Nelson Goodman, whose lectures formed the basis of his book *Fact, Fiction and Forecast*, a notable contribution to the set of problems centred on inductive inference, by the American philosopher Wilfrid Sellars, and by the Dutchman L. E. J. Brouwer, whose exposition of intuitionism in mathematics, a theory of which he was himself the principal architect, I found too difficult to follow. I myself gave the lectures when I had left London to return to Oxford and whatever is of value in my contribution is to be found in my book *Probability and Evidence*.

The chief benefit to myself of my founding the Metalogical Society was that it led to my forming quite a close friendship with Bertrand Russell. As I have related in *Part of My Life*, in the late 1940s he was living in North Wales with his third wife Patricia Spence, and was a neighbour and friend of Arthur and Mamaine Koestler and still more of the Crawshay-Williams. After he was divorced from Patricia Spence, who retained custody of their son Conrad, he took a house in Richmond, in the neighbourhood of Pembroke Lodge, where his grandmother had brought him up, and shared it with his eldest son John Amberley, John's wife Susan, a daughter of Vachel Lindsay, the American grass-roots poet, and their two small daughters. John, the son of Bertrand Russell's second wife Dora Russell, clearly had a great admiration for his father and himself had a vague idea, which never came to fruition, of writing a book about politics. When Bertrand Russell married Edith Finch they continued to live in Richmond and found themselves obliged to take care of his grandchildren when John and Susan, neither of whom had any sense of responsibility, suddenly went off without them. Eventually Bertie and Edith returned to an attractive house in North Wales, where they lived happily together, maintaining a flat in Millbank for their occasional visits to London, and the two little girls passed into the care of Dora Russell.

I saw most of Bertie, as I finally brought myself to call him – though when we corresponded we used each other's surnames – during the period when he was living in Richmond. Although there was a difference of nearly forty years in our ages, our friendship was personal as well as professional. This was partly due to his having outlived many of his contemporaries, partly, I think, to a preference that he had for younger company. Nevertheless the mainstay of our friendship was professional. In 1948 he had published *Human Knowledge: Its Scope and Limits*, a book of over 500 pages which he saw as a distillation of his thinking about the main problems of philosophy over a period of fifty years. The book did not encroach upon the domain of mathematical logic, in which Russell had originally gained his great distinction, but he declared in the preface that logic was not part of philosophy. That Russell had high hopes of the book comes out clearly in Rupert Crawshay-Williams's memoir. He was seriously disappointed. It was not just that the book received one or two frankly hostile reviews; it was rather that the general tone of its reception by professional philosophers was one of polite indifference. What recommended me to Russell was not that I admired this particular book, which in fact I thought inferior to the William James Lectures which he had delivered at Harvard in 1940 and published as *An Inquiry into Meaning and Truth*, but that I was at least disposed to take it seriously. I shared its philosophical approach.

The trouble for Russell, and indeed for me also, was that the theory of knowledge had gone into a temporary eclipse. There had been a turning away from the view that it was the business of philosophy to assess and if possible to justify our claims to knowledge. Wittgenstein's *Philosophical Investigations* was not published until 1953, two years after his death, but his conception of philosophy as turning on the bewitchment of our intellects by the spell of language had been in fairly general currency since the 1930s. Gilbert Ryle's *Concept of Mind*, which came out in 1949, with its celebrated attack on the traditional view of the mind as 'the ghost in the machine' also worked against Russell by depriving his edifice of knowledge of its sensory basis. Least of all to Russell's taste was the fashion which J. L. Austin spread at Oxford, in the late 1940s and throughout the 1950s, of treating philosophy as the meticulous investigation of ordinary linguistic usage. This was not the position of G. E. Moore, whose conception of philosophy came closer to Russell's own, but his practice sometimes seemed to favour it and his insistence that the common-sense view of the world was known for certain to be true put Russell's scepticism out of court.

Though the balance has now been largely altered, Russell's reputation at that time was lower than that of Wittgenstein and Moore and I think that he resented this. He retained his respect for the early work of both these philosophers but he thought that Wittgenstein's *Investigations* were sterile, just as Wittgenstein in his turn coupled Russell with H. G. Wells as thinkers who had run out of problems, and he was repelled by the naïveté of Moore's defence of common sense. 'The trouble with Moore,' he once said to me, 'is that he believes everything that his nurse told him.' The respect which Ryle had for Russell was not reciprocated and there was the foolish episode of the refusal by Ryle, who had succeeded Moore as editor of *Mind*, to allow any review of a book by Ernest Gellner, in which linguistic philosophers were personally attacked in a somewhat strident fashion, to appear in the journal. This offended Russell because he had written a laudatory preface to the book. He was also offended by an article 'On Referring', impugning his cherished theory of descriptions, which Peter Strawson published in *Mind*; not so much indeed by the original article as by Strawson's failure to publish a reply to Russell's rejoinder. Philosophically I think that Russell may have had the better of the argument but he was quite wrong in supposing that Strawson would knowingly subject him to a personal affront. Russell was quite incapable of seeing any merit in 'ordinary language philosophy' and did not even try to take it seriously. Thus in a paper on the subject which he read to the Metalogical Society he pointed out that when a charwoman says 'I ain't never done no harm to nobody' she does not mean 'There is at least one moment at which I was injuring the entire human race.'

All this may suggest that Russell became tetchy in his old age but that would not be true. He had always been vehement in his opinions, and perhaps not always entirely fair to his intellectual and moral adversaries, but at the time of which I am writing, when he was in his late seventies and eighties, and indeed in all the years that I knew him, he retained his keenness of intellect and readiness for entertainment; and his wit, the breadth of his knowledge, and his astonishing memory, not least for the experiences of his youth, made him the best of company. He was indeed capable of being mischievous. For instance I remember a party in my flat to which the actress Bunty Howard, who had worked with me in British Security Co-ordination during the war, asked whether she might bring a young protégée of hers whom she had selected for a leading part in a film. The girl was still being educated at a convent and the nuns were doubtful as to whether she should be allowed to attend a party at which so wicked a man as Bertrand Russell would be present. In the end they gave her permission but supplied her with a list of questions to put to Russell if she conversed with him. The girl, who was remarkably pretty, arrived with her list of questions and managed to corner Russell. Some moments later his dry voice rose above the hubbub of conversation. 'The Pope,' he was saying, 'the Pope! He is paid his salary for telling lies.' I never discovered whether this was reported back to the nuns.

Of all the philosophers who came to the meetings, Karl Popper was the one with whom the scientists felt the greatest affinity. Or rather, this was certainly true of Peter Medawar and I suspect of the others as well. Yet I do not remember that he contributed much to our debates. Though in theory he was in favour of critical discussion, he required it to be on his own terms. When I advised my pupils to attend his seminars, they complained that he did not allow them to criticize his views. Personally, he and I were friendly. I used to lunch with him at the LSE, his company atoning for the ugliness of the place and its material discomfort, but I had the feeling that he never took me very seriously as a philosopher.

How absorbing our discussions could be was shown by the evening when John Young set my flat on fire. My telephone was in my workroom across the passage from my sitting room where the meetings were held. Making a telephone call before he left, John inadvertently dropped a lighted cigarette butt into my wastepaper basket. The three or four of us who remained were still lost in argument when suddenly firemen broke into the flat. Some passer-by, seeing smoke coming out of the window in the next room, and assuming the flat to be unoccupied, had summoned the fire brigade. Taken wholly by surprise, we left the place free for the firemen to operate. The passer-by asked me whose flat it was. When I replied, 'It's mine,' he said, 'Goodness, you're very philosophical,' and walked on. Fortunately, the passer-by had acted so quickly that the fire had not spread very far, and the damage was slight. Some curtains were ruined, a picture blistered, but not beyond restoration, and some books were charred. Unfortunately, they included numbers of *Polemic* which I am sorry not to have been able to keep. A set of them is however accessible in the London Library.

I had kept up my friendship with the Zuckermans and used frequently to stay with them at their house in Edgbaston. Solly had retained the contacts with persons in high places which he had acquired during the war and spent the major part of his time in Whitehall, where he became the government's chief scientific adviser. This did not lead him, as it might have led a less energetic man, to retire from his professorship of anatomy at the University of Birmingham. He worked there assiduously at the weekends and supervised an active corps of researchers. He had Peter Medawar as a colleague until Peter accepted a Chair of Zoology at UCL in 1951.

A friend of Solly's called Robin Whitworth, who worked for the BBC, had the fruitful idea of reviving the eighteenth-century Lunar Society over which the chemist Joseph Priestley had presided in Birmingham. The Society originally owed its title to the fact that it held its meetings at the time of the full moon, when its members were in least danger of being waylaid by footpads. The nucleus of the twentieth-century Society consisted of Solly, Peter Medawar, Julian Huxley and myself with persons such as Charles Madge, the poet, Mass-observer, and Professor of Sociology at Birmingham, Dr R. H. Thouless the psychologist, and Dr S. G. Soal, the experimenter in what was claimed to be psychical research, as occasional guests. The meetings, which were held in Solly's house, not necessarily on the nights of the full moon, were broadcast under the overall title of 'Scientists Talking'. There were four or five of them in all and they covered such subjects as the future evolution of man, the credentials of psycho-analysis and the genuineness of telepathy.

Another society in which I was enrolled by Julian Huxley at about that time was one in which we were invited to plan a more liberal version of his brother's *Brave New World*. Its most assiduous member was Max Nicholson, the naturalist. I supplied it with its secretary, Glyn Seaborn Jones, a graduate pupil of mine who was strongly interested in psychiatry. He subsequently made a career for himself as a lay analyst. Meetings of this society were fairly frequent and a great many memoranda were circulated, mostly written by Julian Huxley himself, but I do not think that we contributed anything much, even in the form of blueprints, towards the progress of civilization. Julian Huxley was an excellent naturalist and a genuine lover of the arts but his attempts to humanize the natural sciences faced greater obstacles than he was willing to reckon with.

The BBC was very indulgent to philosophers, especially on its Third Programme, and I made a considerable number of broadcasts in the decade following the war. In one of my earliest efforts, which I think was directed overseas, my talk was produced by John Arlott who showed me how to read from a script. Being naturally disposed to gabble, I greatly profited from his tuition. Two or three of the overseas broadcasts in which I participated took the form of discussions in French, where I had to acknowledge that my friend Dr Weightman's fluency in the language exceeded my own. Among the Home Service talks that I gave was one on 'Science and Philosophy' in a series on the Ideas and Beliefs of the Victorians, one on John Stuart Mill, one in commemoration of the six hundredth anniversary of William of Ockham, author of the famous maxim, known as Ockham's razor, that entities are not to be needlessly multiplied, and a review of Gilbert Ryle's *The Concept of Mind*, in which Ockham's razor was boldly applied; too boldly indeed for the taste of Lord Samuel who debated the question on the wireless with Gilbert Ryle and myself, and not so much too boldly as too carelessly for my own taste.

A broadcast debate which gave me more pleasure was one in which I was pitted against Father Frederick Copleston of the Society of Jesus in June 1949. In the previous year Father Copleston had held his own with Bertrand Russell in a broadcast debate on the existence of God, and this was effectively a return match with myself as a substitute for Russell. It was billed as a discussion of logical positivism, but although we had some talk about the verification principle and about my characterization of the necessary propositions of logic and pure mathematics as tautologies, both of these issues on which I now see that I was vulnerable, I contrived for the most part to carry the debate to my opponent, obliging him to try to make a case for his acceptance of metaphysics and more specifically for his theism. I thought that on the whole I had the better of the argument and no doubt he thought the same of himself. The text of our debate is reproduced in an anthology called *A Modern Introduction to Philosophy*, edited by Paul Edwards and

Arthur Pap, and published by The Free Press in New York, first in 1957 and then in a revised edition of nearly eight hundred pages in 1965. In our common unworldliness we let them have the text for nothing.

A happy result of this encounter was that Father Copleston and I became good friends and have remained so to this day. When Heythrop College, of which he became the Master, moved to London I used often to dine with him there. Even as Master, he had only a small bed-sitting room to live in, but he seemed inured to this austerity without making any show of asceticism. Some years after our original broadcast we were set to debate the problem of free will on Welsh television. Something was amiss with the apparatus and we were plied with so much drink while we were kept waiting that when we were finally able to appear we were both incoherent. This caused no remark in the studio and I dare say that it equally escaped the notice of our audience.

If inclusion in the large *Oxford English Dictionary* is a sufficient condition for being an English word or expression, then another result of our original debate was that I introduced a new word into the English language. It came about in the following way. In an unsuccessful attempt to induce Copleston to admit that it had to be true of any entity of which it made sense to speak that there should be some possible way of telling whether it existed, I coined the word 'drogulus' to stand for an alleged entity which failed to satisfy this condition. My contention, in short, was that if I said 'There is a drogulus over there' but then went on to say that it was unobservable and that its presence had no physical effects of any kind I had failed to give the word 'drogulus' any meaning. My colleague, Lionel Penrose, who listened to this debate, was experimenting some years later with pieces of wood which he shaped in such a fashion that when they were placed in a trough and shaken together they combined in a way that satisfied the standard criteria of biological reproduction. Finding his experiments of sufficient interest to write about in *Nature*, and needing a word to designate his peculiar artefacts, his inaccurate memory of my debate with Copleston led him to christen them 'droguli', with an acknowledgment to me. In the discussion that followed the publication of his article the word obtained some scientific currency. The result was that it gained entry into the large OED, defined in accordance with Penrose's usage of it, but with its coinage credited to me, although I never intended it to have the meaning that Penrose gave it, or indeed to have any meaning at all.

I think it was in 1949 that I began taking Valerie to the Edinburgh Festival as part of my summer holiday. She would then have been thirteen. It was Renée's idea and Renée made the practical arrangements. We stayed in boarding houses, where I vainly tried to acquire a taste for porridge. Valerie was more musical than I but I enjoyed going with her to concerts to which it would never have occurred to me to go by myself. I do not remember that we saw anything outstanding at the theatre, except a production of Ben Jonson's *Bartholomew Fair*. I grew to like Edinburgh very much, though I do not think that I should have cared to spend the winter there. I paid a pious visit to the site of David Hume's dwelling and I also called on Professor Norman Kemp Smith who had written what I still consider to be the best commentary on the philosophy of David Hume. I think that he underestimates Hume's scepticism but his thesis that Hume was mainly concerned to vindicate the claims of 'natural belief' is very ably sustained. I found Kemp Smith a very courteous old gentleman, though we did not embark upon any philosophical discussion.

It was at about this time that I began to take a more active interest in professional football. As I mentioned in the book to which this is a sequel I became a supporter of Tottenham Hotspur in the years 1919–21 when they successively won promotion from the second to the first division of the Football League and won the Football Association Cup, defeating Wolverhampton Wanderers in the final by a single goal scored by Jimmy Dimmock, their outside left. The Wembley Stadium had not yet come into existence and the match was played on Chelsea's ground at Stamford Bridge. I did not actually watch it and indeed watched very few matches before the war though, having originally chosen to support the Spurs for no better reasons than that they were a London team, that they were currently successful and that I was attracted by their name, I followed their fortunes in the newspaper reports and cared about their vicissitudes. I became a regular spectator of their home matches, however, in the season 1949–50, going early, sometimes by myself but more often with a friend to make sure of getting seats, and four or five years later obtained a pair of season tickets which I have renewed annually at increasing cost ever since. The result is that except when I have been abroad, on holiday or lecturing, I have watched very nearly all the matches played at White Hart Lane, the Spurs' home ground, over a period of thirty years.

No doubt a large part of the reason why I started to form this habit in 1949 was that the club was again enjoying success. Under the management of Arthur Rowe, who had played centre-half for Tottenham in the 1930s, the club first won promotion in 1949–50 from the second division, to which it had been relegated in 1935, and in the following season 1950–1 won the League Championship for the first time in its history. It was known as the push-and-run team, because it was trained by Rowe to rely on short passes with players releasing the ball quickly and running quickly into open spaces. His conception of the game was summarized in the telegram which he sent to Pegasus, the team of former Oxford and Cambridge players which won the Amateur Cup during the period of his success with Spurs: 'Make it simple. Make it quick.'

Journalists and television producers who learn of my interest in professional soccer tend to regard it as consorting oddly with my calling as a philosopher; they treat it as an eccentricity, if not as an affectation. The result has been that I have very frequently been asked to write about it or take part in televised discussions, invitations which I have sometimes accepted but also often refused when it seemed to me that the object in my being asked was not a display of my expertise but rather the exposure of my oddity. My enthusiasm may be eccentric in the sense that not many academic people, and perhaps an even smaller percentage of philosophers, share it, but it is certainly not an affectation. Nor, as I am often expected to say, is my interest primarily aesthetic. I do think that the game, when played adventurously, is aesthetically satisfying; I am excited by the possibilities it offers of quick reversals of fortune; but predominantly I am like any other supporter. I want my team to win.

This does not apply only to professional soccer. I described in *Part of My Life* how my interest in county cricket, and allegiance to Middlesex, survived the disappointment of my childish hopes of myself excelling at the game. Only on two or three occasions since the war have I actually gone with a friend to Twickenham to see Oxford play Cambridge at Rugby Football, but I try to make sure of watching the match on television and care about the result. I also watch international matches, where perversely I identify myself with the Welsh fifteen, though I remain loyal to England in international soccer.

Whenever I watch any sort of sport I tend to make what is often an arbitrary identification with one of the contestants; otherwise the spectacle fails to captivate me. For the most part I do not find this difficult to achieve. Curiously, however, tennis, which is the only out-door game at which I was still a better than average player after the war, is one in which I now take little interest, just because the leading players appear so disagreeable that I cannot identify with any of them. This was not true of an earlier generation. For instance, I have never met Ken Rosewall, but I have always regretted that he never won the Wimbledon Championship.

On New Year's Eve 1949–50 I went to a party by myself at Bunty Howard's and, coming down a flight of stairs on the stroke of the new year, I kissed a small, dark, very pretty girl who was standing at the foot of the staircase. She turned out to be an Australian painter called Jocelyn Rickards, about twenty-four years of age, who had emigrated to England not very long before. She was sharing a house with three other Australians, a photographer called Alec Murray, with whom I was also to make friends, an art dealer and a designer. The house had the unusual name of the House of the Sons of God. Later she and Alec Murray separated from the other two Australians, who contin-ued to live together, and took a flat in Eaton Square, which they shared with Peter Williams, the ballet critic and editor of *Dance and Dancers*. It proved a satisfactory arrangement for all three of them.

When I first met her Jocelyn was nurturing an unrequited love for some country gentleman, and though we quickly became friends and saw each other often it was some months before we became lovers. After that, though we kept our separate addresses, we were con-stantly in one another's company. We usually dined out in restaurants, though Jocelyn liked to cook and did it very well. I owe to her an appreciation of good food that I had not learned before. After dinner we would often go to dance at the Gargoyle in Soho, now an ordinary night club, but then the resort of writers and artists and their friends. It was in a large room with glass walls, said to be the work of Matisse. The owner was David Tennant and if one stayed late enough one could often see him being helped by the waiters up to his flat above. Food was served as well as drink and the prices were reasonable. The band, led by a perky Mr Alexander, was not very good but it played, almost continuously and with gusto, tunes like 'Bye-Bye Blackbird' or 'Melancholy Baby' to which I particularly liked to dance. Cyril

Connolly was often to be seen there, as was Humphrey Slater, lavishly entertaining anyone who came to his table; Philip Toynbee, perhaps getting drunk with Donald Maclean or less frequently Guy Burgess; the legendary Brian Howard and the art critic Douglas Cooper, both waspish in their different ways but neither to me; Raymond Carr and Tony Crosland from Oxford, then seldom sober; the painters Francis Bacon, Robert Buhler and Rodrigo Moynihan; Johnny Minton, who killed himself; and the inseparable Colquhoun and McBride.

Renée knew of my attachment to Jocelyn and subtly tried to undermine it. Jocelyn naturally resented this, and understandably thought it ridiculous that I should be so much under the thumb of a woman from whom I had been divorced for nearly a decade. It may also have been that I unconsciously nurtured my feeling for Renée as a safeguard against my emotions. Otherwise Jocelyn and I might very well have married. As it is, we have maintained our friendship, our large community of taste and our pleasure in one another's wit for over thirty years, despite all the other attachments that we have formed.

About this time I was approached by Penguin Publications with the proposal that I should edit a series of original books for them on philosophy, appearing under their Pelican imprint. The plan was that it should cover the history of philosophy, up to F. H. Bradley, with volumes devoted to individual philosophers, and that there should also be books on general topics such as logic, ethics and politics. The length of the book might be anything from 200 to 300 pages and their authors were set the difficult task of producing something which would be of interest to the professional philosopher while not being so difficult or technical as to discourage the general reader. Financially I made a bad bargain, consenting to receive a fee of £50 per volume for the work of choosing the author, setting a dateline to which I had to try to make him adhere, going through his manuscript when he delivered it, and writing a general introduction, a practice which I discontinued for the later volumes.

The series began well, with the appearance in 1951 of Bryce Gallie's *Peirce and Pragmatism* and Stuart Hampshire's *Spinoza*, and continued throughout the 1950s and early 1960s, incorporating my own *The Problem of Knowledge*, about which I shall have something to say later on, as well as the general topics of ethics, which I entrusted to P. H. Nowell-Smith, and political philosophy, which T. D. Weldon tackled from a linguistic standpoint, and covering nearly all the great philosophers from Thomas Aquinas, of whom Father Copleston as a Jesuit was able to write without too much reverence, to F. H. Bradley, to whom Richard Wollheim was unexpectedly sympathetic. The last volume to appear under my aegis was Patrick Gardiner's excellent book on Schopenhauer which came out in 1963 but I can also claim credit for commissioning Bernard Williams to write a book on Descartes, though I did not edit the text. This did not make its welcome appearance until 1978, by which time the control of all the Penguin output of philosophy had passed into the hands of Dr Ted Honderich, who joined the department of UCL as a lecturer after I had left it.

The series contains some lacunae for which I am not wholly responsible. It should have become obvious to me sooner than it did that James Thomson was never going to write the book on logic which I had commissioned from him and I should have made an effort to find a replacement for him. It was I too who rejected the book which I had asked Ernest Hutten to write on the philosophy of science, as being unsuitable for the series, and then entrusted the task to Johnny Watling, which he has not yet fulfilled. I also failed to persuade Professor Herbert Hart to produce the book on Jeremy Bentham which he is uniquely qualified to write. On the other hand it was the publishers who turned down, on the ground of its length, the book on Plato which I had asked Ian Crombie, my successor at Wadham, to write for the series. It did run to two volumes and I arranged for them to be published in the International Library of Philosophy and Scientific Method which I edited for Routledge and Kegan Paul in the 1960s. It took me a long time to find anyone who would undertake Aristotle and when I finally persuaded Professor Abraham Edel to adapt to our needs a study of Aristotle which he had published in America, Penguin refused it. They also rejected two books on Hegel that I successively sponsored, one by Professor J. N. Findlay, my colleague at King's College, London, for many years, and the second by Professor Charles Taylor. I was not surprised by their thinking Professor Findlay's book too difficult for their readers but Professor Taylor's would have suited us very well. Both books were well received when they were published as hardbacks. When Penguin went on to reject a book that I had commissioned on aesthetics and another on the philosophy of religion, I decided that they had ceased to treat me seriously as an editor and renounced what had become a merely nominal office. I should have done so earlier than I did.

Philosophy was not the only subject to be made the topic of a Pelican series. There were half a dozen others, including the classics, presided over by E. V. Rieu whose translations of Homer proved exceptionally popular. At an early date, when I was still in good standing as an editor, Allen Lane had the notion of having a picture painted of all his Pelican editors, himself and some of his senior staff, united in a single composition. It might have been called a conversation piece if any of us had seemed to be conversing. The work was entrusted to Rodrigo Moynihan. I sat for him several times, without our establishing much *rapport*. I am, however, recognizable in the picture, which served its purpose well enough as a whole. I believe that it is still hung in the Penguin boardroom.

In 1950 I fulfilled a youthful ambition by being elected President of the Aristotelian Society for the session 1950–1. The Aristotelian Society, which was founded in the nineteenth century by an amateur philosopher but ardent empiricist called Shadworth Hodgson, had known better days in the years preceding the First World War, when philosophers from Oxford and Cambridge were disposed to make the journey to London to attend its meetings even when they were not themselves the principal speakers. In the period between the wars the emphasis shifted to the annual sessions, at a different university each year, which the Aristotelian Society held jointly with the Mind Association. After the Second World War it was still possible to obtain speakers from Oxford and Cambridge but the audience, never very large, consisted almost exclusively of members of the philosophical staffs of the London colleges, together with a sprinkling of enthusiastic amateurs. The proceedings, comprising about fifteen papers, were, and still are, published annually, with the symposia in which the Joint Session consists appearing as a supplementary volume.

My presidential address was entitled 'Statements about the Past'. Its most controversial thesis was that there was no such thing as a class of statements about the past as such. Whether a significant statement was about the past, present, or future, depended on the temporal relation of its utterance to its factual content, that is to say, the state of affairs which it affirmed to obtain, and whatever this relation, its factual content would remain the same. If the time of the state of affairs in question could be fixed in another way, say by the employment of a system of measurement, the use of tenses became superfluous: one could convey the same information by stating that the utterance of the statement was earlier or later than, or simultaneous with, its factual content, as the case might be.

This procedure has the merit of helping to free the sense of one's utterances from dependence upon context and for this reason has been accepted by such other philosophers as Goodman and Quine, but I have to confess that I am no longer entirely satisfied with it. I am now inclined to think that there is a sense in which temporal demonstratives serve a purpose which cannot be effected by descriptions. To use an example, devised by the late Arthur Prior, someone who says 'Thank God that's over' after a visit to the dentist is not expressing relief over the eternal fact that the extraction of a tooth at time t precedes a reference to the event at a later time $t+n$. There is, however, a price to be paid for taking this line. One has to admit that temporal talk is incurably subjective.

From 1950 to 1952 I was Dean of the Arts Faculty at University College. So far as I can remember, my administration was distinguished only by the speed with which meetings were concluded. No doubt I was fortunate in the absence of contentious issues, but I also acquired some skill in spotting those committee members who enjoyed holding up the proceedings, on whatever score, and foiling them by passing rapidly to the next question.

In alliance with Hugh Trevor-Roper, I was myself an obstructive element at the first meeting of the Congress for Cultural Freedom which was held in 1950 in West Berlin. The purpose of the Congress, which was financed by the CIA, was to channel funds to a set of periodicals such as *Encounter* in England, *Preuves* in France and *Der Monat* in Germany, which would combine the expression of liberal sentiments with hostility to Communism. I had no objection to this aim and thought that there were many worse uses to which the CIA might and indeed did apply its funds. The choice of venue seemed to me strange but I was glad of the opportunity of a free visit to Berlin, where I had not been before and have not been since. What irritated both Hugh and myself was the hysterical atmosphere in which the Congress was held, orchestrated as it was by revengeful ex-Communists, *imprimis* Arthur Koestler. Little thought had been given to the structure of the debate, with the result that I found myself opening the proceedings with what I admit to have been a namby-pamby paper on the limitations of tolerance, addressing myself to the question how far John Stuart Mill's conception of liberty could still be reasonably upheld. This was not at all to the taste of my audience. '*In unserer Zeit*,' I was told, '*hilft nicht* John Stuart Mill.' What was helpful in our time was left unsaid, but it was evidently something more polemical.

There were some other speeches, the content of which escapes my memory, but most of the time of the Congress was occupied in drafting a resolution, to which Hugh and I, with one or two followers, raised what were mainly mischievous objections. For some reason the musicologist Nicholas Nabokov, a cousin of the writer, played a prominent part in the affair, confirming the dislike which I had already taken to him when I met him in company with my friend Isaiah Berlin. On the other side, I offended not only Arthur Koestler but also Melvin Lasky who as editor of *Der Monat* felt a personal responsibility for the success of the Congress, which Hugh and I were undermining. I do not think that Arthur ever wholly forgave me, though he was kind enough to take me to the celebrated match at Wembley in 1953 when Hungary defeated England by six goals to three, the first time that England had lost to a European country at home. The football played by the Hungarians was of an altogether higher class. In spite of his political beliefs, I think that Arthur was proud of them, as he had every right to be. With Melvin Lasky I eventually made friends, after he had exchanged the editorship of *Der Monat* for that of *Encounter*. His notorious denial that *Encounter* was financed by the CIA did not shock me, as I did not see how he could possibly expect anyone to take it seriously; I still do not understand how it could have deceived anyone who had anything to do with the Congress for Cultural Freedom.

At the outset *Encounter* was edited by Stephen Spender and an American called Irving Kristol. My friendship with Stephen was of long duration but I did not take to Irving Kristol and liked him still less when without consulting me he changed the title of a sober article which I had written on 'Nihilism' to the vulgar 'Philosophy at Absolute Zero'. I have been interested to note that since his return to America he has ceased to make any pretence of liberalism. Probably Stephen Spender exercised more control over the earlier numbers, which contained nothing objectionable except for one disgraceful article by an American called Fiedler, mocking the Rosenbergs for expressing a love of baseball during the period that they were awaiting execution. Even if it had in fact been clear, as it has turned out not to be, that the Rosenbergs were properly convicted of espionage and that they deserved the death penalty, the article would have been in execrable taste. This was, however, an isolated instance. I have not been at all a frequent contributor to *Encounter* throughout the years, but have not avoided writing for it as a matter of principle.

On 29 October 1950 I became forty years old. I find it hard now to understand why this affected me so severely as it did. I felt that it meant farewell to youth and all its pleasures, that it heralded the decline of my intellectual powers. In fact these fears were not justified in the following decade. They may have been justified since, but the onset of age has never again so deeply troubled me.

4 *Travel and Philosophy*

1951 was the year of the Festival of Britain, the year of the defection of Burgess and Maclean, the beginning of thirteen years of Tory government, and for me the occasion of my first visit to South America. The University of San Marcos at Lima in Peru, which was founded on 12 May 1551, claimed to be the oldest university in the Americas, a claim which I believe to be contested by the University of San Domingo. To celebrate the four hundredth anniversary of its foundation, and to eclipse San Domingo, the University of San Marcos organized a philosophical congress, to which it invited a number of philosophers from Central and South America, one or two from the United States, of whom the most memorable was Professor Elizabeth Flower of the University of Pennsylvania, and a handful from Europe. I was the only English representative, but there were two from France, Professor Gaston Berger from the University of Aix and Gabriel Marcel, a Catholic existentialist, better known perhaps as a playwright, and the first Spanish philosopher that I had met, Julian Marias, a disciple of the celebrated Ortega y Gasset. One or two of the Central and South American representatives were exiles from Spain but they were civil to Professor Marias in spite of his having come to terms with Franco. So also was I.

This was before the McCarthy era but the Committee for Investigating un-American Activities was already in being and I was given just a small hint of things to come. I broke my journey to Lima by spending a night in New York and had therefore to pass through Immigration. When the official asked me what my profession was, I said that I taught philosophy. '*Socialist* philosophy?' he asked very sharply. I was tempted to point out that not all socialists were Communists, and anyhow that if one was going to condemn Marxism one should at least have studied it, but he did not strike me as a promising pupil. 'I teach logic,' I said, 'not political philosophy,' and was admitted without further ado.

My journey down to Lima was enlivened by our flying through a thunderstorm but we arrived without mishap. I had already met Francisco Miro Quesada, an enlightened young Peruvian philosopher, on a visit to Rome where we happened to be staying at the same hotel. I knew something of Peruvian politics which I had studied during the war when I was working for British Security Co-ordination in New York and I was sympathetic to the Aprista party, led by the erratic Haya de la Torre. After a brief tenure of power the Apristas had given way to a military dictatorship. The members of the congress were presented to the Dictator, General Odria, who surprised me by seeming more Indian than Spanish, in a country where I had been given to understand that the old Spanish families had kept their hold upon power, with very little admixture of Indian blood. My friend Francisco, or Paco as I called him, belonged to one of those families, who owned the principal newspaper in Lima. The fact that it was allowed to express liberal views lent some support to the claim made to me that this general's rule was mild by South American standards. At least the students in the gallery of the hall where the congress was held were not inhibited from bestowing enthusiastic applause on an impassioned intervention on behalf of political liberty which I made in the course of a debate. All the same, Paco Miro Quesada found the atmosphere sufficiently restrictive to accept an opportunity of exchanging his academic career for diplomacy. He represented his country as Ambassador in Paris before the installation of a Christian Democrat regime made him feel free to resume his university post.

I am reminded by old press cuttings that besides taking part in the debates I gave a lecture to the congress on 'The Existence of Other Minds' and also addressed the Anglo-Peruvian Cultural Association on 'Contemporary British Philosophy'. My Spanish had grown a little rusty in the last ten years but I could still make a fair showing with a prepared text and deal adequately, at least so far as the language went, with any questions that were put to me.

Not that the philosophers in my audience had much sympathy with my ideas. Paris was still the intellectual capital of most countries south of the United States, and existentialism was much in vogue. I remember that one of the more prominent members of the congress, Professor Zea from Mexico, read a paper entitled '*El Ser del Hombre Mexicano*', the Being of Mexican Man, as though Mexicans were essentially different from the remainder of the human race. Both because of his provenance and his philosophical standpoint the greatest deference was paid to Gabriel Marcel. He was an amiable old gentleman, excusably vain, who attached more importance to the spiritual message embodied in his notebooks or his plays than to any form of philosophical argument. I do not know whether his work still commands much interest in France.

As in nearly all South American countries, the gap between rich and poor in Peru was shockingly wide. It was rumoured that on some of the large inland estates the Indian workers were given supplies of the coca shrub in lieu of wages, mainly for the reason that chewing the shrub had the dual effect of dulling men's wits and enabling them to labour at high altitudes. I had no opportunity to verify whether this was true, though the Indians whom I saw did exhibit both hardiness and lassitude, and it is notable that such movements as there have been for radical social reform have received their main impulse from liberal elements of the Spanish aristocracy.

Apart from the inevitable slums on the outskirts, Lima was an attractive city, with some very good examples of the baroque architecture which Spain bequeathed to its colonies. I was more interested, however, in the local museum which had a very fine collection of Indian figurines, two or three of which I bought. I was told that they were not the workmanship of the Incas, who were a martial tribe, reminiscent of the Spartans, but of the coastal people whom the Incas had conquered some four hundred years before Pizarro and his handful of Spaniards conquered them.

I acquired a taste also for the local spirit, pisco, the Peruvian equivalent of the Mexican tequila and about as powerful. Besides its alcoholic purity, it had the merit of being relatively cheap.

After the congress, the party of philosophers was flown to Cuzco, the old Inca capital. The ascent was steep and the aeroplane so primitive that we had to wear oxygen masks. My mask was faulty so that I lost consciousness, but I was revived before I suffered any serious injury. The air at Cuzco was so rarefied that for the first day or two one had to pause at every step while going upstairs. The place was made picturesque by the profusion of Indians with their coloured shawls coming to market from the neighbouring villages with their llamas as beasts of burden. If I remember nothing of its buildings, it is because of the much stronger impression made on me by Machu Picchu, a lost city of the Incas, to which we were next taken. It was a sacred city, built for the purpose of sun worship, at a very high altitude within a forest, in an area where the heirs to the Inca throne took refuge with their soldiers, priests and holy women in the 1530s. In 1572 the last of them was lured by the Spaniards into the plain and killed, his subjects died out or fled, their city was abandoned and the forest enveloped it. Its location was forgotten even by the Indians until it was rediscovered by an American explorer, Hiram Bingham, in 1911. It took a long time for the Peruvians to clear away the forest and the place was only beginning to be exploited as a tourist attraction by the time we went there. We went by train from Cuzco to the foot of the mountain and by bus up a narrow road. That day we were the only visitors.

The uninhabited city was the strangest that I had ever seen and the most grandiose. It occupied a series of terraces with houses constructed of enormous granite ashlars, not held together by cement, which the Incas did not possess, but carved so that they fitted into one another. The Incas had not discovered the wheel but they worked on the principle of the inclined plane. They had no written language, but used knotted cords, called quipus, in different colours, for the purposes of reckoning according to a decimal system. In this way the rulers kept an account of all the common property. The society was hierocratic but the priests enforced an egalitarian regime. They built good roads and maintained a system of communications throughout the empire by relays of foot runners. Having no horses, they mistook the Spaniards on horseback for centaurs and were terrified when they came apart. Their art shows that they used mutilation as a form of punishment but they did not, like the Aztecs in Mexico, appear to have indulged in human sacrifice. The Spaniards took their gold and brought them Christianity. It is not obvious that they gained by the exchange.

After seeing Machu Picchu I was invited to join in an expedition through the jungle to Lake Titicaca and wished that I could have done so, but I was already committed to a lecture tour under the auspices of the British Council. I refused to lecture in Argentina because I disapproved of the dictatorship of Peron. Rightly or wrongly I believed it to be a worse regime than that which I had countenanced in Peru. I therefore saw no more of Buenos Aires than its airport, at which I had to stop in transit from Chile to Uruguay. The flight over the Andes was some compensation.

The only other country which I visited was Brazil. In Chile and Uruguay I lectured in Spanish; in Rio de Janeiro, since I do not speak Portuguese, I lectured in French. Politically and philosophically, I felt most at home in Chile. It had been very largely colonized by German exiles, after the failure of the revolutionary movement in 1848, and Santiago seemed to me to have something of the atmosphere of a Central European town. Its philosophers were not then openly Marxist, if they were so at all, and several of them displayed an interest in the philosophy of science. Montevideo I found very strange, full of ambitious buildings which were capriciously left unfinished. It was said that rich people were selecting it as a place of refuge from the atomic war which they believed to be forthcoming, but if so they were not as yet disgorging their wealth. Rio was beautiful with its magnificent beach and sugar-loaf mountain, but with only the British Council's representative and his wife for company, I fell into a fit of melancholy, friendly as they were. I did discover in Professor Carnabrava a philosopher who looked northwards to Harvard rather than to Paris. He was, however, all too clearly an isolated figure.

The Brazilian aeroplane in which I returned to London made frequent stoppages, not all of them official, shedding most of its passengers en route. The last straw for many of them was a two days' sojourn in the clammy squalor of Dakar. Only I and one other passenger, an official from the Brazilian Embassy in London, remained loyal throughout and were eventually rewarded with a safe arrival.

By now it was summer and no doubt we talked in a desultory fashion about the disappearance of Burgess and Maclean, which had taken place in the spring. Their whereabouts was still officially unknown, though hardly anybody doubted that they had taken refuge somewhere behind the Iron Curtain. Guy Burgess, who was a few months younger than I, was at school with me at Eton and was one of the Oppidans with whom I had a casual acquaintance. I do not think that I saw him while he was an undergraduate at Cambridge and I at Oxford, though we had common friends who spoke to me about him. I must have developed some sympathy for him in the years before the

war since Renée and I did little entertaining in London yet I remember
his coming to our flat in Foubert's Place. I saw more of him after the
war, mainly because he was a great friend of the Halperns who had
returned to London from New York and they frequently invited us
together. I was willing to concede that he had charm but was not myself susceptible to it. This was partly the result of his treating me to
long political discourses which ended by boring me. In the last month
that I saw him they consisted very largely in denunciations of the
United States. It puzzled me in retrospect that a Communist agent
should have so paraded his left-wing views. Perhaps it was a kind of
double bluff.

Though I had known him much less long, I was much more a friend
of Donald Maclean's. He was a close friend of Mary and Robin Campbell and I probably first met him at Stokke. I found him sympathetic
and intelligent. Much has been written of him as a sober Dr Jekyll and
drunken Mr Hyde but I only twice saw him drunk, once at the Gargoyle when he was indeed alarmingly violent, and once at the end of
a party which started in Whitehorse Street and ended in Cyril Connolly's house, where Donald collapsed peaceably under a console
table piled with our coats in the hall. This was only a day or two before
he vanished and it may have been my last sight of him, though we had
a sober lunch together at about the same time. We talked quite often
about politics and he appeared to hold sensible radical views. I did
not know that he ever had been a Communist and even if I had known
it I should have assumed that in his case, like that of his friend and
drinking companion Philip Toynbee, it was something that he had
outgrown. Again, while Guy Burgess made no secret of being a preda-
tory homosexual, I had no grounds at all for supposing that Donald
was similarly addicted and indeed some evidence to the contrary.
Certainly it was not for this reason that he was having trouble in his
marriage. Altogether his defection took me completely by surprise.

I did not know Kim Philby and had only a nodding acquaintance
with Anthony Blunt. The only other Cambridge Communist of the
1930s whom I can claim as a friend is John Cairncross, whom I first
met when he as a young Fellow of Trinity and I as a Student of Christ
Church were examining the boys at Westminster School in classics, a
task for which he was far better equipped than I. Since he lives in
Rome, we see each other rarely but we keep up a friendly correspondence and sometimes exchange our works. The last book of his that

I received from him is a very scholarly history of Christian polygamy.

The Festival of Britain must be chiefly remembered for the Battersea funfair which it left as a legacy to London and perhaps for the architectural boldness of its 'skylon'. It probably has been forgotten that it also included an exhibition of books arranged by the National Book League at the Victoria and Albert Museum. Divided into more than twenty sections with such titles as The Countryman, The Scientist, The Thinker, The Playwright, The Poet, The Storyteller and The Historian, it was supposed to represent the cream of English literature throughout the ages. Of the thirty-seven items coming under the heading 'The Thinker' my *Language, Truth and Logic* was one. I am embarrassed now to see that I was a member of the advisory panel, but I am sure that I had no hand in choosing my own book. Each exhibit was supposed to be a first edition but I found that my own small stock of copies of the first edition of *Language, Truth and Logic* had disappeared during the war, so that I had to borrow one from Professor Henry Price, whose excellent book *Perception* was included in the same section.

There were seventy-five items under the heading 'The Storyteller' and one of them, deservedly, was Graham Greene's *The Power and the Glory*. I had proudly taken Jocelyn to see my book on show and it happened that Graham Greene was visiting the exhibition, perhaps for a similar reason, at the same time as ourselves. I do not remember meeting him before but we introduced ourselves to one another. It was obvious that he found Jocelyn very attractive and that she returned his interest. I did not feel jealous because my relationship with Jocelyn had reached a stage where we believed that it was immune to what we chose to regard as passing infidelities. On the contrary I took a liking to Graham which I think was mutual. He even invited me to see if my rational arguments could undermine his faith and we actually embarked on the experiment which I probably took more seriously than he did; at least, he very soon showed that he did not wish it to continue. We remained on good terms until a friend of his who wished to strike at Jocelyn through me made mischief between us. I bear him no ill-will for this and still think well of him as a person and even better as a writer. I enjoy not only the serious books like *The Power and the Glory* and *The Human Factor* but also the entertainments like *The Comedians* and *Our Man in Havana*. In the case of

Our Man in Havana, I find it hard to choose between the book and the film, with its magnificent performances by Alec Guinness and Noël Coward. I still put Graham Greene first among living English novelists.

My interest in politics had declined since the war, inasmuch as I did not engage in any active party work. I once allowed my name to be put on a list of Labour candidates for the Victoria Ward in a local election for the Westminster City Council, but I did no personal campaigning and the Conservatives won with ease, as they always did in Westminster except in Covent Garden and Soho. Nevertheless I strongly supported Attlee's government and approved of its development of the Welfare State. I still consider it the best administration that this country has had in the present century, with the possible exception of Campbell Bannerman's Liberal government of 1906 and its early continuance under Asquith. I thought it a mistake for Attlee to call an election in the autumn of 1951 and was appalled when the Conservatives were returned with a small but working majority of seats, though Labour had the overall majority of votes. I tried to console myself with the thought that the Labour ministers were tired and needed a period out of office to restore their energy. It never occurred to me that we might be condemned to anything like as much as thirteen years of Conservative rule.

In the summer of 1952 I was invited by the British Council to make a short tour of Italy. I lectured at Rome, Florence and Milan. I can read Italian fairly well, but when I try to speak it I find myself speaking Spanish instead, so I lectured in English and French. This was my first visit to Milan, which impressed me far more favourably than I had expected. It lacks the charm of Rome and the beauty of Florence but it has greater vitality than either. Nor is it aesthetically to be despised. Quite apart from Leonardo's famous 'Last Supper' and the splendid cathedral, there is the Brera gallery, with a bitter crucifixion by Mantegna which remains in my memory. This is the picture which Aldous Huxley mocked Ernest Hemingway for mentioning ever so casually in Hemingway's *Farewell to Arms*. I had the good fortune too to attend a performance of Rossini's *Barber of Seville* at the opera house of La Scala, surely the prettiest in Europe.

Philosophically, the Italian scene had become a patchwork. I could not discover any dominant tendency. The school of mathematical logic which had flourished under Peano and Burali-Forti at the turn of the century had vanished without trace. The influence of Croce could still be detected in the work of Ugo Spirito and Augusto Guzzo, who gave it a religious tinge, but neither commanded any powerful following. The Neapolitan, Franco Lombardi, was a man of wide learning and an entertaining companion, but philosophically detached. Guido Calogero, who for some years combined being a professor in Rome with running the Italian Institute in London, was a follower of Croce in politics, once Croce had distanced himself from Fascism and emerged as a liberal, but not so much in philosophy. A convivial man, with an attractive personality, he had arrived at a position according to which philosophy essentially consisted in the persistence of a dialogue; what the dialogue was supposed to be about was not made clear.

In Turin the religiosity of Guzzo was offset by a little group of existentialists headed by N. Abbagnano. F. Battaglia practised the philosophy of law at the University of Bologna, where some years later I spent a most agreeable week giving one or two lectures and going by car on May Day to see the superb Byzantine frescos at Ravenna. Since the area was Communist the route was made all the more picturesque by the display of red flags. Under the guidance of Togliatti the Communist Party was steadily increasing its power in Italy, but it had produced no significant contribution to Marxist theory since the death of Antonio Gramsci in 1937 at the early age of forty-six. The eclecticism of the Italians allowed them also to embrace analytical philosophy, which had some following in Rome and a stronger representation in Milan, but their activity consisted rather in the translation of books by foreign authors, such as Gilbert Ryle and myself, than in the accomplishment of any original work of their own.

The year 1952 was also made memorable for me by my election to the British Academy. This institution, not to be confused with the Royal Academy of painters, was founded in 1903 as a belated counterpart to the Royal Society. It was thought unfair that workers in the area of the humanities, such as classical scholars, economists, historians and philosophers, should not be eligible for a distinction comparable to that which had been available for nearly 250 years to those who were eminent in the natural sciences. The Academy was divided into sections, representing the different subjects which it embraced. The sections, meeting twice a year mainly for the purpose of considering and choosing candidates for Fellowships, submitted their nominations to a council on which representatives of different sections served for a limited period. The council habitually accepted one or two of the candidates most strongly recommended by their sections, though at the outset the total number of Fellows was not allowed to exceed one hundred. By 1952, the year in which I was elected, this limit had risen to two hundred and it now stands at three hundred and fifty. This rise in numbers has diminished the pleasure which many Fellows took in the meetings, since it has made it more difficult for them to keep their personal enemies out. Otherwise the sections were invited to vote money for various projects, the most important of which were archeological, and to choose persons, not necessarily themselves Fellows of the Academy, to deliver a medley of subsidized lectures. These were marketed separately as pamphlets, and appeared also in the proceedings of the British Academy which came out one or two years later. In my experience, the most interesting feature of these proceedings has usually been the obituaries of the Fellows who had died in the course of the year in question. They have nearly always contained information of interest and though they have had to be adulatory, they have seldom suffered from excessive piety.

Unfortunately, in the eighty years of its existence, the British Academy has never come near to achieving the same prestige as the Royal Society. This was partly due to the manner of its original formation. With the numbers limited to a hundred, the tendency was to elect elderly persons, professors who had been long established in their Chairs or senior Fellows of colleges rather than younger men who might already have shown themselves capable of contributing more to their subject, and this tendency has persisted in spite of the increase of numbers. Thus, while a specialist in one of the natural sciences may well consider himself a failure if he has not been elected to the Royal Society by the time he is forty, my election to the British Academy at the age of forty-one set me among the youngest of its two hundred Fellows. Neither, to the best of my recollection, has any philosopher been elected since that time at a younger age.

When I first became a Fellow, the Academy offered no entertainment apart from the lectures, which were anyhow open to the public, and the annual excitement of the elections. It was for this reason that the excellent Cambridge philosopher, John Wisdom, refused to accept a Fellowship after enquiring from me what he would be getting for his outlay of an entrance fee of ten guineas and an annual subscription of three guineas, figures which have since risen to £10.50 and £20 respectively. Gilbert Ryle had already declined even to be considered, not, I think, from the same motive but rather because he disapproved of the way in which the Academy was constituted or perhaps because he did not see it as fulfilling any useful purpose. Since 1958 there has been an annual dinner thanks to the munificence of Arthur Goodhart, once Master of University College, Oxford, who made provision for it in his will. The dinner has taken place at one of the City Halls or more often at one of the Inns of Court and has at least provided better food than that supplied by the Lord Mayor at his annual banquet to representatives of the arts. The speeches which have inevitably followed the dinners have seldom risen above, or indeed fallen below, the level of mediocrity. I was once charged with welcoming the guests and made some jokes about the Civil Service which resulted, rather to my surprise, in infuriating its Head. The only other speech that I remember at all clearly is one made some time in the middle 1970s by Harold Wilson at very great length, exclusively about himself.

In the autumn of 1952 I paid my first visit to Scandinavia. I lectured first of all in Copenhagen and then at the Swedish universities of Lund, Uppsala and Stockholm. It was the fashion then to prefer Copenhagen to Stockholm, mainly because it was reputed to be livelier. I did not find it so, though I was entertained by the members of one of the Danish student societies, much resembling their German counterparts in their regalia, consumption of beer, and general heartiness though they stopped short of engaging in the ritual of duelling. I made two friends among them, a physicist called Arne Petersen who worked closely with Nils Bohr, and a philosopher called Peter Zinkernagel who held views resembling those which were coming into fashion at Oxford in their deference to ordinary usage and to common sense. I was responsible some ten years later for having a book of his published in England under the title of *Conditions for Description*. Unfortunately, the translation, made by a Danish friend of Zinkernagel's, was as cumbersome as such translations are apt to be, and the book attracted less attention than it merited.

The leading philosopher at the University of Copenhagen was Jørgen Jørgensen, who had been an ardent positivist in the 1930s. During the war, during which he had played a part in the Danish Resistance, he had been even more thoroughly converted to Marxism.

This meant that we no longer had much common ground for a philosophical discussion, but we talked politics without rancour and I admired his character. We paid the ritual visit to Elsinore which, apart from its association with Hamlet, was not especially remarkable.

So far as philosophy went, and no doubt in other respects as well, the best of the Swedish universities was Uppsala. It is also one of the oldest universities in Europe. I had already heard of Professor Marc-Wogau with whom I felt particular sympathy because he agreed with me in upholding the sense-datum theory of perception, which affects to trace knowledge of the world around us back to its origins in sense-experience. It was, however, a revelation to me that the emotive theory of ethics, with regard to which I had believed myself to be one of the pioneers, was no novelty in Uppsala, belonging to a tradition in moral philosophy of which Professor Hedenius was the leading current representative. I found the Swedes almost embarrassingly formal in their manners until they had had a good deal to drink, at which point they threw away their inhibitions. Fortunately, they nearly always did have a good deal to drink. I enjoyed myself particularly in Stockholm which I also found aesthetically attractive. It is the only city other than New York which skyscrapers have seemed to me to embellish rather than deface. The University also boasted an excellent philosopher in the person of Professor Wedberg who combined a mastery of logical analysis with an exceptional command of the history of philosophy.

In England the death of George VI and accession of his daughter Elizabeth II prompted the magazine *Picture Post* to devise a feature entitled 'The New Elizabethans', carrying brief biographies of persons who might become prominent in the coming reign. I was included among them, at the suggestion of my old friend Sylvain Mangeot, to whom I had to give a succinct account of the main tenets of logical positivism. After the demise of *Picture Post*, Sylvain worked for the *News Chronicle* and eventually for Reuters, achieving an expertise in foreign affairs. Though susceptible to women, he never married but took care of his father the violinist André Mangeot, who lived to a great age. Sylvain was an exceptionally good cook, and a good conversationalist so long as he remained awake. Like the economist Nicky Kaldor, he was apt to fall asleep during the course of a meal. This has happened to me but not yet often enough to have stopped my finding it embarrassing.

Another old friendship which I renewed at about this time was that with Goronwy and Margie Rees. Goronwy had ended the war as a colonel, helping to administer the British zone in Germany. I have already related that he was then taken into partnership in the firm of Pontifex Limited by Henry Yorke, the novelist writing under the pseudonym of Henry Green. It was reputed that the partners did not apply themselves very strictly to business, but the firm remained prosperous, and Goronwy turned the experience to good account when he was elected Bursar of All Souls, finding means to increase the very considerable wealth which the college already possessed. At that time he and Margie, with their five children, were living in the country at Sonning, which was one reason why I saw next to nothing of them. Goronwy was very much upset by the defection of Guy Burgess who had been his closest friend. Already in the 1930s Guy had confessed to him that he was a Communist, but Goronwy had dismissed the confession as a drunken fantasy. Before he absconded with Maclean Guy made a long and incoherent telephone call to Margie from the Reform Club. Characteristically, he omitted to pay for it, so that the club put his debt on public record, with the result that for weeks the Rees's house was besieged by journalists. What the journalists hoped to achieve by this is not clear. They can hardly have supposed that the Rees's were harbouring the fugitives. In fact Goronwy had immediately got into contact with MI5. I never learned what he told them but, from hints that he dropped, suspect that he implicated Anthony Blunt, though probably not Kim Philby. In any event, MI5 took no further action at that time.

The defection of Burgess and Maclean had ceased to be news when Goronwy accepted an invitation to become Principal of the University College of Aberystwyth, one of the four colleges that make up the University of Wales. Though he had grown up in Aberystwyth I think he had forgotten to what a narrow-minded community he would be giving himself as hostage. The fact that his father had been a celebrated local preacher influenced him, as well as the fact that Aberystwyth was chiefly a setting for its college, so that the Principal of the college was locally a most important man. I frequently went to stay with them and for the first two years at least found them pretty well contented with their form of life. Perhaps Margie never felt wholly at ease in her strange surroundings, but she supported Goronwy loyally, as she did throughout their marriage, and she was contented with their house which stood on a hill above the town with a fine view of the coast. There were drawbacks, such as the veneer of local temperance which led to my having to order their drink for them when they wanted to replenish their supply, but at the outset at least these were only minor irritants, and Goronwy enjoyed his attempt to cast the college into a more liberal mould, resisting such suggestions as that all undergraduates should be obliged to study the Bible in Welsh. The children too adapted themselves well to the change. The two eldest of the five were girls, then came twin boys, one of whom had Guy Burgess for a godfather, and finally my own godson Matthew. I already had another godson, William Pugh, the second son of David and Margaret Pugh; David, a former air force pilot, having been an undergraduate at Wadham when I was Dean. In neither case was I required to take part in any ceremony or give any religious undertakings, which I could not conscientiously have done. That I should have by now lost track of both my godsons is rather to my discredit, but I did at least perform the offices of a benevolent uncle to them while they were young.

I had read and admired the novels of Henry Green long before I identified him as Goronwy's partner. I never became a very close friend of his but he and his wife Dig used to come to the parties which Jocelyn and I frequently gave at her flat in Eaton Square. Henry made no secret of his attachments, which indeed were only thinly disguised in his novels, and I remember overhearing him at one of our parties denouncing me to the beautiful Kitty Freud as a notorious seducer and pleading with her not to go out with me. Her husband, Lucien Freud, the painter, and I disliked one another but our dislike, which was almost instinctive, had nothing to do with his marriage. I cannot help admiring his technique as a painter but, perhaps owing to personal prejudice, receive little pleasure from his work. Kitty was a daughter of Jacob Epstein and subsequently married Wynne Godley whom I had first met staying with the Campbells at Stokke. He was not then the severe economist that he has since become but the player of an oboe in an orchestra. He played solos beautifully and my image of him as Pan has always prevented me from taking his economic theories as seriously as I am sure that they deserve.

Henry Yorke had a strange career as a writer. Born in 1905, he published his first novel *Blindness* at the age of twenty-one, just after coming down from Oxford where he claimed to have spent most of his time playing billiards. His novel *Living*, which was the fruit of his experiences while he was working as an apprentice in Pontifex's factory at Birmingham, came out in 1929. He then published nothing for ten years before the novel *Party Going*, describing quite a different social milieu, followed a year later by the autobiographical *Pack my Bag*. During the war he served, like Stephen Spender, in the Fire Brigade, finding time to publish the novel *Caught* in 1943. Five more novels, all written under the pseudonym Henry Green, and with one-word titles, appeared at roughly two-yearly intervals, ending with *Doting* which came out in 1952. This was the last of his publications though he lived for another twenty-one years. He toyed with the idea of writing a second volume of autobiography and dictated a few pages to Jenny Rees, the eldest of Goronwy's children, but he soon wearied of the project. He became more and more detached from social life in any form, making over the management of Pontifex to his son, seldom venturing out of his attractive house in Kensington except to visit the local pub, after some years not even doing that but having his bottle of gin sent in, spending his days watching television in the soothing company of his wife. I seldom see his name mentioned by contemporary critics but his novels do not deserve to be forgotten.

A feature of Henry's style is that his novels consist almost entirely of dialogues. In this he resembles Ivy Compton-Burnett, but whereas Henry's personages subtly reveal their different characters and social status by their different turns of speech, Ivy Compton-Burnett tends to make her whole cast, high and low, old and young, employ the same elaborate idiom. The attraction of her novels, for which I have a high regard, lies in their wit, their density, and the way in which she masks her melodramatic effects. I met her only once at dinner with Renée and Robin Fedden, himself the author of a book on suicide and an intrepid traveller, and found her intimidating. She was notorious for enjoying her food and left it to her neighbours, of whom I was one, to open a conversation if they wished. After a time I broke the silence with the jejune question, 'Do you mind people talking to you about your books, Miss Compton-Burnett?' 'Not if they have anything interesting to say about them,' she replied, tartly. This kept me quiet for a time until I decided that I did have something interesting to say. 'One way in which you are unlike other novelists,' I said, 'is that you allow your characters to get away with petty crimes. In novels, evil-doing is almost invariably punished, and the villains who do not come to grief, like Thackeray's Marquis of Steyne or Disraeli's Lord Monmouth are portrayed as grandees, but you allow quite ordinary people to do such things as destroying wills which would disinherit them and profit by their wickedness. One looks for a retribution which never comes.' 'Well,' she said, 'isn't that exactly like life?' I had to admit that it was.

Philip Toynbee used to tell a story against himself of being invited to dine with Ivy Compton-Burnett and her companion, an expert on furniture, Margaret Jourdain. There were no other guests. As often happened when he came to London he had had too much to drink and he passed out with the soup. When he came to several hours later he found that no further notice had been taken of him. The ladies had proceeded quietly with their dinner, had spent their evening as though nothing untoward had happened and had gone to bed, presumably at their usual hour. Instructions had evidently been given that Philip was not to be disturbed and he was left to find his own way out of the house.

Robin and Renée Fedden were neighbours in Kensington of Martyn and Pinkie Beckett. I cemented my friendship with Martyn, which had been renewed on our expedition to the Isle of Wight; Pinkie was a sister of Lionel Esher, who as Lionel Brett had been junior to me in College at Eton. The Becketts were friends of the Rees's and also of Arthur Koestler. When Koestler invited me to watch the Hungarians play at Wembley he also invited Janetta Jackson, a clever and attractive girl with whom I shared many friends before we became lovers. Janetta had been married to Humphrey Slater and to Robert Kee and was then married to Derek Jackson, a friend of Philip Dunn the tycoon, equally rich and even more reactionary, an outstanding amateur jockey and, much more surprisingly, a first-rate spectroscopist. He and his brother had been the prize pupils of Professor Lindemann at Oxford.

Staying in the country with friends of Robin Fedden, I rediscovered 'Lizzie' Lezard of whom I have already written in *Part of My Life* as having become one of my closest friends, and in particular as having shared my interest in watching cricket and football. I remember with pleasure an expedition we made to Scotland to spend a few days with the collector and patron of the arts, Lord Crawford, at his house north of Edinburgh, Lizzie driving me all the way there in his small car. I had never been to Scotland before or indeed to the north of

England, except to take ship from Liverpool, and I was very much taken with the beauty of the north-eastern countryside.

The social circles which I frequented interlocked at many points. I came to know and admire the painter Matthew Smith through his being the lion of the salon presided over by the sculptress Cathleen Mann, the wife of John Follett, another friend of whom I have written in connection with the Welsh Guards. A prominent member of this circle was Polly North, working as a journalist under her maiden name of Polly Peabody, whose attraction for me was enhanced by her being the daughter of Caresse Crosby who, with her husband Harry Crosby, had formed a legendary couple in pre-war café society. I met Caresse Crosby two or three times and was pleasantly surprised to find her wholeheartedly devoted to the cause of World Government, displaying an optimism that I only wished that I could share. In a rather different vein, part of the attraction which I felt for Pam Peniakov was due to her being the widow of Colonel Peniakov, the eponymous organizer and leader of Popski's Private Army, a famous group of desert raiders in the war. Pam was later to marry Tom Matthews, a former editor of *Time* magazine for which Raimund von Hofmannsthal worked in London, thus completing another loop in the circle. I often spent part of my summer holidays staying with Raimund and Liz at their house in Austria at Zell-am-See, playing tennis with Liz and their son Octavian, whom I vainly tried to coach in arithmetic, and finding that my skill as a tennis player had not wholly deserted me.

My relationship with Jocelyn withstood our mutual infidelities. We were very much like an easy-going married couple, except that we did not live under the same roof. She was understandably vexed when someone did come to live with me. This was an actress called Alvys Maben, whom I had met through my friendship with another actress to whom indirectly, through our common friendship with the Stahls, I owed the discovery of my flat. Alvys was the daughter of a prosperous man of business in Birmingham, who had named her after his car. She had been briefly married during the war to a man who had been attached to the air force in some medical capacity and after divorcing him had entrusted the upbringing of her son to her own parents. She was a moderately successful actress, playing a leading part in the wireless soap opera *Mrs Dale's Diary*, and featuring in many of the plays that were shown in those early days of television.

I remember too her playing Gloria in a London production of Shaw's *You Never Can Tell*. She was fair and handsome and coped well with Renée who might have made a stronger effort to separate us had she not had troubles of her own. I was happiest with Alvys when she kept her own flat in Brompton Gardens. I used to take her to watch the Spurs and afterwards she drove me back to her flat and we had tea in front of the fire and played canasta. When she came to live in White-horse Street we could not recreate the same atmosphere of domesticity. I am afraid that I still subconsciously resented the invasion of my privacy, and she was too sensitive not to respond in kind. We went to Paris together for a short holiday and I introduced her to my friends there, one of whom, a French diplomat, immediately fell in love with her. Not long afterwards she left me to marry him. We remained on good terms until her death, some ten years later, in a motor accident.

5 *Philosophical Congresses, Berkeley and Wittgenstein*

The eleventh World Congress of Philosophy which was the first that I attended was held at Brussels in 1953. I have not investigated the origin of these congresses, which may well have persisted throughout this century; I did not come to learn of their existence until 1948 when the first post-war congress was held in Amsterdam. I was not able to attend it because I had already gone to the United States. Since the war the congresses have been held at five-yearly intervals, always at the end of August or the beginning of September and always in a different country. The proceedings have regularly been published, though always belatedly and not always in full.

Since the war at least the responsibility for deciding on a venue for the congresses has been assigned to an organization known by the acronym FISP standing for *Fédération Internationale des Sociétés de Philosophie*. This organization came under the aegis of UNESCO in Paris, from which it drew a modest subsidy. The planning of the congress was entrusted to a joint committee consisting in roughly equal parts of members of the executive committee of FISP and philosophers representing the country in which the congress was to be held. This committee selected a central theme for the congress, to which it never found the means of enforcing any strict adherence, and always had more papers submitted to it than it could fit into the time available for anything but the most perfunctory discussion of them. The most that the committee could do was to arrange for the delivery of some special lectures and organize two or three limited debates. There was a fee charged for admission to the congress which was

never enough to cover the cost of all the secretarial work, the shoulder-
ing not only of the expenses incurred by members of the committee at
all the preparatory meetings as well as at the congress itself, but also
of those incurred by the principal speakers, let alone the publication
of the proceedings. Since it was also the custom to provide entertainment for attendants at the congress in the form of concerts, parties,
banquets and excursions at uneconomic rates, the honour of acting as
host, and thereby securing for one of its professors the presidency of
FISP for the next five years, was purchased by the country in question
at rather a high price. Nevertheless there has never yet been a shortage
of countries that have been willing to pay it.

Apart from the organization of these world congresses, the only
function of FISP, at least at the time when I first became aware of its
existence, was to channel funds from UNESCO to the *Institution
Internationale de Philosophie*. The IIP, which had, and still has, its headquarters in Paris, was composed of philosophers from different
countries who were individually elected. There was a quota for each
country which, so far as I can ascertain, would never have exceeded
seven but for the fact that members over the age of seventy were
exempted from it. In the same way the total membership was restricted
to one hundred, a figure that has never yet been attained theoretically,
but would long ago have been exceeded if the ever-increasing number
of members over the age of seventy were counted in. The Institute
which was founded before the war by a Swedish philosopher Äke
Petzäll, who was sympathetic to logical positivism, and the French
philosopher Raymond Bayer, has always aimed at a wide geographical
coverage and has gone a considerable way towards achieving it,
although its membership has always been predominantly European.
No political bias has been shown, though the President of the Institute
has been instructed on various occasions to protest against the mal-
treatment of some philosopher, most often by a Communist regime
but also sometimes in Central or South America. For a long time the
admission of Soviet philosophers to the Institute was prevented by a
dispute about the method of their selection, the Institute maintaining
its right to make its individual choice, while the Soviet Academy of
Sciences insisted on installing its own nominees. In the end a formula
was reached which effectively gave the Russians what they wanted
without the Institute's having to appear to compromise its principle.
A similar difficulty in the case of Bulgarian philosophers was more

easily settled. The membership now extends so far as to include a philosopher from China, not a Marxist but an expert on the thought of Lao-Tse. I do not know that he has ever attended any of its meetings.

Ever since I joined it in 1953, the Institute has held an annual congress, occasionally in the spring but most often in late August or early September, so far as possible always in a different country and never in the same country in successive years. In the years when a World Congress was held, the Institute organized its own congress at the same time and place. Its meetings took the form of three or four symposia, with a principal speaker on each occasion and someone designated to open the discussion. An overall theme was fixed beforehand, but the choice of subjects for the particular debates was left to the hosts. So was the choice of speakers, who were not limited to members of the Institute. Almost invariably the discussions were recorded and the proceedings subsequently published, after an opportunity had been given to the participants to recast their remarks in grammatical form and perhaps even to sharpen their content. I think it can fairly be said that the philosophical level of the proceedings was superior to that of the proceedings of the World Congresses, but I should not wish to claim that it was exceptionally high. I attended these congresses assiduously, missing no more than three in the twenty-five years that followed my election to the Institute, and I cannot now recall any contribution to our debates that was of outstanding philosophical importance.

Probably the greatest utility of the Institute lay in the work of its committees. This does not apply to the committee over which I briefly presided, which was supposed to organize the translation of contemporary books in English, French, Italian or German into one or more of the other languages. We were unable to find publishers who were prepared to take the risk of losing money on the translations and we had no subsidies to offer. I believe that when Philippe Devaux took my place he did succeed in getting one or two English books translated into French but that was all. This was in contrast to the committees which were responsible, respectively, for the annual production of an international bibliography of philosophical books and articles, and for the translation of edifying choices like Locke's *Letter on Toleration* into such languages as Japanese. Both these committees were presided over by Raymond Klibansky and it was chiefly to his ardour that they owe their success. He was also responsible for bringing out two vast surveys of the state of contemporary philosophy, each in four large volumes, the first set covering the period from 1948 to 1955 and the second that from 1956 to 1967, with articles written in English, French or German. He coaxed money out of UNESCO to subsidize these publications, found a reputable Italian firm to undertake them, and persuaded many well-known philosophers from countries in all parts of the world to contribute the articles. I am ashamed to say that I never accepted his invitation to join their company.

To find his contributors Klibansky saw that he had to look beyond the IIP and in fact it must be admitted that when it was revived after the war the members of the Institute were at no great pains to choose the best philosophers in any given country to be of their number. It was rather a question of finding persons of some official standing who were both willing to join and also not averse to travel. There was no great harm in this except that the existence of the quota blocked the subsequent admission of philosophers of greater repute. The deficiency was perhaps most clearly marked in the cases of England, France and the United States. When I was elected, the other English representatives were Dr Ewing, Professor T. E. Jessop of Hull University, a most good-natured man and a lonely traveller, whose chief claim to philosophical distinction was his collaboration with Canon Luce of Trinity College, Dublin, in producing a fine edition of the complete works of Bishop Berkeley, and Professor L. J. Russell of Birmingham, a competent historian of philosophy who suffered perhaps through comparison with his namesake. Though no longer young, he was a resolute hiker and he and his equally elderly wife would arrive almost anywhere in Europe with knapsacks on their backs. Later I was able to strengthen the British representation by securing the election of Gilbert Ryle and Richard Braithwaite, and later still that of Peter Strawson and Bernard Williams, but the improvement was mainly nominal since, unlike their humbler predecessors, these more distinguished philosophers were not much addicted to travel, at least for such a doubtful purpose, and their attendance was at best spasmodic.

The French contingent included Jean Hyppolite and the philosopher of science A. Koyré, but it did not include Jean-Paul Sartre or Maurice Merleau-Ponty. If I remember rightly an invitation was extended to Sartre but disdained by him and this may have been one of the matters in which Merleau-Ponty was content to follow Sartre's lead. As for the United States, for many years its only active representative appeared to be Richard McKeon, a professor at the University of Chicago, best known as a translator and expositor of the works of Aristotle. He was reputed to have made life difficult for Rudolf Carnap, when Carnap accepted a Chair at the University of Chicago in 1936 rather than continue to face an uncertain future in Prague, but age had mellowed him and his lengthy contributions to our debates generally took the form of an attempt to show that the various disputants were fundamentally in agreement. In recent years the list of American members has become quite impressive, though it does not include either Nelson Goodman or W. V. Quine. In fact, Quine was elected many years ago but he never attended any meetings and fairly soon resigned.

Since I have said that the most useful work of the Institute has been accomplished by Raymond Klibansky, counting as a Canadian representative in virtue of his long occupation of a Chair at McGill University in Montreal, I should in fairness add that the Institute has been managed, for as long as I can remember, by Henry Dumery, by now a professor at one of the many universities of Paris, and that without his unobtrusive management the Institute would not have functioned at all.

An obstacle in the way of these international gatherings was the existence in nearly all countries of national organizations which might also hold annual meetings. I have already referred to the Joint Sessions of the Mind Association and the Aristotelian Society which took place early in July at the beginning of the summer vacation at a different university every year. Normally these meetings would be held at British universities of one sort or another, but in 1953 we broke our rule to the extent of foregathering at Trinity College, Dublin. The reason for this was that this year was the two hundredth anniversary of George Berkeley's death. Bishop Berkeley, as he eventually became, was born near Kilkenny and was buried at Oxford, in a chapel of Christ Church Cathedral, but he received his main education at Trinity College, Dublin, which he entered as a 'pensioner' in 1700 at the early age of fifteen, being elected to a Junior Fellowship in 1707, and it was in his early years as a Fellow that he wrote the works for which he is most famous: *An Essay towards a New Theory of Vision, Principles of Human Knowledge* and *Three Dialogues between Hylas and Philonous*, all published before he reached the age of twenty-nine.

Trinity College was then and long remained a Protestant enclave and Berkeley's preferments, first to the Deanship of Derry in 1724 and then ten years later to the Bishopric of Cloyne were in the Anglican church. It is perhaps not inconsistent with his always having been regarded as an Anglican rather than an Irish philosopher that Trinity College, Dublin, should lay a special claim to him.

This claim was most tenaciously sustained by the long-lived Canon Luce who pretty well succeeded in turning the philosophy department of Trinity into a centre of Berkeleian studies. He wrote a very readable life of Berkeley as a companion volume to the edition, running to nine volumes, in which Professor Jessop played the greater part in editing the philosophical and political texts, and he published a separate commentary in which he stresses and embraces Berkeley's 'immaterialism' as the confounding of 'sceptics and atheists' which Berkeley intended it to achieve. In fact, Berkeley's denial of the existence of matter is much less deserving of Boswell's description of it as an 'ingenious sophistry' when it is not so interpreted as to require the introduction of a deity as a universal sensorium. There are passages in Berkeley's works which would entitle him to be regarded as the originator of phenomenalism, concisely summarized by John Stuart Mill, who espoused it more than a century later, as the doctrine that material things are 'permanent possibilities of sensation'.

In this century, the doctrine was absorbed into the theory of neutral monism, adopted by William James and for a time by Bertrand Russell, according to which both mind and matter are logical constructions out of the sense-data and images which constitute the flow of our experiences. Subsequent writers made it clear that they took this to be a semantic theory. What they meant by saying that material things were logical constructions out of sense-data was that sentences about material things were translatable into sentences exclusively about sense-data. This was the thesis that I propounded in *Language, Truth and Logic*, and though I weakened it slightly in *The Foundations of Empirical Knowledge* by allowing that exact translations were not obtainable, owing to the fact that the sense-data in any given instance would belong to an indefinite and infinite range, I still maintained that in speaking of material things one was not doing anything other than express what would be mainly hypothetical propositions about sense-data. It was only in a lecture published in the proceedings of the Aristotelian Society for 1947–8, under the title of 'Phenomenalism' that I formally renounced the doctrine, on the ground that the obstacles in the way of giving even the outline of a translation were logically insurmountable. Nevertheless I remain sufficiently close to Berkeley to maintain that our common-sense conception of the external world can be exhibited as a warranted theory on the basis of something not very far removed from what he had understood by 'sensible qualities'.

Of the Joint Session itself I remember very little except that the Polish logician, Jan Łukaciewicz, made a speech, having been recruited in his old age not by Trinity but by a rival Catholic university in Dublin, and that an honorary degree was bestowed on Henry Price, at the time still Professor of Logic at Oxford. In view of the care and ingenuity with which he had handled the theory of sense-data in his book *Perception*, this seemed to me a particularly suitable award.

This was my first visit to Dublin and I admired the city, though it did not quite come up to my high expectations. For no special reason, I formed the impression that it was living on its past glories. I must, however, admit that I did not have the leisure to explore it at all thoroughly. After the congress, I stayed for a short while in a country house nearby, which belonged to some friends of the Crawshay-Williams' and of Robert Kee. Robert drove me round the countryside and I remember his annoyance when, instead of attending to the scenery, I started wondering how far sheep were conscious.

I believe that it was at this Joint Session in Dublin that I first made friends with Morris Lazerowitz and his wife, Alice Ambrose, though, as they were frequent visitors to England, it is possible that I had met them before. They had both studied at Cambridge and had a particular admiration and affection, which he no doubt returned, for G. E. Moore. Indeed, it was because of their initiative in securing a visiting professorship for Moore in 1940 at Smith College, a college for girls in Massachusetts, where they were both themselves professors, and the willingness of other American colleges to follow this example, that Moore, who had retired from his Cambridge Chair in 1939, was able to come with his wife to America during the war and so to prolong his university career. He remained in America till 1944, continuing to edit *Mind* until 1947 when he relinquished the office to Gilbert Ryle, having held it for twenty-one years. Though he lived until 1958, dying a few days short of his eighty-sixth birthday, I hardly saw anything more of him. His health prevented him from attending philosophical meetings and I did not feel that I knew him well enough to call on him at his house in Cambridge. I remember his presence at the Joint Session in Manchester in 1946, but otherwise my memories of him, which remain very fond, all go back to the 1930s.

Not only did I like the Lazerowitzes personally but I think that I am indebted to them philosophically. This is because of their insistence, itself prompted by their reflections on Moore's defence of common sense, that philosophers who make such statements as that nothing moves, or that time and space are unreal, or that no one can know that there are physical objects, or that there are experiences which are not their own do not literally mean what they appear to be saying. They are not asserting anything which is testable by observation so that Moore's appeal to common sense does not confute them. Neither are they concerned with the implications of ordinary usage. They are not suggesting that someone who claims to know that there are physical objects is misusing the English language. What then are they doing? According to the Lazerowitzes they are making linguistic proposals. They are suggesting that we drop the use of tenses, that we forego any talk of things being extended in space, that we talk no longer of knowing, but only at best of believing that other people have such and such thoughts and feelings. And Morris Lazerowitz at least has suggested that the desire for these changes issues from unconscious motives which psychoanalysis might bring to light.

I said that I was indebted to the Lazerowitzes because I think that they helped me to see that Moore's procedure somehow missed the point, and also contributed to my persuasion that one needed to do something more than merely discard metaphysics as nonsensical, though here the work of John Wisdom may have had a stronger influence upon me. On the other hand I have never been able to accept the Lazerowitzes' solution of their problem. So far as I know, they have never produced any evidence that philosophers are bent on the revision of linguistic usage; and where they might seem to be so I think it is usually because they have unearthed a logical difficulty, as in the case of Zeno's paradox. Obviously Achilles does catch the tortoise but the argument that by the time he reaches the tortoise's position the tortoise will have advanced a fraction further and so *ad infinitum* cuts deeply into our concepts of space and time and motion. Neither is it easy to see what unconscious motives could be at work. John Wisdom's cousin, J. O. Wisdom, has indeed published a small book in which he links Berkeley's denial of matter to his childish concern with his faeces, but even if the truth of this hypothesis could be established, I do not think that we should be relieved of the task of coping with Berkeley's arguments.

Alice Ambrose had been a favourite pupil of Wittgenstein's and one of the two to whom he dictated the notes which constituted the so-called *Brown Book* in which he developed the concept of language games. The lectures were delivered in 1934–5, and copies of the notes circulated in even greater secrecy than copies of the so-called *Blue Book* which contained accredited notes of lectures which had been delivered the year before. Both *Books* were published posthumously together in 1958. As I have indicated in *Part of My Life* Wittgenstein was easily affronted, especially by those whom he could regard as philosophically indebted to him, and he quarrelled violently with Alice Ambrose when she published an article in *Mind* on the philosophy of mathematics, which he regarded as a perversion of his ideas. So far as I know this breach was never healed.

Wittgenstein died in 1951 and his *Philosophical Investigations*, translated by Elizabeth Anscombe, appeared in 1953. As in the case of the *Tractatus*, the German text and its English translation appeared on facing pages. The work is divided into two parts of which the first and by far the longer was complete by 1945 and was intended by Wittgenstein to be published very largely in the form in which we know it. The second part was written between 1947 and 1949 and it is stated by the editors, Elizabeth Anscombe and Rush Rhees, that if Wittgenstein himself had published the book he would have substituted the sayings of this second part, with some additional material, for 'the last thirty pages or so of Part I'. In Part I the paragraphs are numbered, but not after the fashion of the *Tractatus*, where the use of decimals to as many as five places was designed to mark a logical sequence of thoughts. As Wittgenstein put it in his preface, the nature of his investigation which 'compels us to travel over a wide field of thought criss-cross in every direction' prevented him from following that precedent. He had to be content with a set of philosophical remarks which 'are, as it were, a number of sketches of landscapes which were made in the course of these long and involved journeyings'. He implied that this did not satisfy him and that it was only the plagiarism and misrepresentation from which he had suffered that induced him to publish the book at all. In fact he allowed nearly six more years to pass without publishing it, but perhaps he would have allowed it to appear in something like its present form if his life had been prolonged.

I have related in *Part of My Life* how strong an impression the *Tractatus* made on me when my tutor, Gilbert Ryle, introduced me to it in my last year as an undergraduate. By the time I finished writing *Language, Truth and Logic* three years later, I had come to the conclusion that if philosophy were to serve any theoretical purpose, apart from the banishment of metaphysics, it needed to devote itself to the logic of science. The rational course for me to pursue at this point would have been for me to try to acquire some expertise in one or more of the natural sciences or at least to improve the rather superficial understanding that I had gained of the intricacies of formal logic. In fact I did neither of these things. I continued to worry about problems in the theory of knowledge. *The Foundations of Empirical Knowledge*, which I published in 1940, was the measure of my success in solving them, but I did not flatter myself that it was devoid of error, still less that it left no further work to be done.

Though the manner of his disowning me, which I described in *Part of My Life*, may have lessened my personal respect for Wittgenstein, it had not detracted from my admiration of him as a philosopher. I had looked forward eagerly to the appearance of his *Philosophical Investigations* and hoped that I should find in it at least some important clues to the solution of the philosophical problems on which I had been working. In this I was disappointed. This is not to say that I did not, and do not still, consider it a brilliant piece of work. When I dip into it, as I quite often do, I find almost every passage absorbing; when I try to recall what I have learned from it, I find that the gold dust which I thought that I was amassing has somehow slipped through my fingers. If the book has a central theme it is set out in the following passage which occurs in paragraph 109 of its first part.

We may not advance any kind of theory. There must not be anything hypothetical in our considerations. We must do away with all *explanation*, and description alone must take its place. And this description gets its power of illumination – i.e. its purpose – from the philosophical problems. These are, of course, not empirical problems; they are solved, rather, by looking into the workings of our language, and that in such a way as to make us recognize those workings: *in despite of* an urge to misunderstand

> them. The problems are solved, not by giving new information,
> but by arranging what we have always known. Philosophy is a
> battle against the bewitchment of our intelligence by means of
> language.

I think that my failure to profit from the later work of Wittgenstein
goes together with my inability to acquiesce in this account of the
scope and limits of philosophy. If asked what I should put in its place,
I should be at a loss for any simple answer. The best I could achieve
would be to put my own work in evidence; and I am doing this to some
extent in the course of this book.

In 1953 the Knightbridge Professorship of Moral Philosophy at
Cambridge became vacant, owing to the retirement of C. D. Broad,
and I wondered whether I should apply for it. Admittedly, my contributions to moral philosophy were slight, consisting as they did
only in my trenchant but brief exposition of the emotive theory of
ethics in *Language, Truth and Logic*, a more soberly reasoned article 'On
the Analysis of Moral Judgements', sustaining much the same view,
which I had published in *Horizon* in 1949, the 1948 essay on 'The
Principle of Utility' which I mentioned earlier as my contribution to a
book entitled *Jeremy Bentham and the Law*, and my 'Freedom and
Necessity', contributed to *Polemic* in 1946, which still seems to me to
have commanded more respect than it deserves, but I assumed that
the titles of their Chairs did not weight more heavily on philosophers
in Cambridge than they did in Oxford and I knew that Broad himself
had not been much of a moralist, in spite of his characteristically brisk
survey of the field in his book *Five Types of Ethical Theory*. Accordingly
I wrote to my friend Richard Braithwaite at King's to ask whether he
thought that it would be worth my while to apply for the Chair. He
answered that it would not be absurd for me to enter but that in his
wife's opinion he himself was *much* the strongest candidate. Since I
concurred with this judgement, I gave up any thought of entering
and Braithwaite was in fact elected. He did not set up as a moral
theorist, beyond investigating the application to moral conduct of
the theory of games.

If I had wished to move to Cambridge, it would have been more
sensible for me to apply in 1951 for the other philosophical Chair,
which had become vacant first through Wittgenstein's deciding in
1948 that he disliked being a professor, leaving the way open for von

Wright to succeed him, and then through von Wright's own decision to return to his native Finland. At that date, however, I did not consider leaving London, and in any case should not have thought that I stood a chance against John Wisdom who had long been part of the Cambridge scene and was in fact deservedly elected. I have always been a great admirer of John Wisdom's work, especially the series of articles 'On Other Minds' which made up the greater part of the book that he published under that title in 1952. He is generous in acknowledging his debt to Wittgenstein but both in *Other Minds* and in his later collections of essays his style is very much his own.

I have already claimed to be a fluent French speaker but so far as I can recall the only article that I have originally published in French is one called 'L'Immutabilité du Passé' which I contributed to a review called *Les Etudes Philosophiques* in the first quarter of 1953. Though I never published an English version of it, it could be taken as a sequel to my Aristotelian Society address, 'Statements about the Past'. Its main thesis was that, so far as fixity went, the past and future were symmetrical. There is no changing the past; what has been has been: but equally in that purely logical sense, there is no changing the future; what will be will be. This is not to subscribe to fatalism. The future depends upon the present, in the sense that if things were different from what they are, if, for example, we were to be acting differently from the way we do, things would often be different from what they will be: but in this sense the past also depends upon the present, for if such and such present effects were not occurring the relevant causes would not have occurred. The point is that if causes are equatable with sufficient or necessary conditions or both, then they operate in either temporal direction. That causes should not succeed their effects appears an arbitrary stipulation. And yet it seems absurd to talk of trying to affect the past and quite sensible to talk of trying to affect the future. I was at a loss to account for this discrepancy otherwise than by suggesting that it might be due to our being endowed with memory and not, or only in exceptional cases, with precognition, and consequently knowing a great deal less about the future than we do about the past.

I sent an off-print of this article to Henry Price who characteristically fastened on to the question of precognition. He had no doubts about its occurrence but objected to my drawing a parallel between it and memory on the ground that whereas one could properly speak only of remembering one's own past experiences, one could precognize the future experiences of other persons as well as one's own. He suggested that if I wished to sustain the parallel I should have to enlarge the sense of 'memory' so that it embraced what the parapsychologists call 'retrodiction', that is, a process subjectively akin to memory but collecting experiences that had not in fact been one's own. I had no objection to this, nor did I doubt that retrodiction could occur as in George IV's 'remembering' that he led a charge at Waterloo. Price also remarked that to allow causality to work backwards in time might mean admitting the possibility of action at a distance, which he did not find unacceptable, though others might, and he suggested that 'the plain man' would find my argument much easier to accept if I spoke of the future as 'determining' rather than 'causing' the past.

By the autumn of 1953 I found that I had published enough articles during and since the war for it to be worth my collecting them into a book. I dedicated the book to Julian who was by then an Oppidan at Eton in the house of my old Eton and Christ Church friend, James Parr, and offered it to Macmillan who had published *The Foundations of Empirical Knowledge* in 1940. They were pleased to accept it and brought out a well-printed edition in the following year. The essays, which ranged in date from 1945 to 1954, were twelve in number and included the contributions to the Aristotelian Society and the ventures into the field of moral philosophy to which I have already referred. Thirty years later, there is none of them that I should wish to repudiate with the possible exception of an essay concerning 'One's Knowledge of Other Minds', originally published in the Swedish journal *Theoria* in 1953, where my attempt to buttress the argument from analogy by claiming that it is only a contingent fact that descriptions which are satisfied by other persons are not satisfied by oneself no longer seems to me felicitous.

The book was well received. I was especially pleased that it elicited a favourable review from Bertrand Russell, who remarked incidentally that he wished that he had written *Language, Truth and Logic*. This was an expression of his regard for me, rather than a mark of his conversion to logical positivism, to which he maintained a quite friendly opposition, regarding it as a much lesser evil than the Oxford cult of ordinary language. But he never adhered, for example, to the principle of verifiability. Thus in a letter to Elizabeth Crawshay-Williams,

The author in the early 1950s

Angelica Weldon

Jocelyn Rickards

At the Pekin Academy of
Sciences, 1954

Alvys Maben

Valerie Ayer, 1954

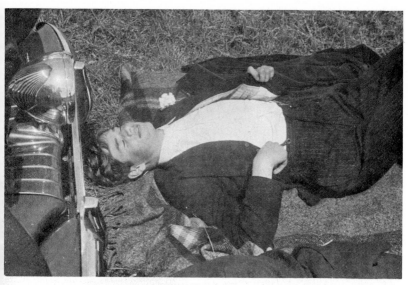

Julian Ayer at the Fourth of June, Eton, 1954

With Elizabeth von Hofmannsthal at Zell-am-See, 1957

Playing tennis at Zell-am-See, 1957

With Dee and Gully at 13 Conway Street, 1960

The Brains Trust, 1961. From right to left: Norman Fisher, Alan Bullock, Robert Bolt, Jacob Bronowski, the author

With Bertrand Russell on his ninetieth birthday, May 1962

With Raymond Carr and Hugh
Trevor Roper, 1962

Front row: the author with
John Bayley and Anthony
Quinton, New College, 1962

reprinted in Rupert's *Russell Remembered*, he complained that the date of an October meeting of the Metalogical Society was 'a secret locked within the breast of Professor A. J. Ayer'. 'If he were to die to-morrow,' he continued, 'there would be no way of ascertaining what date he had decided on & therefore, on the verification principle, he would not have decided on a date, which is absurd.' This may not be a knock-down argument, but it does underline the difficulty for the upholder of the verification principle of deciding whether to admit the paradoxes which result from making verifiability depend upon the identities and spatio-temporal positions of the speakers in question or whether to invoke the use of an ideal observer, whose powers it would not be easy to circumscribe.

I paid several visits to the Crawshay-Williams in their cottage at Portmeirion, mostly after Russell had left the area, but Patrick Blackett, the physicist, was still there as well as John Strachey and Clough and Annabel Williams-Ellis. I made little headway with John Strachey, despite his evolution from a theorist of Communism into a Labour minister, but I enjoyed the company of Patrick Blackett, and admired Clough Williams-Ellis as a work of art, much more so indeed than his pretentious rococo hotel. I did the Crawshay-Williams a bad turn through collapsing with jaundice on the very first evening of the weekend for which they had invited me and remaining as a patient, needing to be taken care of, in their cottage for a fortnight or more. The fault was mine in that I was already feeling so ill before I left London that I should not have inflicted myself upon them. They never took the risk of inviting me again though I remained friends at least with Rupert who quite often came to see me. I do not think that Elizabeth was hostile but she was sensitive about her deafness which set up a barrier between her and any but her closest friends.

Throughout 1954 I made a series of broadcasts on the Third Programme, which at that time was at its most hospitable to philosophy. By then I had largely overcome my shyness in the presence of the microphone though I preferred taking part in a discussion to reading from a script. Judging by a letter which I received from John Wisdom, a debate on the theory of knowledge which I conducted with members of my department came across well. I learned something about early Indian philosophy from a discussion into which I entered with an expert from the School of Oriental Languages. It appeared that there were interesting Indian schools of logic which petered out by about the ninth century AD, to be replaced by arcane varieties of metaphysics. I spoke on my own about free will and took part in a series which appeared as a small book under the rather over-confident title of *Revolution in Philosophy*. My contribution was a talk on the Vienna Circle.

By this time Valerie was working at the BBC. After leaving Wychwood she had spent some time with a family in Paris, attending lectures designed for foreign students at the Sorbonne. She enjoyed being in Paris but did not take the work too seriously. When she returned to England she took a secretarial course and went to work for an elderly lady of Russian origin, called Miss Kallin, who had become a BBC producer, concerned mainly with the Third Programme. Renée had given up her flat in Dolphin Square and taken another smaller house in Hampstead, which Valerie shared. This was not an entirely happy arrangement, mainly because Valerie needed to develop away from her mother's overpowering influence. The problem was solved by Miss Kallin who found Valerie a position with one of the main broadcasting companies in New York. The position was only temporary, but Valerie had never lost the romantic feeling for the United States which she had acquired in the years she spent there as a child, and I suspected that she would remain there for as long as she could make it possible.

6　*Visit to Russia and China*

In the summer of 1954, a few hours before I was due to leave London to stay with friends in France, I received a telephone call from a biologist at University College, with whom I had a nodding acquaintance. 'Would you care to visit China?' he said. 'The Chinese Government is inviting you.' When he had convinced me that he was serious, I said that I was very sorry but that I had already made arrangements for my summer holiday which it was now too late for me to cancel. He said that need not be an obstacle, since the Chinese invitation was for September. It was timed to coincide with the fifth anniversary of the Communist Revolution and those who accepted the Chinese Government's invitation would be taking part in the celebrations in Peking. Not wishing to enrol myself in a group of fellow-travellers, in the political sense of the term, I asked who else had been invited. Among the persons mentioned the only one whom I already counted as a friend was the architect, Hugh Casson, whose political opinions I knew to be Conservative. Telling my interlocutor that I needed a little time to consider his proposition and that I would shortly ring him back, I immediately rang up Hugh. 'Have you been invited to go to China?' I asked him. He said that he had and that like me he had temporized. 'Well,' I said, 'it is an astonishing windfall. I'll accept if you will.' 'All right,' he said. 'I was thinking just the same.' And so we both committed ourselves, leaving me at least to wonder why the Chinese had picked me out.

In fact, what had happened was this. Some months before a letter had been circulated expressing good-will towards the Chinese people. Though presumably drafted by Communists, its contents were of an extremely innocuous character, effectively saying nothing more than that the signatories respected the ancient culture of China and hoped that any political differences that might arise between our respective governments could be settled by peaceful means. The draft was sent to almost everyone of any note in the domains of the arts and sciences and some seven hundred of them signed it, many of them persons of international eminence, those eminent persons who always do sign things, as someone sourly put it to me. The organizers of the affair then sent the letter, with its impressive list of signatures, to the Chinese People's Society for Cultural Relations with Foreign Countries, the Chinese equivalent of our British Council. Not knowing, perhaps, how easily such signatures were obtained in England, and possibly also over-estimating the political influence of the kind of persons who supplied them, the Chinese authorities offered to pay for five of the signatories to come to Peking, to deliver the letter to the Chinese Academy of Sciences, and to spend up to a month in China as their guests. I do not know how the five were selected. Presumably the greater luminaries found it inconvenient or impolitic to embark on such a venture; not all of us may have been even among the second choices, but naturally this was not revealed to us. In the end the party consisted of Hugh Casson, the painter Stanley Spencer, the writer Rex Warner, Professor Hawkes of Bedford College, London University, whose subject was geology, and myself. John Chinnery, a young lecturer in Chinese at the School of Oriental Studies, accompanied us as secretary and interpreter. We were told that the delegation had to have a leader and Professor Hawkes, a tall, calm, good-humoured elderly man appeared to be the obvious choice.

Considering that, except for Hugh Casson and myself, we had not come together by choice and that we were constantly in one another's company for over a month, occasionally in trying circumstances, we got on very well. I formed a particularly close friendship with Rex Warner, a discerning epicurean a few years older than myself. I already admired him as a novelist before coming to like him as a man, and in spite of its allegorical flavour, which would normally not appeal to me, I still consider his book *The Aerodrome* to be one of the best English novels to be written in the 1930s. Rex is an accomplished classical scholar who has produced among other things a very good translation of Thucydides and I do not know why his novels *The Young Caesar* and *Imperial Caesar*, published in 1958 and 1960, and written ostensibly by Julius Caesar in the first person, have never achieved the same popularity as Robert Graves's similar novels about Claudius. I am sure they would be equally worth dramatizing.

If there was an undercurrent and sometimes more than an undercurrent of friction in the party, it arose from the dislike which Stanley Spencer and I quite quickly came to feel for one another and did not always make much effort to conceal. I did not, and still do not, question his skill as a painter, though I tend to be repelled by the mixture of eroticism and religiosity that appears in much of his work, but he remains in my memory as the most self-centred man that I have ever met. His gnome-like appearance was not unappealing and I could bear with his minor eccentricities, such as his taking pains to look dishevelled and his wearing pyjamas as underclothes. It was his conversation that wore me down. He lived at Cookham, a small town on the Thames which was the locus of many of his paintings, and he had served in Mesopotamia in the First World War, and he could hardly utter a sentence without referring to one or the other. He also had the habit, which I found maddening, of assuming that we were familiar with all the details of his private life, referring to various women by their Christian names and recounting episodes in his biography as if we had taken part in them. If in turn I gave him reason to dislike me, it was mainly because I sharply contradicted the statements he made about the meaning of life and even about aesthetics. As a man nearly twenty years my senior and a much greater celebrity he felt himself entitled to more respect. I know that he also got on Hawkes's nerves but Hawkes was too nice a man to show it. Hugh and Rex were sometimes irritated but chiefly amused by our propensity to squabble.

It had been arranged that our route to China and back should take us both times through Russia. I should have liked to savour the experience of travelling by the Trans-Siberian railway, but we did not have the leisure for that, especially as Professor Hawkes and I had to be back in London for the beginning of the autumn term. As it was I earned a mild rebuke from Ifor Evans for being several days late. Accordingly, with one exception in China, which I shall come to in its place, we did all our travelling by air. Even this took up a considerable portion of our time. The Russian aeroplanes in which we traversed Siberia made frequent stops. According to the record which I kept at the time we made twenty-five separate flights in the whole course of our expedition and spent a total of seventy-nine hours in the air. This leaves out of account the hours spent loitering in aerodromes. I had brought with me several volumes of the Everyman edition of Gibbon's *Decline and Fall of the Roman Empire*, which I had never previously read. Hugh Casson bet me that I should never get through them, but I just managed it by an intensive course of reading on our return journey.

It was already possible to fly directly from London to Moscow, but we chose to break our journey at Prague. I had paid a brief visit to Prague in 1933, when I had admired the beauty of the old city and received a general·impression of middle-class contentment. On this occasion, the impression made on all of us was very different indeed. Five or six years had passed since the death of Jan Masaryk and the purge of Slansky and his followers but an air of listlessness, of hopeless depression, greeted the visitor like a clammy southern wind. Presumably some people were thriving under the current regime and others bravely engaging in clandestine opposition but there was no mistaking the general sense of defeat and despair. Even the beauty of the city had been marred by the erection, in white marble, of a gigantic monument to Stalin and the Red Army, which was so placed on the heights of the city that it seemed to meet the eye at every turn. One of the few good results of the abortive Czech rising in 1968 was the destruction of this monstrosity.

We spent twenty-four hours in Prague, which confirmed our resolve not to revisit it on our return journey. We expected to be flown from there directly to Moscow, but Russian civil aircraft at that date were not allowed to fly unless the weather conditions were perfect, and since that was not the case we had to spend a night in Minsk before reaching Moscow. I cannot explain why the name 'Minsk' still has a romantic sound for me. It draws no support from anything that we discovered in the city.

We had expected to spend only a short time in Moscow, but in fact we remained there for five days. The delay was due to our having low priority among the delegations that were making their way to Peking to take part in the anniversary celebrations. The Chinese authorities, who took charge of all our expenses, had arranged for us to stay at the Metropole Hotel, an old-fashioned place with an agreeable echo of Edwardian luxury. The waiters in the hotel restaurant, which was always full, looked like survivors from the *ancien régime*. The service was extremely slow but we were too busy gorging ourselves on caviar to care. I am told that the pollution of the waters where the sturgeon breed has since turned caviar into a luxury, even in Moscow, but then it was plentiful and popular. The rest of the menu was less appetizing, mostly scrawny chicken and goose.

Stalin had died the year before and his body was ensconced with Lenin's in the mausoleum in Red Square, from which it was later to be removed. Already his portrait was little in evidence in Moscow, though we were to find it still prominently displayed in provincial aerodromes. No single successor to him had yet emerged, with the effect that there was a comparative dearth in shops, hotels and other public places of photographs of any members of the Politbureau. This was in contrast to Prague where pictures of the leading Czech Communists greeted us everywhere, in conjunction with those of Malenkov whom the Czechs had wrongly forecast as Stalin's successor. Though the Russians may have been wondering what was next in store for them, it was obvious that in Moscow at least Stalin's death had produced an atmosphere of détente.

This was my first visit to the Soviet Union, I do not speak Russian, we had no official standing during our five days spent in Moscow, and no access to any special source of information, but I think that the impressions which I then reached may still be of some interest. The people of Moscow did not appear downtrodden like the Czechs, or exuberant as we were to find the Chinese, but much like the people to be seen on the streets of any modest provincial city in the West. One thing that particularly struck us was the drabness of people's clothes, the absence of any attempt on the part of either sex to cut any sort of dash. We were told that good clothes were made in Russia but that it suited the current production programme that they be very expensive, beyond the means of any but a privileged minority. This was the year for buying refrigerators. The turn of clothes would come later. In general, so far as we could tell by looking at the shops, there seemed to be a fair supply of consumer goods, perhaps not of the very best quality. It was difficult for us to judge of prices. Translated into pounds at the official rate everything was fiendishly expensive, but the official rate was wholly artificial and we did not venture into the black market. Compared with other goods food and drink seemed reasonably cheap.

Since we were visiting Moscow only in transit, nobody took much notice of us. We were left free to wander about as we pleased. This rather surprised us as we had been led to expect that foreigners were kept under close surveillance. Perhaps there was some discreet sur-veillance or perhaps we were not considered of sufficient importance to be watched. The Intourist agency did put cars at our disposal and, when we wanted, an English-speaking guide. We travelled a short distance on the Moscow underground, which was a source of local pride. Its stations were decorated like Lyons Corner Houses. Aesthetically we were most impressed by the Kremlin and the Bolshoi Theatre, where we saw performances of Verdi's opera *Aïda*, and Prokofiev's ballet *Cinderella*. The stage of the Bolshoi, itself a very handsome eighteenth-century building, seemed exceptionally wide and deep, making the appearance of the Egyptian army in *Aïda* un-commonly effective, the decors were impressive in their realistic way and the lighting superb. Evidently no expense was spared. We judged that these performances were extremely popular. The house was packed on both occasions and people approached us outside with offers to buy our tickets. The part of Cinderella was taken by Lepeshinskaya who then ranked third or fourth in the hierarchy of Russian ballerinas. I am not a connoisseur of the art of ballet, but for what my opinion is worth I thought she danced as well as anyone that I had ever seen. I had once seen Pavlova perform in London but only at a time when she was past her best.

The Kremlin was a surprise to us. Because of its associations I had expected it to be a grim, sinister fortress. The appearance it actually presented was that of a bright, fantastic set of buildings, freshly painted in yellow, white and green with golden Byzantine cupolas. Most of it was open to the public and it was daily thronged with parties of what can best be described as pilgrims, reverently listening to, and in some cases writing down, every word that their guides had to say about the very costly but for the most part very ugly objects acquired by various Tsars with which the museum was filled. What we most admired in the Kremlin were three small churches containing a number of very fine medieval ikons, which had been most com-petently restored. We were told that the whole complex was soon to be a museum. The Government had resolved to evacuate it and instal itself in one or more of the new skyscrapers which were in the process of being built.

These skyscrapers, of which there were to be five or six in all, were being erected at suitably chosen points as part of a plan to raise the skyline of Moscow. Three of them were already finished. The largest, and the greatest source of pride, was the new science building of the University. As in Birmingham at the same date, the humanities were allowed to remain in the old University; in Moscow's case, a modest but attractive eighteenth-century building in the centre of the town. The new science building, on the outskirts, was a very large Gothic skycraper and architecturally, it seemed to us, most unattractive; there were, however, said to be those who liked it. At least it was very handsomely equipped. We had no means of appraising the educational standard, but the length of time which we were told that it took to get a degree would suggest that the level of entrance was lower than in the best English universities. An undergraduate course was said to last five years. After that, if one wanted to do research, one spent three years before one achieved the status of being a candidate for a doctor's degree, and then another five years before one could obtain a doctorate, a total of thirteen years study. This seemed to us a great deal, but we may not have been correctly informed; or it may be that the doctorate had an unusually high value. We were told that it was not a requisite even for university teaching, any more than it used to be in England.

The speed with which such buildings were erected was extraordinary. The unskilled labour force seemed to consist mainly of women, who worked like the sturdy peasants that they appeared to be. There was a gang of them whom we could watch from the windows of our hotel as they tossed bricks around from dawn till dusk. The building on which they were working seemed to go up before our eyes, like the buildings in film cartoons. This is hardly an exaggeration. When, on our flight from Moscow to Peking, our aeroplane landed at Novosibirsk, we walked on duckboards to a shack which served as an aerodrome. On our way back, less than four weeks later, we found an asphalt path and a new three-storey aerodrome, not beautiful indeed – what aerodrome ever is? – but solid and well-appointed.

Our overall impression of Russia at that time was that on the surface it was very like Victorian England. There was the same expanding economy, the harsh conditions of labour, a comparable jingoism, a similar sanctimoniousness and moral earnestness, the same predilection for social realism, contemporary Soviet painting being very like English academic painting of the mid-nineteenth century, and the furnishings in public rooms, which were all that we saw, being mid-Victorian down to the antimacassars. Later experience has revealed that there were elements of the same romantic, destructive, nihilistic undercurrents, but these we were not in a position to detect any more than we were made aware of the repression that survived Stalin's death.

Flying across Siberia was a wearisome business. My chief impression was that of the immense size of the country. It occurred to me that if Napoleon or Hitler had ever made such a journey they would have been less ready to embark on their invasions. Moscow is almost on the frontier. Our aeroplane, more of a rattletrap than the newer model with which we were supplied on our return, was not equipped for long distance flying. The places at which we landed every two and a half hours had names that I found romantic – Kazan, Sverdlovsk, Omsk, Novosibirsk, Krasnoyarsk, Irkutsk – and I conceived an arbitrary affection for Omsk, but in fact there was little to choose between the aerodromes, the apsects of the cities from the air or the stretches of country in between.

At Irkutsk on the shores of Lake Baikal, described by Gibbon as an expanse of water which disdains the appellation of a lake, we were held up for forty-eight hours, and were lucky that it was not longer. The trouble was that the runways in Peking were not yet equipped for the reception of aeroplanes except in daylight. To arrive at Peking in daylight it was necessary to leave Irkutsk at dawn. Our aircraft would not take off unless the sky was clear. Irkutsk in September was nearly always enshrouded in an early morning mist arising from Lake Baikal. Our spirits dropped to their lowest point in the whole expedition. Since Irkutsk was in a fortified zone, we were not allowed to leave the airport. We were amazed to read in the visitors' book an entry by Hewlett-Johnson, the Red Dean of Canterbury, beginning 'I have spent three useful days in Irkutsk'; we wondered what a useless day in the Deanery could be like. But presumably Hewlett-Johnson was at least allowed to visit the town. Caviar and vodka were indeed available to us but the roubles with which the Chinese had provided us to cover incidental expenses were running short. On the whole our tempers stood the test well. Stanley and I were even too dispirited to quarrel. I spent most of the time playing picquet with Rex, finishing by owing him a very large notional sum. Then suddenly, early on the third morning, there was a break in the mist. The whole airport came frantically to life. We rushed to collect our belongings and scampered to the plane. A couple of hours later we were breakfasting on yoghourt on the outskirts of Ulan Bator, the capital of

Outer Mongolia, watching a camel caravan make its way slowly towards us across the Gobi desert.

The sensation of flying over the Gobi desert and the mountains that governed the western approaches to Peking was matched in my experience only by the sensation of flying over the Andes. There is even a parallel between the terraced agriculture of North China and Peru. I can still remember the excitement with which I caught my first glimpse of the Great Wall of China, stretching out below us, of which Gibbon wrote: 'This stupendous work which holds a con-spicuous place in the map of the world, has never contributed to the safety of an unwarlike people.' Shortly afterwards we landed at Peking aerodrome. I was astonished to hear a band playing and to see what I thought I recognized as the leaders of the Chinese Government waiting to greet us. I happened to be the first to get out of the aero-plane. I had not taken more than a few steps before the band stopped playing, the dignitaries retreated, and our aeroplane was hastily shunted to a remote corner of the aerodrome where five men in horn-rimmed spectacles stood waving small Union Jacks. What had happened was that the aeroplanes had arrived in the wrong order. We had usurped the place of the Roumanian Government's delega-tion. Our own reception committee made us welcome with cups of tea and escorted us to our comfortable hotel.

I came to think of Peking as the most attractive city that I had ever visited but its charm was not immediately obvious. It did not have the direct appeal of Paris or New York. As we drove into it from the aerodrome it seemed rather ramshackle. It had in fact been built to a plan, three cities enclosing one another, like a series of Chinese boxes, but the plan was not evident, except possibly from the air. The build-ings were low and none of them stood out. It was only when we had the opportunity to explore the city, to visit its temples and palaces, its pagodas and lakes and parks that its fascination made itself felt. It was impossible for us to determine the age of any of the public monu-ments. They were all built of wood, perfectly proportioned according to strict rules, governed largely by astrology, with curiously curved roofs, decked out with images to repel evil spirits, brightly painted in colours that gained lustre from the astonishing blue of the sky. When such buildings had burned down accidentally or through enemy action they had been rebuilt as before. Much of their attraction, for me at least, came from the parks and lakes and gardens by which they were surrounded. The lakes particularly gave to this bustling city of what were then three million people, but now must be many more, an air of extraordinary serenity. The parks and gardens were full of what looked like sculptures by Henry Moore but were in fact stones which had acquired their shapes naturally. They were much sought after and had been brought to Peking from all over China. The Chinese seemed to have a taste for what might be described as natural deformities, though there were other social reasons for their practice, abandoned since the Sun Yat Sen revolution, of binding women's feet. A great many of the trees, for example, were groomed so as to look like the trees in their paintings. It was though they had been persuaded by Oscar Wilde to try to make nature imitate art. Even the goldfish, of which there were a great many on show in the public parks, were bred for strangeness. They were large and beautiful and of almost every colour besides gold.

At that time Peking was still in the main a medieval town. The Forbidden City, so called because it had been reserved for the Emperor and his court, had a splendid boulevard, said to date back to the time of Genghis Khan, running past its main entrance, but the outer cities displayed a cluster of alleyways and courtyards, narrow streets where the shops were all devoted to a single trade, so as to form the street of the antique dealers, the silk merchants, the cobblers or whatever, markets where people seemed to sit for hours sipping tea and listening to story tellers or watching jugglers and acrobats. We also saw the jugglers and acrobats performing on the stage, to which they are probably by now confined. These troupes were more skilful than any others that I have ever seen.

Whether inside or outside Peking there were very few good roads. Those outside were so dusty that if one drove on them it was advisable to wear a mask. The wearing of such masks was a custom introduced by the Japanese, and almost the only evidence of their former presence in China. Altogether there was very little motor traffic: a few trams crowded to the brim at all times of day, a few cars put at the disposal of officials or of visitors like ourselves. When the occupants were very important, more so than we were judged to be, the cars had curtains to shield them from the public gaze. Members of the Labour Party delegation, led by Mr Attlee, whose visit overlapped with ours, took exception to this practice but I doubt if it was anything more than a continuance of the imperial tradition.

Bicycles were among the few machines that the Chinese themselves produced in any quantity and there were a great many of those. They were used to pull rickshaws, of which we saw greater numbers than there appeared to be customers for them. I saw one hand-pulled rickshaw in Shanghai, none in Peking and we were told that no new rickshaws were being manufactured, though the rickshaw men, who were all owner-drivers, were to be allowed to continue their trade so long as they could keep their vehicles in repair. The goods that came into the city were mostly brought in mule and donkey carts. I even saw camels at the outer gates.

The city I am describing is the Peking of thirty years ago, which I have never revisited. My information as to its present condition comes mainly from Sir John Addis, a pupil of mine at Christ Church before the war, who was Chargé d'Affaires at the time of my visit, entertaining me handsomely at his house in the Old British Compound, and became our Ambassador to China after diplomatic relations had been officially resumed. He told me that the old gates and many of the old houses have been pulled down and that the modernization has conformed to the depressing pattern of socialist realism. A redeeming factor is that the Forbidden City has been preserved. This accords with the intention, frequently expressed to us, of maintaining at least the aesthetic values of the past. Our guides were constantly informing us that monuments and temples which had been allowed to fall into disrepair during the Kuomintang regime were now being faithfully restored. We were told also that the geologists who were digging up the soil of China in a search for mineral deposits were accompanied by teams of archaeologists on the quest for objects of cultural and historical interest. We saw an impressive exhibition in Peking of items which had been discovered in this way in the previous eighteen months. The exhibition which went on tour in Europe some years ago allows one to hope that in spite of the ravages of the Cultural Revolution this practice has not been wholly discontinued.

We were attracted not only by the physical aspects of Peking but by the spectacle of its inhabitants. I do not know how it came to be thought that the Chinese were inscrutable. They had, in the main, the gayest, most animated, most expressive features of any people that I had ever come across. They were inscrutable, especially to me who did not speak their language, only in so far as one was sometimes left wondering what all the animation, the apparently spontaneous air of friendliness, might conceal. Not that we had any reason to mistrust their appearance. There was an almost complete uniformity of dress: blue coats and trousers for the ordinary citizens, both men and women, blue or grey uniforms for persons in official positions. There were occasional variations of colour, and a few old people wore traditional costumes. We saw a fair number of people in Shanghai wearing Western clothing, but hardly any in Peking. Surprisingly, the uniformity of dress did not produce an impression of drabness. This was partly because the people themselves were so full of life, partly because so many of those that one saw in the streets were small children, in blue rompers unbuttoning at the back, the most attractive children that I have ever seen. In the light of this profusion of children, in Peking alone, I can well believe that the population of China, which was estimated at six hundred million when we were there, has risen to a thousand million in the last thirty years.

We saw the people of Peking *en masse* on 1 October, the date of the celebration of the fifth anniversary of the proclamation of the new republic. There was a parade lasting four hours in which a quarter of a million of them took part, an exhausting spectacle, since we had to stand to watch it, but very impressive in its way. Only a fraction of it was military. In the main it consisted of groups of factory workers carrying banners, standing on floats and waving paper flowers, so that for most of the time the whole vast square in front of the entrance to the Forbidden City, where Mao Tse Tung, flanked by members of his Government and foreign, principally Russian, delegates stood taking the salute, was a sea of paper flowers, also of groups of children, letting loose balloons and doves of peace, of athletes, male and female, showing off their skills, of dancers whirling past with a fluttering of scarves and fans, with each group, as it passed the saluting point, shouting out slogans of fidelity to the regime, or to Mao Tse Tung himself and hostility to their enemies, principally the United States. The whole affair, including the marshalling of the spectators, was perfectly organized; every phase began and ended at the appointed time; and in the evening there was a two-hour display of fireworks which, after all, the Chinese invented, and dancing in the streets. For all the stage management, even the late-night dancers tending to march away in groups, I was left in little doubt that the enthusiasm displayed was genuine, that the loyalty of the people, or at least the people that we had seen, had been very largely captured by their present government. It must be remembered that this was the period at which the Government was at its most liberal, the period when it was building up to the fatal experiment of the hundred flowers. The brutality of the Cultural Revolution, its almost equally disastrous aftermath, and the cynicism which these traumas bred all lay in the future.

The leader of the Russian delegation was Khrushchev, who had not yet emerged as the successor to Stalin. We had to listen to his making a very long fraternal speech in Russian, a language which none of us understood, and then to its being interpreted at equal length into Chinese. Fortunately, when the interpreter began to speak, I spotted a door leading into a garden into which I was able to escape.

I am tempted to claim that I met Khrushchev but it would not be true. He and I were present at a party distinguished also by the presence, among many others, of Mao Tse Tung, Chou En Lai, the Dalai Lama and the Panchen Lama, but I did not speak to any of them. The Dalai Lama looked like an American college boy with a row of pens in his breast pocket for signing autographs. Of our little group only Hugh Casson was bold enough to obtain one.

Our own ceremony was conducted without fanfare. The President of the Chinese Academy of Sciences, accompanied by members of his council, received our letter with its impressive list of signatories. We signed our own names over again in a special book. Professor Hawkes made a short speech in which he thanked the Academy for its hospitality, and the President made an equally short and suitable reply. Both speeches were interpreted, though several members of the Chinese Academy spoke quite good English. The proceedings concluded soberly with our drinking cups of tea.

Sobriety was not the keynote of our social relations with our Chinese hosts. The Mandarin cooking in our hotel, and in the restaurant in which we were served our farewell banquet, was superb, better than any Chinese food that I have eaten anywhere outside Peking. We were also liberally supplied with a beer, not unlike lager, which the Chinese make themselves and drink in large quantities and with a fiendish spirit called mao-tai, similar to vodka but stronger and coarser. When challenged with the word 'ganbi' one was supposed to drain one's glass of mao-tai at a gulp. Rex and I were quickly identified as the drinkers in our party, so that we were frequently challenged and never failed to respond. I am proud to say that we always emerged with honour.

Western food also was served at the hotel. If one wanted it one sat at a rectangular table; the tables at which Chinese food was served were circular. We usually preferred Western food for breakfast, though not for any other meals. Once or twice Stanley Spencer made the mistake of sitting at a circular table at breakfast and became very angry when he was denied his eggs and bacon, berating the Chinese waiters in pidgin French. He was also apt to be curt with our guides, but they did not seem to resent it. He was old and eccentric, both of them qualities which had traditionally been accorded respect in China, and perhaps are still. They also admired his style of painting, which bore some similarity to their own. He stayed on in Peking to paint after the rest of us had left to return home.

Mao's notorious Little Red Book had not yet been published, but copies of his essays, translated into English, were put beside our beds in the hotel, like copies of the Gideon Bible in hotels in the United States. I was particularly interested by his pamphlet entitled 'Contradiction', in which he claimed to have discovered a new Marxist principle, namely the principle of the particularity of contradiction. What it amounted to was that all processes were dialectical, in as much as all change took place through the conflict of opposing forces, but each process was dialectical in its own way. It followed that there were no dialectical laws in any strict sense; the same initial conditions might be coupled with different results. Politically, this could be taken to mean that the Chinese were not obliged to imitate the Russians. Philosophically, it constituted not a modification of the dialectic but its abandonment. For a law of nature, as classical Marxists previously took their law of contradiction to be, which cannot cover any instance without *ad hoc* interpretation, is no law at all. When treated in this fashion, Marxism becomes a framework into which you try to fit your observations, not a theory about the character of the events which you might expect to observe. The Chinese have always had a reputation for being a practical people, and in giving their Marxism an empirical twist Mao was being true to this tradition.

The local philosophers, whom I mischievously tried to persuade that Mao was less of a Marxist than a pragmatist, clearly had to make at least a show of disagreeing with me, but in fact they were not very much interested in Marxism. Their pupils were obliged to study it, but the main burden of teaching it fell upon a Russian who had been specially imported for the purpose. What the Chinese professors chiefly cared about was formal logic. The first question put to me was: What had Gödel most recently written? Almost without exception, they spoke good English and had in many cases worked at English or American universities. The philosopher of whom I saw most was a disciple of G. E. Moore's. He visited me a year or two later in England and said that he was arranging for one or two of my books to be translated into Chinese, but this was no longer possible after the failure of the hundred flowers. At the time we were there, there was in Peking even a positivist professor who had attended meetings of the Vienna Circle. The history of Western philosophy was part of the curriculum as well as the study of ancient Chinese philosophy. I cannot believe that this continued throughout the Cultural Revolution, but I am glad to know that both the positivist and the leading expert on Taoism have survived.

I gave a lecture at Peking University on contemporary British philosophy. It was not altogether a success, first because the audience was kept waiting for a very long time through a rare failure of organization, which was no fault of mine and secondly because I had to break off every ten minutes to make way for my interpreter, which made it difficult for me to develop my theme in a coherent fashion. All the same, my performance was politely received.

We talked to a number of writers, who seemed already to be in a worse position than the philosophers, no doubt because they were thought to cater for a larger public and therefore were more harassed by the nascent official doctrine that literature should serve the interests of the people. We were given several volumes of recent novels and short stories to read in translation and found them depressing. A typical short story might relate how such and such a private in the Red Army finds the hardship of a march too great and is tempted to drop out, but then one of his comrades or the political commissar reminds him of all that Chairman Mao and the Government and the Party are doing for him; he marches on, distinguishes himself in battle and is allowed to join the Communist Party as a reward. Or else, it might depict an office worker who attempts to tyrannize his wife and daughter. His colleagues at the office intervene with their criticism. They explain to him the workings of the new marriage laws: he becomes aware of his error and behaves differently in future. Not all writers, however, were yet reduced to working at this level. The Chinese classics were still closely studied and much foreign literature was being translated. Among English authors Fielding and Dickens seemed especially popular, as well as Shakespeare. I met one man who was engaged in the heroic task of translating Hamlet into Chinese verse.

Apart from having to make good our claim to be a cultural delegation, we were treated as slightly privileged tourists. We made a special excursion to the Great Wall of China, from which I abstracted one or two pebbles as a souvenir, long since lost, and another to visit the Ming Tombs, the finest monuments that I had seen since Machu Picchu. They are approached by a long avenue flanked on either side by large statues of animals. Hugh Casson stopped for a minute in front of a statue of a camel and said that he was attracted to women who looked like camels 'That's why I married my wife.' I did not take him altogether seriously.

We were taken to the theatre often enough for me to acquire a taste for Chinese opera. There were several varieties of it. The most important were the Peking opera in which traditionally all the parts had been taken by men, as in the Kabuki theatre in Japan, though in the Peking opera women had recently been allowed to perform, and the Shanghai opera, in which all the parts were still taken by women. The Peking opera, like the Kabuki theatre, contains a very large element of miming: it is almost a ballet, with passages of recitative. The Shanghai opera is almost wholly recitative. The words are sung or spoken in a curious falsetto, common to both sexes, and the music strikes very strangely and at first rather unpleasantly upon a Western ear. I found, however, that I quickly became accustomed to it and I was enchanted by the wit and grace of these productions, the movement of the actors, the elaboration of their gestures with fans and sleeves. The themes of these operas were mostly drawn from ancient folk-tales. Of the six pieces that I saw only one was propagandist. It was an interesting and fairly successful attempt to fit a modern didactic story, that of the victimization of a peasant girl by a wicked landlord who is finally brought to retribution, into a traditional mould. This opera, called *The White Headed Girl*, appeared to be very popular, but not more popular than others without a moral. One of the charges later to be levelled against Chiang Ch'ing, Mao's widow and a member of the Gang of Four, was that she had suppressed the ancient folk-tales in favour of new and inferior pieces of propaganda.

After spending rather more than a fortnight in Peking we were flown to Shanghai, a Westernized industrial city of some seven million inhabitants, a number which I believe has since been almost doubled. In the two days that we spent there we found nothing that was particularly attractive and comparatively little that was distinctively Chinese. From Shanghai we were taken south by train to Hangchow. A special coach was added to the train, with a compartment for each of us in case we wanted to be alone. Not only that, but an opera company travelled from Shanghai for the especial purpose of giving a performance for our benefit in Hangchow on the following evening.

Hangchow must be, or anyhow have been, one of the most romantic places in the world. It lay on the shores of the Western Lake, a favourite venue for Chinese painting. All over the lake were little islands with crooked bridges, like those to be seen on Chinese plates, and tea-houses where they served the most delicious green tea. The hillside all around was dotted with Buddhist temples and painted caves. The inhabitants with whom we conversed were rightly proud of their city. Some of them spoke English and I had a lively discussion with a local teacher about Heisenberg's principle of indeterminacy.

The two or three days that we spent in Hangchow were the climax of our expedition. Nothing untoward happened to us on our return flight across Siberia. This time we did not linger in Moscow and broke our journey home at Stockholm rather than Prague. We were struck by the opulence of the goods on display in Stockholm as compared with those in Moscow.

We were each given a farewell present on leaving Peking. Mine was a statue of a medieval warrior, presumably a modern copy of an ancient piece, but still very attractive. I nursed it all across Siberia, through Moscow and Stockholm and dropped it on the asphalt at London airport. Fortunately it broke cleanly into three pieces and I was able to have it repaired so that the lines of breakage do not show. I cherish it still.

Our visit must have been accounted a success, since similar groups were invited from England to visit China in the following four years. The last group to go included Graham Greene and Hugh Trevor-Roper who were rumoured not to have had such a smooth passage with their hosts. Possibly for this reason, more probably because of the change in the political climate of China, no further attempts were made for many years to establish even a cultural liaison with the West. Now tourists are made welcome but they go at their own expense.

For some years after my return I was invited, together with other members of cultural delegations and persons thought to be politically sympathetic to the Chinese, to attend an annual reception at the Chinese Legation in London. I thought that I detected a slight air of disdain in our hosts as their guests made a bee-line for the food and drink abundantly provided. It was very good but never quite matched my memories of what I had enjoyed in Peking. In the course of this period I joined an Anglo-Chinese friendship association but became critical of the way it was managed and signed a letter to that effect which Hugh Trevor-Roper had drafted. Thereafter my name was removed from the list of those whom the Chinese officials in London thought it profitable to invite. It makes me sad to think that I am never likely to see Peking or Hangchow again.

7 *Philosophical Questions*

The International Institute of Philosophy was invited by Professor Theodorakopoulos, its only Greek representative, to meet in Athens in 1955. As I have already said, these meetings normally took place at the end of August or the beginning of September, but because of the Greek climate we met on this occasion in the spring. I can remember nothing of the discussions, which were on the topic of Dialogue and Dialectic, but I do remember that this was the first appearance of any philosophers from behind the Iron Curtain, Tadeusz Kotarbinski and Adam Schaff both arriving unexpectedly from Poland. Kotarbinski, already an old man, was the doyen of Polish philosophers. He was a materialist in so far as he believed that the fundamental constituents of the world are material bodies in space and time, but an upholder of classical logic rather than any form of dialectics, and he maintained this position under the Communist regime just as he had adhered to his political liberalism during the Nazi occupation. His wife, who was also a philosopher, had been imprisoned in Auschwitz and had been one of the very few to survive. Schaff was a subtle Marxist who had re-entered Poland with the Russians and been installed by them in a position of power. He was not liked by the senior Polish philosophers, but they had reason to be grateful to him, as even in the short period following 1949 when Polish culture was subjected to strong Marxist pressure he ensured that they retained their salaries, although they might be confined to teaching logic, and placed some of them safely under the umbrella of the Polish Academy of Sciences. Almost inevitably he took an interest in analytical philosophy, and published quite a good and open-minded book on the topic of semantics.

An unusual feature of our Athens congress was the interest taken in our proceedings by the Greek royal family. We were summoned to the palace, given plenty to drink, and closely interrogated by Queen Frederika, of Hohenzollern descent. Like my Chinese friend in Hangchow, she had read about the principle of indeterminacy and was interested in its philosophical implications. She had drawn her own conclusions and seemed more concerned with imparting them to us than in discovering whether they could withstand our criticism. For some reason, I bore the brunt of the discussion, which was animated if inconclusive.

There was an amusing sequel to this episode. In March 1961 King Paul and Queen Frederika came to London and the Queen asked the Greek Ambassador, the celebrated poet George Seferis, to organize a luncheon party for her to meet a number of leading English intellectuals. I was invited together with my second wife Dee Wells, an American journalist whom I had married the year before. The other guests, about twenty in all, included Graham Greene, Freddie Ashton, Osbert Lancaster, Lord Adrian, the eminent physiologist, and Harold Nicolson, who recorded the affair in his diary. The Queen recognized me but was struck by a change in my appearance. 'What have you done,' she asked, 'with all your curls?' I was unable to account for the fact that my hair had grown straighter. Dee pretended to believe that she was alluding to my marriage and that the question was 'What have you done with all your girls?' In any event the topic was not pursued. Conversation was general at lunch, Dee finding herself next to King Paul who talked to her amicably about sailing, which appeared to be his main source of pleasure. After lunch we were made to sit in a large semi-circle converging on Queen Frederika who proceeded to harangue us for nearly two hours on the philosophy of science. Graham Greene made an intervention which was brushed aside. I made several ineffective attempts to argue in what Harold Nicolson described in his diary as my 'exquisite manner'. I have always suspected that this phrase was ironical. Afterwards I remonstrated with Lord Adrian for his remaining silent on a subject on which he was so much better qualified to speak than I, but he merely thanked me for protecting him.

The principal advantage of belonging to the IIP consisted, as I have said, in the opportunities that it provided for travel, and this was never more clearly illustrated than on our expedition to Greece.

There is always the danger that a famous work of architecture like the Parthenon will prove a disappointment when one sees it for the first time, but this was not so in my case. Very much the contrary. I also enjoyed the amenities of Athens, the *mezes* and the ouzo, the fish served in a restaurant in Piraeus, the vitality of the people. We went as a group to visit Delphi and the theatre at Epidaurus, with its marvellous acoustics, and across the Isthmus of Corinth into the Peloponnese. We stopped at the site of Mycenae. I persuaded myself that the place was numinous, but I doubt if I should have had that feeling if I had not read the *Oresteia*. Apart from having to teach Plato and Aristotle to a few Christ Church pupils in the 1930s and to those reading Greats at Wadham during the short period that I held a fellowship there after the war, I had done nothing to keep up my knowledge of ancient Greek. About enough of it remained with me for me to be able to make out the gist of a newspaper article. On the other hand I could neither speak nor understand demotic Greek. I learned how to ask politely for hot water but that was about all.

After the congress ended I went to the island of Hydra to stay in a house belonging to the painter Nikko Ghika. Hydra is one of the most attractive of the Greek islands, partly because all motor traffic is forbidden there. Ghika's house was high up on the island with a splendid view from the terrace. My friends Paddy Leigh-Fermor and Joan Rayner were staying there. This was one of the periods at which I was an enthusiastic chess player and Joan and I were very evenly matched. In London I used to play regularly also with Humphrey Slater, who was a stronger player than I but not so much so as to rob our games of zest. Towards the end of the 1950s he borrowed a small sum of money from me, when he was going to stay with friends in Spain, and insisted on leaving his box of splendid Staunton chessmen with me as security. He died on this holiday in Spain and I still have the chessmen. If I now play rather seldom it is partly because I have no regular opponent, partly because it vexes me that my game shows no improvement. I put this down chiefly to my lack of visual imagery. I cannot form a mental picture of the disposition of the pieces which would result from such and such a series of moves on either side. I have to reason it out: if I move my knight, then he will most probably move his bishop, and then I shall have to protect my queen, but won't that cost me a pawn? I find that I soon run into difficulties with this purely conceptual approach.

I had the good fortune still to be in Hydra at the time fixed for the celebration of Easter by the Greek Orthodox Church. This was the first time that I had taken part in any of its ceremonies and my lack of any religious belief did not prevent my being moved by the procession of candles. I also enjoyed the feasting. The lamb, which was our staple diet, was so young and succulent that I had no complaint about the lack of variety.

In 1955, Ifor Evans decided that it would be beneficial to University College to set up a Communications Research Centre. To inaugurate the centre he arranged for a series of lectures to be given by members of the staff. It was thought appropriate that I, as a philosopher, should open the series. The second lecture, which was delivered by Professor Haldane, gave a fascinating account of the system of communication which governed the migration of bees. This was much more suited to the audience than my own abstract disquisition on the different varieties of signs. Always anxious to secure money for the college, Ifor had invited representatives of engineering firms to listen to my lecture, in the hope that it would induce them to subsidize the research centre. My lecture could hardly have been less suited to such an audience but they listened to it politely, if without much appearance of interest. The whole series of lectures came out in a book entitled *Studies in Communication* in 1955. I waited until 1969 before reprinting my lecture 'What is Communication?' in a collection of my essays entitled *Metaphysics and Common Sense*. The University College Communications Research Centre organized a few seminars but I do not remember that they led to any discoveries of importance. The centre may, however, have achieved one of its purposes in causing different departments of the college to work more closely together, though I am not sure that even this effect lasted very long.

Social life in London in 1955 was enlivened by the presence of Raymond Chandler, whom I greatly admired as a writer of detective stories. Ever since I was a boy I had been a detective story addict, starting like so many others with Conan Doyle's Sherlock Holmes, not disdaining cruder imitators of Sherlock Holmes like Sexton Blake, discovering Simenon's Maigret before the author was much translated into English, faithfully following the exploits of Agatha Christie's Inspector Poirot and Miss Marples, Ngaio Marsh's Inspector Roderick Alleyn, Margery Allingham's Albert Campion, even Dorothy Sayers' Lord Peter Wimsey. If I came to prefer the tougher

American school of which Dashiel Hammett was the founder and Raymond Chandler and Ross Macdonald the outstanding later exponents, I think it was originally because of the excellent films that were made from Hammett's books, notably *The Thin Man* series and *The Maltese Falcon*, about which I have already written in *Part of My Life*. In Chandler's case I preferred the novels to the films in spite of the portrayal of his hero, the private detective Philip Marlowe, by such actors as Robert Montgomery, Dick Powell and Humphrey Bogart. One reason for this was that the attraction of Chandler's writing lay in his style and his creation of atmosphere, which the films did not wholly succeed in capturing, rather than his over-elaborate plots.

Chandler was born an American of Quaker stock but he was educated in England at Dulwich College, like P. G. Wodehouse and G. E. Moore, and though he was in his late sixties when he came to England in 1955 and had spent most of his life in southern California, he retained many of the attitudes of an English public schoolboy of the Edwardian age. He was greatly distressed by the recent death of his wife, a woman very much older than himself, and had taken to drinking heavily. When he was sober he was disconcertingly formal, but still good company. He conceived a romantic attachment for Natasha Spender, Stephen Spender's wife, which extended to Jocelyn. He disapproved of me because he thought that I had treated Jocelyn badly. Both she and Natasha made assiduous attempts to lighten his dark moods. He seemed a happier man when he returned to America but was destined to live only four years longer.

In the summer I went to stay at Bois Normand, a charming country house not far from Honfleur in Normandy belonging to my war-time friend Nicole Bouchet de Fareins. Her sister Francette Drin was also there with her teenage daughter, Christine. I had announced that I wanted to be left to myself for so many hours a day in order to work on a book that I was writing and Nicole, without my knowledge, forbade Christine and her own daughters who were of about the same age to make any noise during these periods. This made me unpopular with the girls throughout my stay, though later we were to make friends. In fact, I should not have minded how much noise they made, as when I am concentrating on my writing, it takes a very great deal to distract me. Even when I am interrupted, I find it easy to resume my train of thought.

The book, which I completed by the end of the year, was published in 1956 under the title of *The Problem of Knowledge*. There had been some trouble about its publication. Penguin Publications wanted it to appear in the Pelican series of philosophy books which I was editing for them, but it had been made a condition for membership of the series that the books should not have been previously published. At the same time Macmillan wanted to publish the book in hardback, but it was customary for books which were published in hardback to appear some time before they were issued in paperback, to give the hardback publishers a chance to recoup their investment before the cheaper paperback edition spoiled their market. In the end it was decided that the book should be published simultaneously by Macmillan in hardback and by Penguin in paperback, with Penguin having the translation rights. Strangely enough, since they had the better of the arrangement, it was the Penguin people who were the more reluctant to agree to it. In fact, the book sold well in both formats and has been translated into Italian, Spanish, Portuguese, Polish, Serbo-Croat, Japanese and Hindi. Its appearing simultaneously in the two formats also gave me the chance to make a double dedication. I dedicated the Penguin book to Jocelyn Rickards and the Macmillan book to Mary and Robin Campbell.

While it may not have the punch of *Language, Truth and Logic* or have become quite so widely known, I think that *The Problem of Knowledge* is the better book of the two. For one thing it is less derivative. Its scope is clearly set out in the preface.

> Having maintained that to say that one knows a fact is to claim the right to be sure of it, I show how such claims may be disputed on philosophical grounds. Though their targets vary, these sceptical challenges follow a consistent pattern; the same line of reasoning is used to impugn our knowledge of the external world, or of the past, or of the experiences of others. The attempt to meet these objections supplies the main subject-matter for what is called the theory of knowledge; and different philosophical standpoints are characterized by the acceptance or denial of different stages in the sceptic's argument.

The cases which I examined were those of scepticism concerning our knowledge of physical objects, concerning our knowledge of the past and future, and concerning the existence of minds other than one's own. I suggested that the sceptic proceeded in every instance by arguing that there was a gap between the premises on which we relied and the conclusion which we wished to reach and that this gap was not capable of being bridged either by deductive or inductive reasoning. From this it was held to follow that our acceptance of the conclusion was not justifiable.

My general procedure was to allow the sceptic to make his points but then take the verdict away from him, like a corrupt referee at a boxing match. I still think well of the book as a whole but if I had to criticize it today, I should say that I gave way too easily to common sense. I now think that there are more elaborate ways of justifying our belief both in the existence of physical objects and in the experiences of other persons. I have developed these ideas in my later books, notably in *The Central Questions of Philosophy*, which reproduces the series of Gifford Lectures that I delivered at the University of St Andrews in 1972-3 and published in 1973.

A point which I have always conceded to the sceptic is that there is no non-circular way of justifying induction. The best we can do is to adhere to procedures that have rewarded us in the past, but this is to assume that what has held good in the past will continue to do so in the future, which is precisely what Hume put in question.

I disagree, therefore, with those who think that the means of justifying induction can be found in the logical theory of probability. A most ingenious version of this view was advanced by my old friend and sponsor Roy Harrod in his book *Foundations of Inductive Logic*, which was also published in 1956, but had been, as it were, rehearsed in a series of lectures which I had invited him to give at University College in 1954. Though famous as an economist, Roy always had a hankering after philosophy and he thought more highly of this book than of any of his contributions to economic theory. It is true that if his solution to the problem of induction had been successful, it would have been of major philosophical importance. I have stated my objections to it in Harrod's festschrift *Induction, Growth and Trade* and reprinted them in my book *Probability and Evidence*.

I made a speech about probability at the ninth symposium of the Colston Research Society, held at the University of Bristol at the beginning of April 1957. It had been assumed by Keynes in his famous book *A Treatise on Probability*, and by many others since, that statements of probability were incomplete, unless the evidence on which they were based was specified. What they then stated was that such and such a proposition was made probable to such and such a degree by such and such evidence, and this was supposed to be a logical truth. I argued that this view could not be correct since we should then have no reason to build up evidence. If the relative probabilities had been assessed correctly all the competing statements would be equally valid. We think it rational to assign probabilities in accordance with the total available evidence, but according to theories of the Keynesian type this yields no better assessment of what is likely to happen than assignments made on a narrower basis. Consequently, such theories are inadmissible as analyses of statements of probability. My speech was published in the proceedings of the symposium and reprinted together with a note on the frequency theory of probability in my book *The Concept of a Person*. In subsequent literature I have quite often found my argument brushed aside but never yet seen it convincingly answered.

A book of a very different character from *The Problem of Knowledge* but which came out in the same year was Colin Wilson's *The Outsider*. I had been introduced to Colin Wilson by Stephen Spender and thought him an agreeable young man but I did not think highly of his book. The title was that of the English translation of Camus's novel *L'Etranger*, but the book had nothing in common with the novel. It was mainly a tissue of not always accurate quotations from such philosophers as Nietzsche and contemporary existentialists. No doubt it was a good thing for us to be reminded of the existence of different modes of philosophizing from those that were currently fashionable in England but this hardly accounted for the rapturous welcome the book received from critics like Cyril Connolly and Philip Toynbee. What I saw as their unwarranted praise made my own review of the book in *Encounter* more hostile than it otherwise might have been. I thought it rather hard on Colin Wilson that when he published a book called *Religion and the Rebel*, which was no more than a continuation of *The Outsider*, in the following year, it met with a lukewarm reception. This has not, however, prevented him from pursuing a successful literary career. I believe that what originally led reviewers like Connolly and Toynbee astray was their unfamiliarity with abstract ideas combined with a middle-class sense of guilt provoked by the work of an autodidact. When its object had become successful this feeling of guilt subsided.

By 1956 Julian, who was then seventeen, had come to terms with Eton and was emerging into prominence as an athlete. He was soon to be playing soccer for the school and ended by winning his school colours for the Field Game and by playing cricket for Eton against Harrow at Lords. As in previous years, in at least one of which I took Valerie with me, I visited him for the celebrations of the Fourth of June. On this occasion I was accompanied by an American economist called Jo Saxe whom I had got to know through his attachment to Francette Drin. In the evening he drove me to Oxford where we attended the annual dance at St Antony's of which my old friend Bill Deakin was Warden.

Neither of us had a partner for the dance, but of course I knew many people there including Iris Murdoch and John Bayley, who had recently become engaged and danced charmingly together. Late in the evening Jo introduced me to Dee Wells, whom he had met at the end of the war when they were both working for the American Embassy in Paris. Dee had been brought to the dance by another American, who had drunk too much and eventually passed out. For some reason, I was wearing a borrowed dinner jacket which did not fit me well and Dee showed no enthusiasm in accepting my invitation to dance. She relaxed, however, when she discovered that I was a competent dancer. After we began making conversation, she asked me what I did. 'I am a logician,' I replied, not wholly accurately, but I did hold a Chair of Logic and it would have been pedantic to say 'I am an epistemologist.' Dee understood me, or pretended to understand me, as saying, 'I am a magician', and asked me to tell her how I created my illusions. I let her go on for a while and then said, rather severely, 'I said "logician" not "magician".' By this time, however, I had aroused her interest and we not only continued as dancing partners for most of the evening, but agreed to meet in London on the following day. I was spending the night in Oxford at the Halbans and travelled to London the next morning by the same train as Dee though not in the same compartment, as she thought she owed it to her bibulous escort to travel back with him. We had anyhow arranged for her to visit me in Whitehorse Street and that night we became lovers.

Dee, who was then thirty-one, fourteen years younger than I, had been born Dee Chapman, in Providence, Rhode Island, where her father's family owned the local newspaper, but had been brought up in the neighbourhood of Boston. She had a brother a year or two older than herself and a much younger brother and sister. Both her brothers and her sister had gone to good universities and it was a sore point with Dee that a temporary decline in the family fortunes had deprived her of this advantage. Instead she went to work in a factory at the age of seventeen and a year or so later joined the Canadian army, rising to the rank of Sergeant Major. She never saw service outside Canada. At the end of the war she was posted to the American Embassy in Paris where she met and married an American career diplomat, Alfred Wells. They had a daughter, Alexandra, who was born in 1950. Al Wells accepted a post in Burma and on their way there when they stopped at Suez the infant Alexandra was so fascinated by the local magicians, known as the Gully-Gully men, that Dee gave her the nickname of Gully, by which she is still known. Dee enjoyed life in Burma but soon became dissatisfied with her marriage, putting up with it only for a year or two before she left, taking Gully with her and an incontinent but appealing dachshund puppy called Monster. The divorce which she obtained in Vienna, where Al had been transferred, gave her custody of Gully but very little money for their joint support. She decided that it would be easier to make a living in England than in the United States and took lodgings for a time in Clapham, on the outskirts of London, working as a freelance journalist.

She was a very gifted journalist and soon obtained a regular position on the London staff of a New York paper. She became their fashion correspondent, attending shows in Paris and in Rome. Later she went to work for the *Sunday Express*, first as a film critic and then as their leading book reviewer. Disapproving of the political outlook of the Beaverbrook press, she moved to the *Daily Herald* as a columnist, continuing when the *Daily Herald* was transmuted by Hugh Cudlipp into the *Sun*, but resigning when the *Sun* fell into the grasp of Rupert Murdoch and became the tabloid that it has remained.

When I met her she had left Clapham and was living with Gully, Monster and an Italian maid in a large house in Holland Park Avenue, belonging to Sue and Basil Boothby. Basil was in the Foreign Office and Dee had met and made friends with them in Burma. He had since been transferred to Brussels and lent Dee his London house while he and his family remained abroad. I saw him once briefly in Brussels but made friends with him in later years. He was interested in philosophy and shared my taste for watching professional football.

Sue, who belonged to the Asquith family, was a woman of character and charm.

Dee had been having an affair with a Cambridge economist but gave him up on my account. I was not as yet sufficiently committed to her to renounce all other attachments, or even to profess to do so. Jocelyn, with whom I had arrived at a friendly *modus vivendi*, disapproved of my taking up with Dee, not out of jealousy but because she did not then like her or think us suited to one another. Renée tended rather to approve of her as a counterweight to Jocelyn. I enjoyed her company, spent a fair amount of time in Holland Park Avenue and let events take their course.

The Joint Session was held this year at Aberystwyth. Dee accompanied me on the long train journey but did not stay for the congress. Goronwy Rees was still Principal of University College but his position was being threatened. The reason for this lay at bottom in his lasting obsession with Guy Burgess. A year or so before, when I was staying with him and Margie, he had shown me an essay that went into great detail about Guy's character and habits, his relations with Goronwy, the peculiarities of the house in which he had lived in London during the war and the persons who had frequented it. The essay was well and soberly written and seemed to me to be a valuable historical document. I advised Goronwy to lodge a copy with the British Museum and he said that he would consider doing so. At that time the whereabouts of Burgess and Maclean were still officially unknown. Then in February 1956 they gave a press interview in Moscow, which naturally attracted very wide publicity. For some reason, which I have never wholly fathomed, Goronwy felt that Guy's official reappearance gave him the right, even the duty, to publish his account of their relations. If he had been content to publish in one of the quality newspapers the piece that he had shown me, all might have been well. Unfortunately, he also saw this as an opportunity to make some extra money and instructed his agent to let the material go to the highest bidder. This proved to be the *Sunday People*, which insisted that the original be rewritten by a member of its own staff in a style to which its readership was accustomed, and that it should appear anonymously as a series of short articles. Again, it is a mystery to me why Goronwy agreed to those conditions. The result was that his style was vulgarized, sensational sub-headings were inserted, and the author was made to appear shocked by Guy's homosexuality and his Bohemian way of life. The coating of anonymity was transparent, and for the benefit of those who had not already guessed it, the name of the author was revealed by a gossip columnist on the *Daily Telegraph*.

The consequences for Goronwy were disastrous. The publication of the articles both offended many of his personal friends, who thought that he ought to have displayed more loyalty to Burgess, and shocked the members of the Aberystwyth establishment, who thought that he should never have had occasion to display any. I discovered how much he minded the charge of disloyalty when I ran into him by chance at a London restaurant. When I went up to greet him, he said 'What, are you still speaking to me?' 'Of course,' I said, 'why shouldn't I?' 'Well,' he answered, 'nobody else is.' This was some way from being true. There were others who stood by him from the start, and of those who had attacked him the ones for whom he cared most soon forgave him.

It was otherwise with his fortunes at Aberystwyth. His enemies succeeded in setting up a commission, consisting of three English academics, all of a Conservative temper, to enquire into the conduct of the Principal. After humiliating Goronwy by the way in which they conducted their interrogation, the members of the committee returned an adverse report. Even so, the council of the college voted by a majority that no further action be taken, but Goronwy's enemies were powerful enough to make his position untenable. He held out for a while but resigned his post in the summer of 1957.

He had not saved any money to speak of, but Margie had some capital from her father and, in partnership with Derek Verschoyle, under whom Goronwy had worked on the literary side of the *Spectator* before the war, they invested their capital in a company designed, if I remember rightly, to market prefabricated doors. They took a small house in Southend where Dee and I went to visit them. Margie was away when we called but she and Dee met shortly afterwards and became and remained very close friends.

It was not very long before the building company failed, and a worse misfortune followed. They had a car, which Margie drove, and once when she had stopped for petrol, Goronwy, who had got out to stretch his legs, was caught by a passing car and dragged alongside it. The accident, which nearly cost him his life, left him permanently a little lame. His experiences in hospital are vividly recounted in the best of his books, *A Bundle of Sensations*, which appeared in 1960. The title is drawn from Hume's theory of the self, which he in fact called 'a bundle of perceptions', but for Goronwy this was not so much a philosophical proposition as the expression of his views of his own personality. The other experiences which the book revived were those of his childhood, his soldiering, and visits to Germany before and after the war. They displayed the unity more than the diversity of his self.

From then on Goronwy made his living as a professional writer. He wrote books of various kinds but, in my view, his best work was autobiographical. Next to *A Bundle of Sensations* I would put *A Chapter of Accidents*, published as late as 1972, in which it is to be hoped that the ghost of Guy Burgess was finally exorcized.

The last six months of 1956 were marked by the Suez crisis, lasting from July when Nasser seized the Suez Canal until December when under American pressure the English and French withdrew their troops from Egypt. Throughout the crisis I supported the position of the Labour Party, as set out by Hugh Gaitskell who had replaced Attlee as leader of the party in December 1955. A false impression of my attitude might have been given by Veronica Hull's novel *The Monkey Puzzle*, in which I appear under a different name but a very thin disguise. On the whole I am portrayed in a fairly hostile light throughout the book and appear at my worst at the very end where I refuse to sign a letter of protest brought to me by one of the author's friends. This refusal is attributed by another of my pupils, clearly modelled on Peter Newnham, to the snobbery of liberal philosophers of my sort. The accusation had some foundation in fact. I did make it a condition of signing a letter that was brought to me that it should be redrafted in certain places and this condition was not fulfilled. What my critics did not know or chose to overlook was that I had already signed a similar, if more temperate, letter of protest which had been published in *The Times*.

If I was not quite so whole-heartedly opposed to Eden in this affair as I had been, say, to his policy of non-intervention in the Spanish Civil War, it was because of the involvement of the Israelis. I had never been an out-and-out Zionist, and am now so less than ever, but for atavistic reasons in any conflict between the Israelis and the Arabs I tend to take the Israelis' side. Had I known or even suspected that the British, French and Israeli governments were acting in collusion, my opposition would have been unqualified, but the details of the plot were not revealed until some time later. Perhaps it was naïve of me not to have discerned them.

Veronica Hull's novel was published by the firm of Arthur Burke of which my old friend Tony Samuel had become Chairman. I had seen little of him since the war but retained an affectionate memory of our sharing an office in British Security Co-ordination in New York. Either fearing that I might bring a libel action against his firm, or possibly merely wishing not to hurt my feelings, he took me out to lunch and showed me the typescript of the book. After glancing through it I said that I had no objection to his publishing it as it stood except that I should prefer the character who portrayed me to be described as a lecturer in the philosophy department rather than as 'the little professor'. He duly made the change.

It was at about this time that I accepted an invitation from a Bristol aircraft company to attend a seminar which had been organized for its executives at a country house somewhere in the home counties. The seminar was scheduled for a weekend and I was invited to speak on one of the afternoons and stay overnight if I wished. If I did stay overnight I was to bring a dinner jacket and would be welcome to attend the evening session. I was not told what the evening session was to comprise but equipped myself to stay overnight in case it proved to be interesting. When I arrived I found that the evening speaker was to be Enoch Powell, whom I had never met, and I decided to stay and hear him. By pure coincidence I had chosen to speak on the subject of racial prejudice, reviewing it in its various forms, and analyzing its causes. I spoke in a low key and held the attention of my hearers without arousing their emotions. The discussion was rational. Even if they were infected with racial prejudice they would have been unlikely to admit it. In the evening Enoch Powell spoke on the subject of democracy. He asked for and obtained the assurance that his speech would not be reported. He then pointed out, what Rousseau and others had said before him, that England was not a democracy in any strict sense of the term. It was an oligarchy of which the members sometimes had to make a show of bowing to the wishes of the people in order to retain their power. He assumed that his audience belonged or aspired to belong to this oligarchy and that their principal motive was one of self-interest. His advice to them was not to allow their motive to become too apparent. I was greatly amused to note that the audience found this shocking. They had conceived of themselves as performing a public service, for which they deserved the privileges that they enjoyed, and were not at all pleased to be shown up as a bunch of self-seekers. I took only a small part in the discussion but enough to make Powell realize that I was probably not a company executive. We have met a few times since without quarrelling. I think that he has done a great deal of mischief but I do not think that he himself is motivated by enlightened self-interest.

In the course of the year I had developed a close, if not monogamous relation with Dee and in May 1957 I took her to Bertrand Russell's eighty-fifth birthday party. The Russells now lived mainly in Wales but had a London flat at Milbank where the party was held. The Crawshay-Williams were there and Alan Wood and his wife, who were both to die within the year. Alan Wood had just published a biography of Russell called *Bertrand Russell: The Passionate Sceptic*, and had begun a study of Russell's philosophy, for which he was, I think, less well qualified. There have been many books written about Russell's philosophy in its various aspects, but so far, apart from the three volumes of Russell's own autobiography, which becomes a little sketchy after the splendid first volume, and autobiographical notes that occur elsewhere in his work, there has not been a better biographical study than Alan Wood's.

Rupert Crawshay-Williams tells an amusing story of a time when Russell was still married to Patricia Spence and they had lent the Crawshay-Williams their London flat. Elizabeth was looking for a place to put Rupert's spare suit and asked the maid who was helping her unpack 'Where does Lord Russell put *his* trousers?' 'He *wears* them' was the answer. Later when he was married to Edith, Russell bought two suits but the change was not easily detectable since the suits were duplicates.

Though we remained friends and corresponded with one another I ceased to see so much of Bertrand Russell in the ensuing years. This was partly because he spent most of his time in Wales, partly because I was not associated with him in the political campaign which increasingly occupied his time and interest. One reason for this is that I disliked and distrusted the American Ralph Schoenman, who had insinuated himself into the position of Russell's secretary and was clearly attempting to manipulate Russell, in the interests of what seemed to be some form of Trotskyism. Another was that I did not share Russell's hostility to Britain's defence policy in so far as it admitted the possibility of our resorting to nuclear warfare. For one thing, I thought it highly improbable that if Britain were to forego nuclear weapons, the United States would follow suit, and even if the United States were to follow suit, I was not sure that I was in favour of unilateral as opposed to multilateral disarmament. This does not mean that I regard the nuclear arms race, as conducted both by the United States and the Soviet Union and their respective satellites, as anything but a dangerous and expensive folly.

As a result of our making two of their members welcome in Greece two years before, the Polish philosophers invited the IIP to hold its annual congress in Warsaw in July 1957. The theme was the relation between thought and action. I was pleased to see Kotarbinski again, and especially pleased to meet Kazimierz Ajdukiewicz who had been in touch with the Vienna Circle before the war and had contributed an important article on meaning to their journal *Erkenntnis*. Like Kotarbinski, he had made no concessions to Marxism. I also made the acquaintance of Leszek Kolakowski, who was then an enthusiastic Marxist but later defected, obtaining academic posts first in Montreal and then in Oxford, and recently bringing out a work in three volumes entitled *Main Currents of Marxism*, which is highly critical of the doctrines it examines, but also a piece of careful scholarship.

Warsaw had been almost wholly destroyed by the Germans before they left and was still very largely dilapidated, but its famous eighteenth-century square had been faithfully restored and the hotel in which we were lodged was comfortable, if not luxurious. The cafés, said to be patronized by writers, painters and film-makers, were full and lively. Some of their patrons spoke English and the political atmosphere at that time seemed to be relaxed.

The deference paid to official visitors in countries behind the Iron Curtain worked for once to our disadvantage. When we set out on a journey by train to Krakow I casually enquired whether there was a dining car on the train. In fact there wasn't but I was told that there would be. The result, which was not at all what I had intended, was that the start of our journey was delayed for over an hour while a dining car was unearthed from elsewhere and attached to the train.

Krakow, when we eventually reached it, proved to be a handsome city, bearing the imprint, I thought, of its Austrian provenance. It seemed to have escaped the ravages of war and, at least so far as its philosophy went, to have eluded the clutches of Marxism. Roman Ingarden, one of the leading European phenomenologists, was left in charge of the philosophy department, with Madame Dambska, also a phenomenologist, as his chief assistant. The tolerance shown at this period did not indefinitely continue and I understand that this school of philosophy has had difficulty in maintaining itself, especially since Ingarden's death.

From Krakow we were taken to see the silver mines at Katowice, which were indeed very impressive, and then made the long journey to Bialystok, near the Russian frontier, where we were shown over what was said to have been Goering's hunting lodge. We also paid a casual visit to Lublin, but from the academic point of view the University did not have the interest for us of either Warsaw or Krakow.

Our most haunting expedition was that which we made to Auschwitz, renamed Oświęcim, which the Poles had preserved as a museum. I was surprised that Madame Kotarbinski joined our party, but it may have been that she hoped to exorcize her memories of what went on there. The mere fact that a railway line had been especially built to go as far as the camp and no further struck the first sinister note. On arrival at the station the prisoners had been divided into two groups: those who were going to be put to work, and those who were going straight to the gas chambers. The second group were told that they were being taken to bath-houses and to further the deception they were issued with bars of soap. I distrust racial generalizations but I could not help thinking it characteristically German that the bars of soap were numbered and a tally kept of the victims to whom they were issued. We were shown the ledgers in which these records were kept. We were also shown the granaries full of women's hair which had not yet been removed for industrial use when the camp was captured. Another set of relics comprised the gold fillings taken from the victims' teeth.

It may be argued that such places should be razed to the ground rather than kept as memorials which can serve only to foster racial hatred. On the other hand, the spirit of the Nazis has not been wholly effaced: there has been a pretence in certain quarters that the story of the holocaust has been in some degree a fabrication. Perhaps it is as well that there should be concrete reminders of the evil that the Nazis perpetrated, not only against the Jews.

8   The Brains Trust

By the end of 1956 my books and the occasional talks that I had broadcast, nearly always on the Third Programme, had earned me slightly more than a purely professional reputation. If in the ensuing years I became something of a public figure, this was almost entirely due to my appearances on television, and these were almost all the result of my taking part in a programme called 'The Brains Trust'.

In its original form, the Brains Trust was a weekly programme, put out on the wireless, and commanding a large audience during the war. It was a panel consisting almost invariably of the same three persons, discussing a series of questions supposed to be chosen by the BBC producer from a stock of questions sent in by the listening public. These persons were C. E. M. Joad, playing the part of a philosopher, Julian Huxley, functioning as a scientific polymath, and Commander Campbell, a retired naval officer, injecting a note of bluff common sense. They made an excellent combination. Whatever his defects, Joad was a quick-witted and lucid speaker; he was not required to probe deeply into philosophical problems, and his giving the impression that the philosopher's stock response to any but the most simple factual question was to say 'it depends on what you mean by' whatever it might be was not intolerably misleading. Julian Huxley, though primarily an ornithologist, was also an expert in the theory of evolution and had sufficient all-round culture to enable him to serve as the first Director General of UNESCO. Commander Campbell added a touch of humour to his ample store of common sense. The programme fulfilled the BBC's ideal of blending education with entertainment.

The Brains Trust was revived after the war but transferred to television. By the time I took note of it, its format had changed. There was now a question master and four panellists instead of three. Moreover, the composition of the panel changed from week to week, though a certain number of persons kept reappearing. Of the original trio only Julian Huxley remained. I did not possess a television set during the time that I lived in Whitehorse Street, and knew next to nothing about the Brains Trust in its new format until I myself appeared on it. I believe that Bertrand Russell made successful appearances on the programme when it was first revived but I never watched any of them and am here relying on the evidence of Rupert Crawshay-Williams's book.

I myself was first invited to take part in the programme in the month of October 1956. The invitation came from John Furness, a mild-mannered man, who was the programme's regular producer. My fellow panellists on that occasion were Noel Annan, the Provost of King's College, Cambridge, and not, I think, yet ennobled, John Betjeman, the poet, with whom I had a slight social acquaintance, and Donald Tyerman who was editor of the *Economist*. The question master, one who most often fulfilled this role, was Norman Fisher who had at that time some position in the Coal Board but later moved into publishing. The usual procedure, then and for a year or two afterwards, was for the panellists, the question master and the producer to meet for lunch on a Sunday at Scott's restaurant in Piccadilly Circus. After a good lunch with a fair amount to drink we were driven to the television studios, made up, which consisted in being given a slight coating of powder and a combing of one's hair, assigned our places on the dais confronting the cameras and rehearsed with one or two dummy questions. Nothing like these questions figured in the actual programme and, contrary to popular suspicion, we had no forewarning of what the actual questions were going to be. It was obvious that some attempt was made to fit the choice of questions to the interests of the performers, and it is possible that when suitable questions had not been forthcoming from the public the producer and his assistants supplied them, but I do not know that this was ever the case. The programme was put out at 4.15 pm and at the time of which I am writing was broadcast live, which had the effect of making the participants more alert. About half a dozen questions were dealt with as a rule; never, I think, less than five or more than seven. A fee of £50 was paid to each panellist, which was generous for those days, especially as the work involved no preparation, and the fee was supplemented by a good lunch, drinks after the programme and free transport home. I also found the work enjoyable in itself.

The questions were seldom purely factual, not often literary, and almost never scientific. Politics might be brought in on an international scale, but party politics were eschewed. Religion was discussable in general terms. Some but not many questions were meant to be facetious. The overwhelming majority of them, at least in the programmes in which I figured, raised abstract or concrete issues of morality. I have discovered a record of those that were put to the team on my first appearance and remember them as being typical. They were seven in number and went as follows.

1. Is it morally right to act upon one's convictions by attempting to convince others?
2. Is UNO Council's veto a good thing and if not what would you substitute?
3. Are there any logical reasons for good behaviour?
4. Which is more effective, a cartoon or a lampoon?
5. Can a couple be happily married when they hold strongly opposed religious views?
6. Is it the duty of a good citizen to be an informer?
7. Would it be desirable for there to be a Ministry of Culture?

This is a heavy set of questions for four persons to discuss at all adequately within the compass of three-quarters of an hour, especially as one had to deal with them impromptu, though most of them raised issues to which one was already likely to have given some thought. The procedure was for the question master to put the question to one of the participants. He or she, for women also took part in these programmes though not with the same frequency as men, was supposed to make his or her original answer brief, so as to give scope to the other participants, and if possible controversial, so as to provoke them to argument. The convention, which was not always strictly observed, was that if one wanted to intervene in the discussion one caught the chairman's eye and waited to be named. This was to protect the listeners from a hubbub of voices. The question master was supposed to see that each speaker held the floor for roughly an equal amount of time, but this was hardly feasible. In my memory of that first occasion, Tyerman hardly figures at all, John Betjeman was chiefly concerned with making jokes and most of the serious discussion was carried on by Noel Annan and myself. I do not remember how I answered this series of questions, but I assume that, in the case of the third question at least, I held fast to my theory that there is no going outside morality to discover a foundation for one's choice of moral principles.

It was two months before I was asked to appear again. This time my fellow performers were Rebecca West, the Reverend Mervyn Stockwood and Dr Jacob Bronowski. All three were impressive in their different ways. Bronowski, in particular, could lay claim to being the programme's star performer. He appeared more often on it than anyone else, with the possible exception of Julian Huxley, and while Huxley may have had the greater range of knowledge, Bronowski excelled him in his powers of exposition. Like Fisher, he was connected with the Coal Board and had invented some form of smokeless fuel. Previously, he had held a university post as a lecturer in mathematics. He had a good working knowledge of all the physical sciences and also an interest in the arts. He had, for example, written a good book about William Blake. I had thought that he would be an excellent choice for the Chair of the History and Philosophy of Science at University College, London, when it became vacant in the mid-1950s, on the retirement of Professor Herbert Dingle, but practising scientists like John Young were distrustful of scientific popularizers and Bruno, as his friends called him, had a cocky manner which alienated those who did not know him well. University College then had the brilliant idea of approaching Dr Joseph Needham, renowned among other things for his monumental history of Chinese science, but the external 'experts' on the London University committee, activated, I believe, by political prejudice, presumed to question his scholarship and prevented his election. The Chair passed into the hands of some worthy member of the department and when he retired was accepted by Dr Feyerabend, a well qualified philosopher of science, but as much of an academic pluralist as an eighteenth-century bishop, with the result that he was very seldom seen in London. The professorship was then abolished, which has always seemed to me a pity. Bronowski eventually migrated to America and spent the remainder of his life in the comfortable embrace of a Californian institute.

I admired Rebecca West both as a writer on her own account and because of her old association with H. G. Wells but I disliked what I, perhaps mistakenly, took to be her patronizing manner. She appeared with me again in the following month, this time in company with Julian Huxley and the Oxford historian Alan Bullock, whose biography of Hitler, which still holds its own with any other that I know of, had appeared in 1952. Bullock was also a regular performer on the programme. For once, Norman Fisher did not appear as question master and was replaced by Malcolm Muggeridge, who found it difficult to be as self-effacing as his part required. I had first met Muggeridge in Algiers during the war, when he was serving as an intelligence officer. Afterwards we saw each other socially from time to time. I admired his wit and courage as a journalist, and quite enjoyed his company, once I had accustomed myself to his affected way of speaking. Two things turned me against him; first his allowing his prominence on television to aggrandize his self-esteem, and secondly his increasing religiosity. We finally quarrelled when I rashly consented to appear in a series of religious programmes which he was orchestrating. When I contested his facile assertion that suffering was ennobling by citing some of the obvious counter-examples, he made no attempt to argue but simply resorted to personal abuse. I was so taken aback that I left him in possession of the field. Judging that he was impervious to reason, I declined a further opportunity to debate with him on television. As it happens, we have never subsequently met.

Next to Bronowski, Julian Huxley and Alan Bullock, the most regular performer, at least as an accompaniment to myself, was Marghanita Laski who was quick-witted and knowledgeable. Outside television she was best known as a literary critic. Two women who in their very different ways were no less formidable than Rebecca West were Dame Edith Sitwell and Lady Violet Bonham Carter, both of whom wrote to me after the programmes in which we had appeared together, Dame Edith, whom I had found unexpectedly nervous, saying that if ever she were asked to perform again she would cheat by herself sending in questions to which she knew the answers, Lady Violet once apologizing for having misinformed me about Mr Gladstone's introduction of an Irish Home Rule bill in the 1890s, and once reproaching me for my having said that I was not afraid of putting power into the hands of scientists. Her argument, for which there is indeed empirical evidence, is that 'scientists are curiously fallible in the field of political judgement'. If our discussion were taking place today, she would have difficulty in denying that professional politicians are hardly less so.

The most interesting scientist to appear with me on the programme was Dr Grey Walter, the inventor of mechanical tortoises whose behaviour was controlled by their sensitivity to light. Their conduct appeared purposive in so far as they searched for a source of light when their batteries needed recharging. Dr Grey Walter was a pioneer in the field of artificial intelligence, a field in which such progress has been made in the last quarter of a century that philosophers, especially in the United States, are treating machines of a special type as models for the human mind.

In fact Dr Grey Walter was not given much opportunity to display his expertise, since our companions on the programme were Julian and Aldous Huxley and the questions were almost entirely geared to Aldous Huxley's interests. We were asked about extra-sensory perception, about the claim of mysticism to be a source of knowledge, about the pressure of population on food production, whether in the event of there being a pill which would have the effect of relieving anxiety without impairing judgement one would be justified in taking it, this last question being clearly intended to relate to Huxley's *Brave New World*. I had not met Aldous Huxley before and was very glad to have this single opportunity to do so both in the course of the programme and privately at Julian Huxley's house. I liked him personally but found him less forthcoming in conversation than I had hoped. My attitude towards his work was ambivalent. I very much admired his early novels, *Crome Yellow*, *Antic Hay*, *Those Barren Leaves* and *Point Counter Point*, as well as his short stories and essays of that period, but from the moment he settled in Hollywood and came increasingly under the influence of his fellow expatriate, Gerald Heard, his writing acquired a metaphysical aura which I found wholly unacceptable. I cannot better express my ambivalence than by referring to a long review of his *Adonis and the Alphabet and Other Essays*, which I published in the *Spectator* in November 1956 under the title 'A Lot of Learning'. I do not know whether Aldous Huxley ever saw this review, or had forgotten all about it in the two years that passed before we met, but neither of us made any reference to it. Having started with some quotations which showed how remarkably Cyril Connolly had succeeded in capturing his mannerisms in his parody, reproduced in Connolly's *The Condemned Playground*, of Huxley's novel *Eyeless in*

Gaza, I went on to acknowledge the extraordinary range of topics with which Huxley dealt in his essays and the wit which he brought to his display of knowledge. I said that he possessed in a high degree 'one of the distinguishing marks of the intelligent man: the power to find similarities in things which are apparently disparate'. At the same time I found his incursions into philosophy distressingly naïve, as shown, for example, by his claim to incorporate a number of not-selves, his belief that he could not lift his right hand but could only give an order which was obeyed in an unknown fashion by someone equally unknown and by his metaphysical description of the universe as 'a many-dimensional pattern, infinite in extent, infinite in duration, infinite in significance and infinitely aware, we may surmise, of its own infinities'.

There was a period in 1957 when Norman Fisher was replaced as question master by the Canadian Bernard Braden. This made Dr Bronowski very indignant. He thought that the programme was devalued by being subjected to the chairmanship of a professional comedian and refused to appear on it under that condition. I did not share this scruple, and on the three or four occasions when I appeared with Bernard Braden in the Chair, he proved to be as conscientious a question master as one could wish for, not striking any false note of levity. We made friends, to some extent, outside the studio, and I found that he was typical of many comedians in having serious intellectual interests. Charlie Chaplin, whom I met only once at a party in London where I was introduced to him by Graham Greene, who warned me that I should find him less attractive off the screen, Frankie Howerd and John Cleese, both of whom I count as personal friends, are other notable examples.

I made fourteen appearances on the Brains Trust in 1957, an average of over one a month, and forty-one in all between October 1956 and January 1961, adding a final performance when the programme was brought to an end in November 1961. This final programme was exceptional in that it took the form of a trans-Atlantic conversation between Henry Kissinger and myself in New York, where I had gone to lecture, and Bronowski and an American political scientist called Professor Neustadt in London, with Norman Fisher in London asking the questions. I had barely heard of Dr Kissinger, who was then expressing the sentiments which are said to have made him the model for the character of Dr Strangelove in the film of that name which

appeared in 1963, but I found him less bloodthirsty than I had expected, though clearly not averse to the use of unlimited force. The
questions such as 'Why do the Russians always make the West dance
to their tune?', 'Why do the Americans want to be liked whereas the
French do not care?' and 'What are the possibilities of civil defence?'
were designed to provoke a lively debate but failed to do so, not wholly
through Kissinger's fault but because none of the rest of us was willing
to make the effort to draw him out. I confess that I found him intellectually quite unremarkable and have always been surprised by his
subsequent acquisition of fame and power. Perhaps he had latent
talents, which he had not so far had the opportunity to develop; more
probably this was an occasion on which he made no effort to exert
himself.

The only other occasion on which I took part in the programme
abroad was in December 1958 when John Furness, Norman Fisher,
Alan Bullock and I all went to Paris to be joined by Raymond Aron
and Olivier Todd. Since the programme was broadcast as usual in
English to an English audience, the more obvious course would have
been to bring Aron and Todd to London, but this may have been
inconvenient for the Frenchmen, or the BBC may even have felt that
its regular producer and question master and two of its most regular
performers had earned a brief excursion. I have already spoken of
Olivier Todd and had met Raymond Aron fairly frequently over the
years. His political opinions tended to be to the right of mine, though
I shared his mistrust of de Gaulle, dating back to the war when Aron
broadcast independently from London, and I had and continue to
have considerable respect for his intelligence.

Throughout the four years from the autumn of 1956 to the autumn
of 1960 most of my fellow panellists were writers, including, besides
those I have already mentioned, Lord David Cecil, Cyril Connolly,
David Daiches, Ruth Pitter, Stevie Smith, Goronwy Rees, Margaret
Lane, Harold Nicolson and Pamela Hansford-Johnson. Of these
Lord David Cecil was the most fluent, Cyril Connolly surprisingly ill
at ease. The actors Ralph Richardson and Richard Harris and the
dancer Moira Shearer, with each of whom I appeared once, were not
at home with abstract ideas. The academic administrators, eventually
Lords Maud, Annan, Evans, James and Wolfenden, were safe and
sensible. The Wolfenden Report which recommended, among other
things, that homosexual practices between consenting adult males be

legalized was presented in 1957 but it took another ten years before a bill to that effect, initiated by Lord Arran in the House of Lords, received the Royal Assent. For the greater part of this period I was Chairman of the Society for Homosexual Law Reform, a cause in which I had no personal interest other than a concern for justice. It is easy to over-estimate the influence of societies of this kind but I like to believe that in this instance our propaganda did have a considerable effect upon Members of Parliament not so much directly as through its influence on public opinion.

The effect of any of the Brains Trust programmes upon public opinion is likely to have been evanescent. A possible exception was one put out in August 1957 when Julian Huxley and I confronted Father Martin d'Arcy and Lord David Cecil. The first question put to us was whether we believed in the Devil. 'No,' I said immediately, 'and not in God either,' giving my reasons as briefly as I could. Father d'Arcy responded with less than Jesuitical urbanity and a lively discussion followed in which the Anglican David Cecil joined forces with the Roman Catholic d'Arcy and Julian Huxley gave me his powerful support. Later in the programme we were asked whether we believed in original sin and Father d'Arcy said that he did. I was tempted but forebore to point out that this committed him to belief in the literal existence of Adam and Eve, since the doctrine of original sin is not, as is popularly supposed, that human beings are intrinsically wicked, but rather that the transgression of Adam and Eve has put a stain on all their descendants, with the solitary exception of the Virgin Mary, from which they need to be redeemed if they are to qualify for heaven. The doctrine of the Immaculate Conception, which is commonly confused with that of the Virgin Birth, extends the exemption to the Virgin Mary's mother, St Anne. Father d'Arcy, with whom my personal relations were always good from the time I first attended a class of his at Oxford, admitted after the programme that he would have been embarrassed if I had fastened these doctrines on to him and thanked me for not doing so.

There was an amusing sequel to this programme. It so happened that Father d'Arcy was not again invited to appear on the Brains Trust, and Frank Longford, or Frank Pakenham as he then was, suspected that this was due to my machinations. As he relates in his memoirs, Frank voiced this absurd idea to Father d'Arcy and quotes Father d'Arcy as replying, 'Oh no. Freddie Ayer is a gentleman.'

This is such a trite remark that I strongly doubt whether Father d'Arcy ever made it. What I suspect that he actually did was to quote the saying 'The Devil is a gentleman.' His identifying me with the Devil, in this context, would not have been inconsistent, on either part, with the maintenance of our personal friendship. However the conversation went, it did not prevent Frank Pakenham from making a speech in the House of Lords to the effect that since we lived in a Christian country such atheists as Julian Huxley and myself should not be permitted to appear on television. Characteristically, he then wrote me a letter in which he affirmed his respect for me and asked me not to take his action amiss. Seeing that he had been endeavouring to deprive me of part of my livelihood, I thought this rather cool, but I assured him, truly, that I bore him no ill-will. I might have felt differently if I had believed that there was any chance of his being taken seriously.

Most probably for reasons of economy, our Sunday lunches at Scott's were discontinued in 1959 and replaced by Thursday dinners at the television studios. In accordance with what became the general practice at the BBC the programmes no longer went out live, but were previously recorded, thereby losing some of their sparkle. For a time Michael Flanders, the entertainer, and John Wolfenden replaced Norman Fisher. John Furness was replaced by Jack Ashley and Catherine Freeman, then still Catherine Dove. One improvement was that the number of panellists was reduced from four to three. For one of my last appearances on the programme in England in October 1960, John Furness and Norman Fisher were back in their places and Alan Bullock and Marghanita Laski completed our familiar team.

I have already said that I enjoyed taking part in these programmes and I must also confess that I enjoyed the publicity which they brought me. One of its first fruits was an anonymous profile in the *Observer*, actually written by my old friend Philip Toynbee. It mainly consisted in a summary of my career and a fairly accurate account of my philosophical views, but it also contained flattering remarks on my intelligence and character. A critical comment with which I agreed was that my apparent assurance concealed an inner nervousness.

The profile appeared in September 1957. Rather more than a year later I received the rarer honour of being made the subject of a set of verses in *Punch*, appearing over the signature of E. V. Milner who was and has remained unknown to me. They were prefaced by a quotation from *The Problem of Knowledge* in which I argued that no sense was attachable to the notion that people were individuated as different souls or spiritual substances, and the verses made play with the duality of 'Freddie' and 'Professor A. J. Ayer'.

The point of the verses depended on my being differently identified by two strangers in a train and I am not suggesting that such episodes were typical. What more often happened, or so it seemed to me, was that people found my appearance familiar but could not actually place me. They would come up to me and say, 'Haven't we met somewhere before?' Or more specifically, 'Weren't you in business at Stockton-on-Tees?' I suppose that the kindest thing would have been to pretend that they did know me, but I was reluctant to do that and anyhow was not sure that I could sustain the deception. At the time it seemed rather rude just to say that they were mistaken; it might leave them with the impression that I had known them but had forgotten them. Usually I ended by saying, with some false modesty, 'Perhaps you have seen me on television?' Sometimes this would elicit recognition, sometimes embarrassment, seldom neither one or the other. What I liked best was being recognized by taxi-drivers, and this happened surprisingly often.

I received many letters from strangers, some appreciative, some intelligently critical, others the outpourings of lunatics, a few simply abusive. The most abusive came from professed Christians. In more than one case they expressed the hope that I or my children or anyone that I cared for should be stricken with some incurable disease: that would bring me face to face with their God. Through art and selective quotation one is so impressed with the image of 'gentle Jesus, meek and mild' that one has to read the Bible thoroughly to be reminded how savage a religion Christianity is. I did not answer hysterical letters of this type, nor those of out-and-out lunatics but I answered more than was prudent of those on the lunatic fringe. The trouble was that it often launched me on a correspondence which I felt it impolite to discontinue. The greatest nuisance were the people who sent me manuscripts, sometimes the length of books, with the request that I should comment on them and in some cases, not only that, but also use my influence to get them published. I cannot pretend that I read these manuscripts thoroughly, but I always glanced through them at least and was scrupulous about returning them, even when their authors had failed to provide postage.

I have been told that the reason why the Brains Trust was brought to an end was that a lady called Grace Wyndham-Goldie, who held a position of influence in the BBC, considered it middle-brow. In as much as it was intended both to be serious and to have popular appeal, I should have thought this a reason for maintaining rather than abandoning it, but I was not asked for my opinion. The programmes which replaced it were gaudier affairs with snappy titles like 'That was the week, that was' and 'Not so much a programme, more a way of life'. Some of them were quite fun to watch, but it should have been obvious to me that I was not suited to them. Very rashly, I allowed myself to be persuaded by Donald Baverstock, the producer of 'Not so much a programme' to be one of a quartet which included the singer, Eartha Kitt. I was seated on the left of the semi-circle and she was put next to me. We were asked a question about romantic love and I tried to talk learnedly about the troubadours. Out of mischievousness or boredom she made a show of flirting with me. Instead of bringing my speech to an end, or better still responding in kind, I floundered on and was made to look thoroughly foolish. The producer and the Chairman, my friend Ned Sherrin, pronounced it 'good television', and asked me to appear on the programme in the following week, but I had learned my lesson and declined. At this distance of time I can see that my success on the Brains Trust had given me an uncritical appetite for publicity.

Since then, I have been more circumspect. To be honest, I have not had very many temptations of this sort to resist. At one time, as I have already mentioned, I was quite frequently invited to take part in televised discussions of Association Football, but except on the rare occasions when I could persuade myself that I was being genuinely invited for my expertise, I have made it a rule to refuse. I have also taken to refusing the invitations that I still occasionally receive to take part in religious debates on television. I have nothing new to add to what I have said and written on this topic, and prefer to rely on my writings to win converts to my point of view. I have enjoyed the comparatively little work that I have done for the Open University, and would gladly have done more, and I have enjoyed my occasional appearances on book programmes. I also do not mind being interviewed, so long as the interviewer does not try to put me down, but I have long ceased to be a fashionable subject. In view of the passage of years, there is no reason why it should be otherwise.

As my work for the Brains Trust did not require any preparation, I was not hampered by it in my social life or inclined to devote any less attention to the running of my department at University College. By this time Jocelyn had formed a strong attachment to the playwright John Osborne, with whom I was not altogether comfortable, but she and I remained very close friends. I was increasingly involved with Dee but we were not seen as a couple and I did not regard myself as in any way debarred from making love to other women, though as I entered my late forties I began to think that it was time for me to make at least some effort to settle down. Renée's influence over me had waned, though I still visited her fairly regularly in a small house which she had taken in Hampstead. She mostly lived there alone, as Julian spent the greater part of the year at Eton and Valerie had made her escape to the United States.

The philosophy department was now comfortably housed at 19 Gordon Square. I had a large room on the first floor in which I held my tutorials and classes, including the Monday seminars. It was also the place of meeting for our Philosophical Society. There was a lecture room on the ground floor with a student common room and a room for our devoted secretary, Miss Darling. There were enough rooms on the upper floors for each of the staff who gave tutorials besides lecturing. Richard Wollheim, who had become a Reader, and Johnny Watling were still with me. James Thomson and Peter Long, who had fairly soon followed Thomson to Cambridge, had been replaced by two senior men whom I had also promoted from the department, A. H. Basson, who later changed his name to Cavendish, and Peter Downing. Between the five of us we managed to cover ancient philosophy up to Aristotle, modern philosophy from Descartes to the present century, logic, the theory of knowledge, the philosophy of mind and moral and political philosophy. I gave classes to undergraduates at all levels but now restricted my supervision to graduates. One of them, Timothy Sprigge, who came to me for help with a thesis on ethics which gained him a doctorate in Cambridge, now holds a Chair of Philosophy at Edinburgh; another, Robin Denniston, has become a power in the world of publishing; another, Oliver Stutchbury devised the concept of unit trusts and acted for a time as financial adviser to the Labour Party until he lost patience with Transport House.

Among the most interesting of my graduate pupils were three from

Yugoslavia. Two of them, Mihailo Marković from Belgrade and Gayo Petrović from Zagreb, considered themselves to be Marxists, but they were Marxists of a very flexible kind. Marković obtained a London doctorate with a thesis in the domain of the philosophy of science. Petrović did not work for a degree but spent two years in the department. On returning to their own country both of them obtained Chairs at their respective universities and they were both elected to the International Institute of Philosophy. They were among the founders of the journal *Praxis* which flourished from 1964 until it was closed down by the authorities in 1975. As Kolakowski put it in the third volume of his *Main Currents of Marxism*, 'The *Praxis* group played an important part in disseminating a humanistic version of Marxism not only in Yugoslavia but in the international philosophical world; they also contributed to reviving philosophical thought in Yugoslavia and were an important centre of intellectual resistance to autocratic and bureaucratic forms of government in that country.' I was a member of the editorial board of *Praxis*, though I do not know that I contributed anything to its orientation other than what Marković and Petrović may have learned from me as my pupils, and whatever influence the translation of *The Problem of Knowledge* into Serbo-Croat and lectures I gave in Yugoslavian universities may have exercised. When *Praxis* was banned, the Zagreb philosophers weathered the storm. The Belgrade group, including Marković, were forbidden to teach but they retained their salaries and Marković has been allowed to accept numerous invitations from American universities.

My third Yugoslav was Edo Pivcević. Unlike the others he was too strongly opposed to the regime even to attempt to reform it from the inside. He had previously been to a German university where he had become wedded to phenomenology, as developed by Husserl, about whom he later published an informative book. There was little that I could teach him but we became personal friends and I helped him to secure a lectureship in the philosophy department of Bristol University. A Croatian nationalist, he even induced me to join the Anglo-Croatian Society, though I have never taken any active part in its proceedings.

In 1957 I was invited by the Trustees of the Sulgrave Manor Board to give the Sir George Watson lectures for that year. The lectures, which were given annually, were officially required to be focused on the United States but I persuaded the trustees that this could be taken to cover a comparison of·British with American philosophy. Accordingly, in a series of four lectures under the overall title of 'Pragmatism and Analysis', I attempted to trace the course of the main stream of American philosophy from Peirce and James to Quine and Goodman, alongside that of the main stream of British philosophy from Moore and Russell, to Austin and Ryle. The lectures, which were delivered at University College, were well received, but when I reviewed them with a view to publication I thought them sketchy, especially on the American side. This led me to make a serious study of the work of Charles Sanders Peirce and William James, resulting in a book called *The Origins of Pragmatism* which I published in 1968. It contained an exposition and criticism of what I took to be the principal theses of these two philosophers, making them also a springboard for the expression of my own views. I expected the book to be a success, at least in the United States, but I was disappointed, in spite of a favourable review from Morton White in the *New York Review of Books*. The trouble was that those who might have been interested in my own theories were put off by the historical title of the book, while the professional historians of pragmatism found it insufficiently specialized. The British component of my Sir George Watson lectures resulted still later in a study of the philosophy of Bernard Russell and G. E. Moore, which furnished the William James lectures which I delivered at Harvard in 1970, and appeared as a book in 1971 under the title of *Russell and Moore: the Analytical Heritage*. This had a more favourable reception especially in England, but I myself consider *The Origins of Pragmatism* to be the better book of the two.

9 *East and West*

In the spring of 1958 I accepted an invitation from the British Council to undertake a lecture tour of India and Western Pakistan, the eastern sector of Pakistan not yet having broken away to become the country of Bangladesh. The tour was very extensive. Starting at Calcutta I flew south to Madras, then west to Bangalore, then south west to Mysore, then took the long flight north-west to Bombay and the even longer flight north-east from Bombay to Delhi. From Delhi I flew to Karachi, the capital of Pakistan, and was then driven through the desert by an official of the British Council to Hyderabad, Sind, where the philosophers of Pakistan were holding a congress, returned in the same way to Karachi and then came home. Besides taking part in the Pakistani congress, I gave lectures at the Universities of Calcutta, Madras, Bombay and Delhi and lectured also at Bangalore. From Madras I made an excursion to see the remarkable sculptures at Mahabalipuram and from Delhi I went south to Agra to see the celebrated fort and the Taj Mahal and still further south to visit the temples at Ellora and Ajanta, deservedly famous for their erotic sculpture.

If anyone is antecedently well-disposed towards India and its way of life, I should advise him not to make Calcutta his port of entry. It is not only that it is an ugly, noisy, dirty city, terrifyingly overcrowded. What is most shocking is the calm acceptance of these evils. When I was there, refugees, whom the city had no way to accommodate, were pouring in from the north. Disease had broken out among them with the result that a whole section of the city was simply cordoned off. Inside the fairly grand hotel where I was staying, there were numerous servants in livery who rushed to light one's cigarette. Outside, lying on the pavement, was a row of dying men. If one or two of them died in the course of the night, others quickly took their place. One saw men pulling heavily loaded carts, because their labour was cheaper than that of horses or oxen. I was told that their expectation of life was less than thirty years.

Physically, the most attractive place in Calcutta was the English cemetery. Looking at the tombstones, I was surprised by the preponderance of youthful deaths, not so much the deaths of young children, but of people in early manhood. When I read the memoirs of William Hickey, a fascinating record of life in India in the early part of the nineteenth century, before the Indian Mutiny caused the East India Company to give way to the British Raj and the arrival of the womenfolk of British officials brought about a degree of racial segregation that had not previously existed, I thought that the early deaths were due to the enormous consumption by the English nabobs of food and drink, especially drink, which was fatally unsuited to the local climate. I still think that there is some truth in this but I also reflected that successful traders would be likely to have made their fortunes by early middle-age and would then have chosen to enjoy their wealth in England rather than peter out in India. This was in fact true of William Hickey himself.

I have owned to a slight interest in early Indian logic but I found no one to share it in the universities which I visited. Neither did I discover anyone capable of instructing me in the theories of Vedanta which were funnelled through Hollywood into the United States, an omission which I did not regret. For one thing, professors of philosophy at Indian universities did not read Sanskrit. For another, they were so poorly paid that they had to supplement their salaries by journalism and other means. Consequently they had no leisure to think about their subject. What had secured them their posts was their ability to reproduce what they had been taught, and they required the same of their large number of pupils, mostly women who wanted a university degree as a mark of emancipation and found philosophy an easy option.

What these professors had been taught, and what they were relaying to their pupils, was a version of absolute idealism. This may indeed have harmonized with some aspects of Vedanta or Zen Buddhism, but it was not indigenous in origin. It had been brought to India at the end of the nineteenth century by a set of philosophical evangelists, mainly Scotsmen, who clove to the prevailing fashion of neo-

Hegelianism. The texts which were handed down were the works of F. H. Bradley and T. H. Green. Apart from the reason which I have already given for their retention, they were planted in fertile soil. An inhabitant of a place like Calcutta would have a motive for believing that appearances are not real.

Another factor, which favoured the preservation of tradition, was the respect shown by Indian students for the printed word. This was brought home to me when I lectured on pragmatism and fell into an argument with one of the older members of my audience in the course of the subsequent discussion. The next day he approached me privately and showed me a copy of an issue of *Mind*, going back to the 1890s, in which there was an article supporting his opinion. 'You see,' he said triumphantly, 'I knew that I was right.' 'All that this shows,' I said, 'is that not everything which finds its way into print is true, even in such a respectable journal as *Mind*.' But that was a proposition which I could not get him to admit.

It would be unfair, however, to judge the intellectual life of Calcutta by the standard of its University, or indeed to judge the University by the quality of its department of philosophy. Young Indians of ability were encouraged to take up subjects which had a practical bearing on the welfare of their country. They were to be found in the departments of mathematics, or physics or biology. Among the social sciences, economics was especially favoured. It was, indeed, on this, my only visit to Calcutta, that I first met Amartya Sen, an outstanding young economist who had, if I remember rightly, already been invited to work in Cambridge. For some years now he has occupied a Chair of Economics in Oxford. It was a pleasure for me to converse with him and his friends. It was a pleasure too to renew my acquaintance with Lindsay Emerson, who had been some years junior to me at my preparatory school and in College at Eton. I had last seen him twenty-five years before on a visit to Cambridge where he was still an undergraduate. He had become editor of *The Statesman*, an excellent English language newspaper. He had an Indian wife, a range of acquaintances among Indian artists and writers and an interest in Indian politics, which reconciled him to living in Calcutta and made him very well qualified for the post which he held.

What I enjoyed most of all was calling upon J. B. S. Haldane in his biological institute. He had resigned his professorship at University College at the time of Suez, saying that he refused to live and work any longer in a criminal country. His wife Helen, who was also employed in the department of biology at UCL had followed his example and accompanied him to Calcutta. In his case, the force of his gesture was perhaps diminished by the fact that he was due to reach the retiring age for London university professors anyway in three years' time and had, I think, already made arrangements for continuing his work in India, but he was a man of strong feeling and there is no reason to doubt that his disapproval of the behaviour of the British Government over Suez was strongly felt. He had parted company with the Communist Party when a disciple of Lysenko visited his laboratory and criticized his work on genetics, at which point, so the rumour ran in the college, he had laid hands on the visitor and forcibly ejected him, but his sympathies remained with the left, and the political standpoint of India, at that time, would not have been uncongenial to him. I am sure, however, that his main motive was philanthropic. He agreed with Swift that 'Whoever could make two ears of corn or two blades of grass to grow upon a spot of ground where only one grew before, would deserve better of mankind, and do more essential service to his country than the whole race of politicians put together.' He thought that he had the skill to perform a feat of this kind, and that he could discover Indian pupils to whom to impart it: there could be no doubt that the country needed it.

When I visited him, I was amused to see him wearing an Indian smock, which accentuated his corpulence, but he claimed to find it more comfortable than Western clothing. On the whole he seemed satisfied with his decision to settle in Calcutta. There were things that tried his temper, such as the lack of punctuality shown by some of those with whom he had practical dealings, and still more their habit of telling him what they thought he wished to hear rather than what was actually the case, but he had attracted some able pupils with whose help his own research was prospering, and that more than outweighed any vexations to which he was subjected. I have kept and shall be reproducing two letters which he wrote me in the following year, but I was not to see him again until he returned to England to undergo an operation for cancer of the rectum from the effects of which he died in 1964. Even he could not prevent India from obeying Malthus's law that population rises to the level of food supply, but I am sure that he did as much as any man could to diminish the evil of its consequences.

Aesthetically, Madras was a great improvement on Calcutta. The city itself was more attractive, the atmosphere more relaxed, there was much less evidence of poverty. Excursions to view the remains of Tippoo Sahib's palace and the animal sculptures of Mahabalipuram were both rewarding. What was lacking, at least so far as I could discover, was any intellectual drive. The same was true of Mysore and Bangalore, both of which were very pleasant places to visit. The Maharajah of Mysore was said to be interested in philosophy and was indeed made an honorary member of the International Institute in the following year when the Institute held its annual congress in Mysore, one of the very few between the years 1953 and 1978 that I did not attend; but I fear that the award of his honorary membership may have been rather a mark of gratitude for his patronage than a tribute to his philosophical ability.

A notable feature of all this southern part of India was the pervasiveness and strength of the belief in astrology. Few major decisions were taken, such as that of the date of a wedding, or even the choice of a marriage partner, without consultations with the stars. The theory was not scientific, in the sense of satisfying Karl Popper's criterion of falsifiability: it was not open to empirical refutation. On the other hand, it was not frivolous like the versions that find their way into Western journals. It was not assumed that all those born under the same sign of the zodiac, no matter on what day or in what year, had the same character or were destined to undergo the same fortune. The horoscopes which fuelled the theory were very carefully cast.

Bombay was more garish than Calcutta, though hardly more prosperous. One had the feeling, however, that something might be done about the poverty there, if anyone cared enough to do it, whereas in Calcutta the problem had seemed hopeless. The University was again a disappointment, but I saw more evidence than I had in Madras of a flourishing intellectual life outside it. In particular, I came across a vigorous group of young painters, working, it seemed to me, very much in the style of Rouault.

From every point of view the highlight of my tour was my visit to Delhi and its neighbourhood. Not only did the well-known tourist attractions, Ellora, Ajanta, Agra and the Taj Mahal entirely fulfil their promise but I admired Lutyens' New Delhi itself. It reminded me of the new city of Rabat which Marshal Lyautey had commissioned for the French in Morocco. I was very comfortably housed by the head of the British Council in India and his wife, Henry and Jane Croom-Johnson, who not only introduced me to their most interesting friends, like the writer Khushwant Singh, but also procured me official introductions of which I shall describe the use I made. The only drawback was that Delhi was in one of the parts of India where prohibition was in force. In order to be allowed to consume alcohol in public, one had to register as an alcoholic. Since no evidence was required, I had no objection to doing this, but then found that it enabled one only to drink in rooms, set aside for the purpose, which might contain genuine alcoholics. I tried this once, but found it so gloomy that I preferred to rely on the hospitality of the Croom-Johnsons and their friends who had either circumvented the restrictions or were not subject to them.

The interviews arranged for me were with the President, Radakrishnan, the Prime Minister, Jawaharlal Nehru and the Defence Minister, Krishna Menon. Of these the least satisfactory was my interview with Krishna Menon. He was an important figure in the Indian government of the time, not only in virtue of his office but through the reputation, which he had acquired while living in England, as a theorist of the left. I should have been happy to discuss political theory with him and happier still to learn about the problems with which he was currently dealing, but he appeared to take the view that he had condescended to me sufficiently in granting me an audience. We were constantly interrupted by messengers and telephone calls and I took my leave after little more than an exchange of courtesies.

This was in marked contrast to my reception both by Radakrishnan and by Nehru. With Radakrishnan, whom I already knew slightly, I discussed philosophy. He had held the Chair of Eastern Religions and Ethics at Oxford and embraced a form of idealism which was very foreign to my own way of thinking, but he was more anxious to be informed of recent developments in British philosophy than to engage in philosophical dispute. He complained that his official duties prevented him from paying the attention to philosophy which he would have preferred to do and implied that his assumption of the presidency was a duty which he had not thought it right to evade.

I should not have been surprised or offended if Nehru had vouchsafed me only a formal interview, but in fact he talked with me most freely. He must have given orders that he was not to be disturbed during our meeting, for we conversed without interruption for the best part of an hour. His looks reminded me of Charlie Chaplin's, as Chaplin had appeared to me in the flesh not on the screen, but he gave me an impression of much greater sincerity. We spoke of the Hindu religion which he did not go so far as to condemn outright but clearly found a political liability. He had been a loyal lieutenant to Gandhi but seemed far from sharing Gandhi's cult of the spinning-wheel and all that went with it. He had the practical aim of modernizing India, in the Western sense, but had no illusions about the obstacles to its fulfilment. We did not speak of the prevalence of corruption, though it can hardly have escaped his notice. He complained rather of the reluctance of his subordinates to accept responsibility. He could lay down guidelines but could not occupy every stage in the chain of command in order to make sure that they were followed. I had no ideas that were of any value to him, but I was captivated by his intelligence and charm.

I was sorry to leave Delhi, especially as I had then to proceed to Karachi, which seemed to me even uglier than Calcutta and hardly less poverty stricken. By now it was growing very hot and I pitied the British Council official who had to convey me in a jeep through the Sind desert to Hyderabad and back, and share a bungalow with me for the duration of the philosophical congress. He rightly did not feel obliged to attend its meetings. It was a strange congress, if only because every meeting was preceded by a reading from the Koran. Some pious sentiments were expressed, but I cannot recall there being any philosophical argument. Hyderabad itself had nothing to commend it and I was not disposed or indeed invited to linger in Karachi. I left, therefore, with a very unfavourable impression of Pakistan. It might have been different if I had had the leisure or the opportunity to travel northwards to Lahore.

Not long after I returned to England, I received a telephone call from Valerie saying that she was engaged to be married and asking me to fly over to give her away. The wedding was to take place in Rochester, in New York State, where her prospective husband, Jack Wright, held some junior position at the University. It was never quite clear to me what his subject was: it appeared to hover between English literature, religion and philosophy. I was somewhat surprised to find that the ceremony was to take place in a hotel, even though I knew from watching American films that this was not an uncommon practice. Mrs Godley, Valerie's American foster-mother, was present and seemed to share my instinctive misgivings about my son-in-law. In fact it seemed to me even then that Valerie was not in love with him, but wanted to get married in order to remain in America and put herself at a distance from her mother. Nevertheless she strove to make a success of her marriage, coping as best she could with a husband who came increasingly to resent her. Eventually they agreed upon a divorce. Valerie came back to England, but did not feel at home there and soon found the means of returning to the United States. A few years later she made a second marriage to Brian Hayden, a charming and talented psychologist, and set up house with him in Providence, Rhode Island, becoming assistant curator of the local museum. She lived very happily with him until her premature death in 1981. She had no children by either marriage.

By 1958 Julian had left Eton and gone up to Oxford. He had not been unhappy at Eton but he wanted to get away from Etonians, so that he chose to go to Corpus Christi, an intellectually distinguished but unfashionable college. I had rather hoped that he would get a Soccer Blue, of which I believed him capable, but he preferred to concentrate on reading history, playing games only for his college. After he had taken his degree at Oxford, he moved to Corpus Christi College, Cambridge, to obtain a diploma in education. He found the Cambridge Corpus much more luxurious than its Oxford counterpart and his companions more like public schoolboys. This tallies with my own impression that Cambridge is in general richer than Oxford, more resistant to change, and more enclosed. Julian went on to become a schoolmaster at Dulwich for a short period before moving to the Middlesex Polytechnic, where he first taught history and then established himself as a careers officer. He married an attractive Brazilian girl with whom he lived on a houseboat moored at Chelsea but this marriage, which was childless, also ended in divorce.

Much of my spare time in 1958 was devoted to compiling an anthology of logical positivism. The book, which appeared in the following year under the title of *Logical Positivism*, was commissioned by the Free Press in New York and listed under the Library of Philosophical Movements, with Paul Edwards named as general editor. I wrote a twenty-five page introduction to the book, critically expounding the main doctrines of the Vienna Circle and making some assessment of its influence. I also selected the papers for inclusion, seventeen in all, of which four were written by Moritz Schlick, three by Rudolf Carnap and two by Otto Neurath. They were divided into six sections, comprising, first, Bertrand Russell's 'Logical Atomism', which formed a section of its own, then four papers under the heading of 'Philosophy, Metaphysics and Meaning', two under that of 'Logic and Mathematics', four under that of 'Knowledge and Truth', three under that of 'Ethics and Sociology', and finally three under that of 'Analytical Philosophy'. Almost all the papers in the second, third and fourth sections were taken from early number of *Erkenntnis* and were appearing in English for the first time. For the most part the translators, who had been selected by Paul Edwards, were more fluent in German than in English, so that I had to subject their work to extensive revision. The bibliography supplied to me by Edwards's pupils, for which he thanks them in his preface, was so slipshod as to be almost useless. I supplanted it by a bibliography, largely compiled by Miss Darling, which ran to sixty-five closely printed pages and included works which were either expository or critical not only of logical positivism, in any strict sense of the term, but of every form of modern analytical philosophy produced up to that date. The value of such a bibliography is bound to be ephemeral, but I think that it may still be found of use. The anthology was re-issued in paperback in 1966 and prospered also in a Spanish edition.

The twelfth International Congress of Philosophy was held in Venice in September 1958. It was one of the rare congresses, held on foreign soil, that Gilbert Ryle thought it worth his while to attend. He had planned to motor to Venice with his friend Harry Weldon, a tutor in philosophy at Magdalen, and when this intention was frustrated by Harry Weldon's death, Gilbert invited me to take his place. I accepted with pleasure but also with some trepidation. I suppose that I was his most successful pupil; we had been colleagues at Christ Church for six years before the war, we had been fellow subalterns at the Welsh Guards' training battalion, there was a difference of no more than ten years in our ages, but I still did not feel that I knew him very well. I was not even sure that he altogether liked me, tending, as I think he did, to regard me as more of a café society figure than I actually was. At the same time he may have thought that my cosmopolitanism would add to the interest of our expedition. In fact, apart from my fluency in French, I had little to offer as a guide, being a poor map-reader and having little knowledge of France apart from Paris, which we skirted. I was able to recommend some quite good hotels and restaurants, but nothing that he could not have discovered for himself by consulting *Michelin*. Nevertheless I think that he was pleased to have me for a companion and I enjoyed our journey, though I did not feel that it brought me any closer to him. His conviviality, displayed freely in a college common room or an officers' mess, masked a reserve which I was not the one to penetrate.

I had a happy memory of Venice, which I had visited briefly with Renée in 1935, and liked it even more on this occasion when I took advantage of the periods of leisure allowed us by the congress to explore it more thoroughly. The congress was distinguished by the appearance, for the first time, of a large delegation from the Soviet Union. They kept pretty much to themselves, but several of them seemed to go out of their way to make friends with me personally. I was a little surprised by this as I had received a letter from Bertrand Russell, admittedly dating back to 1952, in which he wrote that in a very long article on him published in *The Bolshevik* in Moscow he had discovered the sentence 'In his slander of materialists Russell outdoes even such full-grown bisons of contemporary imperialist philosophy like John Dewey, D. Santayana and Ayer.' Russell had added 'I am trying to learn to think of you as a bison, in the hope of becoming modern-minded.' I do not know why the bison was singled out for opprobrium, except for its being large, shaggy and American, or why Santayana was given the wrong initial, or why I was moved up into an older generation, but the personal attitude of the Russians towards me suggested that such denunciations were pieces of ritual which did not need to be taken seriously.

The paper which I read to this congress was called 'Meaning and Intentionality'. It was published in the proceedings of the congress and republished by me only eleven years later in *Metaphysics and Common Sense*. Owing a good deal to a thesis which I had supervised by Dr R. W. Ashby, who became a lecturer at King's College, London, it was an attempt to eliminate intentional entities by analyzing meaning in terms of belief and then giving the outline of a behavioural theory of belief. I still have some faith in the first part of this programme, though not in the second, at least in the way in which I presented it. My paper was dismissed by Alonzo Church on logical grounds which were not entirely clear to me, and very bitterly attacked by the Israeli philosopher, Y. Bar-Hillel, because it began with what I still regard as some well-founded criticisms of Carnap to whose work Bar-Hillel was wholeheartedly devoted. Bar-Hillel was magisterially rebuked by Ryle not for the content but for the tone of his speech. In the event it led to no lasting ill-will on either side.

The Cardinal of Venice at that date was Angelo Giuseppe Roncalli who later in the year was elected Pope John XXIII. He had the reputation of being well-versed in philosophy and with the minimum of requisite ceremony attended at least one of the sessions of the congress. I do not recall his taking any part in the discussion. No doubt it is only because he became Pope that his appearance remains in my memory.

By the autumn of 1958 Dee and I had drawn sufficiently close to one another to venture on the experiment of setting up house together. Our understanding was that we would get married if the experiment worked. We had spent part of the summer together in France, taking Gully with us, and staying with Francette Drin and Jo Saxe at a farmhouse which they had rented not far from Paris, and there seemed to be no difficulty over Gully's accepting me as a step-father. The house which Dee found for us in London was at 13 Conway Street, just off Fitzroy Square and within walking distance of University College. It was built in the early nineteenth century, a narrow house with four floors and a basement, so that I had a room for myself to work in and there were bedrooms for Gully and a maid. Conway Street now runs between Fitzroy Square and the Post Office Tower, but at that date the Post Office Tower was not yet built.

While the house was being made ready I accepted an invitation from the Yugoslav philosophers to tour their country. I visited Ljubljana, Belgrade, Zagreb, Sarajevo and Dubrovnik. I earned some dinars from my lectures but had to bank them in Ljubljana, along with the royalties owing to me from the translation into Serbo-Croat of *The Problem of Knowledge*, as Yugoslav currency could not be exported. I did not find much to admire in Belgrade, except for its situation, but I was gratified by the warmth of my welcome, which included my being taken to a football match by Professor Korać. Zagreb was a prettier town, which had retained the impression of its Austrian past, and it had the strongest department of philosophy in Yugoslavia. Professor Filipović, who headed it, was himself a neo-Kantian and he had recruited phenomenologists and existentialists besides such liberal

Marxists as my old pupil Gayo Petrović. The Rector of the University, Professor Vranicki, had written a more conventional history of Marxism but he too could lay fair claim to being a revisionist.

My reasons for visiting Sarajevo were not primarily academic, though I did have the unexpected pleasure of meeting a professor of linguistics who had mastered Welsh. I was surprised to discover the extent to which the Turkish occupation, preceding the Austrian, had left its imprint upon the town. The number of mosques, and the calls to prayer, indicated that it still contained many practising Moslems. It was also a symbol of Serbian nationalism because it was here that the murder of the Austrian archduke Franz Ferdinand and his wife took place in July 1914, provoking the First World War. Casts had been made allegedly of the footprints of the assassin Gavrilo Princip on the corner where he stood to fire the fatal shots, so that tourists could put themselves, as I dutifully did, in his position. Princip himself died in prison but two of the six young conspirators were still alive, both suitably employed, one as the curator of the museum at Sarajevo, the other as a professor of history at the University of Belgrade.

To conclude my tour by visiting Dubrovnik was a piece of self-indulgence. Not only was the railway journey winding slowly through the mountains itself a delight, but Dubrovnik, formerly Ragusa, on the eastern coast of the Adriatic, was as attractive a place for a holiday as any to be found in Europe. A large part of its attraction stemmed from the preservation of the old walled city, within which no motor traffic was allowed.

No sooner had I settled into 13 Conway Street, keeping up the lease of 2 Whitehorse Street which still had three years to run, but allowing Renée to occupy it, than Henry Price resigned the Wykeham Professorship of Logic at Oxford on the grounds of ill health and, after some hesitation, I decided to apply for the post. My motives were mixed. Principally, I think, I was moved by the fact that the Oxford Chair carried more prestige. It would also provide me with a challenge, which I suspected that I needed. The department at UCL was very much my own creation and I felt that I was in some danger of resting on my laurels. I did not care for the type of linguistic philosophy with which Austin was associating Oxford and I hoped that I could do something to counteract his influence. I suspect also that I unconsciously prized the measure of independence which the move would secure for me. The professorship carried with it a fellowship and a set of rooms at New College. Dee's job as a journalist would make it inconvenient for her to live outside of London and she had no desire to abandon the house which we had just moved into. We agreed that if I obtained the Oxford Chair I would spend four days a week in college during term and come home for long weekends. A factor which worked in favour of this arrangement was that the three terms which made up the academic year at Oxford were each of them only eight weeks long.

Not that my election was a foregone conclusion. If the title of the Chair was taken literally then W. C. Kneale, a Fellow of Exeter College, and a rather older man than I, might be thought to have a stronger claim. He had published an interesting book entitled *Probability and Induction* and was known to be at work, in collaboration with his wife Martha, a Fellow of Lady Margaret Hall, on a monumental history of logic. Peter Strawson, a Fellow of University College, had not yet published his brilliant book *Individuals* but he had published his *Introduction to Logical Theory* and was not too young to be eligible for the Chair. I had eminent supporters in the persons of Bertrand Russell and Isaiah Berlin, each of whom readily agreed to supply a favourable reference, but though two references were asked for in the advertisement for the post, I did not think that they would have much influence on the electors, who would be likely already to have made up their minds about the comparative merits of the candidates.

The election, as I afterwards learned, took a slightly strange course. The electors were the President of Magdalen, not himself a philosopher but acting in his capacity as Vice Chancellor, the Warden of New College, Sir William Hayter, a former diplomat who had ended his career in the Foreign Office as Ambassador to Moscow, the philosopher Anthony Quinton, also representing New College, the two other philosophy professors Ryle and Austin, J. D. Mabbott of St Johns, representing the philosophy sub-faculty and, as external expert, Professor John Wisdom from Cambridge. On the first ballot, the two New College electors and John Wisdom cast their votes for me, Ryle and Mabbott voted for Kneale, and Austin for Strawson. There was at least one other applicant for whom nobody voted. The Vice Chancellor, remarking that I already had as many votes as all the other candidates put together, added his own vote to those that I had received and declared me elected. Either Ryle, Austin or Mabbott, or perhaps all three of them, raised the objection that none of the philosophical experts on the committee who represented Oxford University, or in other words not one of themselves, had voted for me and asked that the meeting be adjourned to allow time for further reflection. The Vice Chancellor refused their request on the grounds that even if they agreed on a candidate my four votes would still outnumber his three. The result was that I was invited to occupy the Chair and Ryle, Austin and Mabbott all resigned from the electoral board, a clear instance of locking the stable door after the horse had bolted. It was conveyed to me that their gesture was intended to express disapproval not of my election but of the high-handedness of the Vice Chancellor, but, to say the least, it was open to being misconstrued. Gilbert Ryle wrote to welcome me, adding that he might as well confess, since I was bound to learn it from the grapevine, that he had not voted for me. Austin did not write.

There were others who did. I received the most charming letter from Henry Price, saying that my election had given him great pleasure on philosophical as well as personal grounds, that he considered himself a British empiricist and that it was nice to think that his successor was to be a British empiricist too. Maurice Bowra said that he had always been unhappy about my being in London, and that I was needed back in Oxford where I really belonged. One of my old Eton masters, A. S. F. Gow, Fellow in Classics at Trinity College, Cambridge, A. E. Housman's executor, and one who like myself had been a friend of George Orwell's sent me his compliments and added that his own dislike of abstract thinking was such that it may well have been our respective guardian angels who sent him to Cambridge and removed me at an early age from his tuition. My old Christ Church tutor in ancient Greek history, R. H. Dundas, sent me a characteristically astringent postcard, signed as always simply 'D', and saying in its entirety 'Excellent; what glorifies the Professor sheds a little lunar radiance on the Tutor – All good men go to or fro New College: but I think the wiser go fro. No answer.' He himself had gone straight from New College to Christ Church; I, more indirectly, the reverse.

The most amusing letter I received came from J. B. S. Haldane. It began:

I suppose I must congratulate Oxford on recapturing you. Possibly I should congratulate you. I think you are succeeding

Price. He is one of the people who never quite recovered from me. In 1919 or 1920 I gave him 10 tutorials on the physiology of the human senses and a little about the brain. They were highly misleading and crude, being largely concerned with 'illusions'. He shows little evidence of having learned much more on the subject since then.

I need hardly say that I considered this exceedingly unfair to Price. Haldane then went on to say that he had discovered 'the literary "source" of *le néant* and all that' in a play of Schiller's, *Die Jungfrau von Orleans*, Act II Scene VI, quoting in the original German a passage of which the English translation is '. . . and the only profit we carry away from the battle of life is the insight into nothingness'. He then went on to quote in Latin a passage about the vanity of all pursuits from Bernard's *De Contemptu Mundi*, asking me to find him an edition of this work for which I could pay with money he had left with Lionel Penrose, since he doubted if there was a copy in India. His letter continued:

I certainly have no feeling of 'peremptory nullification' at this moment (to quote Donne's sermon on death) as my young colleague Subodh Kumar Roy has increased the yield of 3 small rice plots by 121% (i.e. more than doubled it) and there seems no obvious reason why he shouldn't do so for the rice growing area of the world.

After remarking that this discovery was an offshoot of a project of Haldane's own which looked as if it might give gains of ten or twenty per cent only, he concluded:

The plain fact is that we don't know anything about tropical agriculture, and the situation is vastly complicated by the hordes of experts who nevertheless get enough done to be an economic asset. This is a paranoiac letter, but suggests that I am not wholly miserable and abject.

I replied, thanking him for his letter, defending my decision to return to Oxford and saying among other things 'How like you to find the reference to *das Nichts* in Schiller.' This elicited another long letter from him, in which he said that he thought I was right to go back to Oxford, but denied that there was anything remarkable about his knowledge of Schiller.

Millions of unfortunate school children [he wrote] must read the passage. But they have been conditioned to think only one thing at a time whereas I am like Macheath 'I sip each flower. I change every hour'. I owe this to my father, who encouraged me to get an all-round education, while all my schoolmasters, not to mention my mother, were against it.'

He again referred to Bernard, of whose book I eventually succeeded in finding him a copy, quoting in the original Latin one of his less felicitous couplets but saying that he nevertheless regarded him as a great poet, 'so how could I help remembering scraps of him?' In my own letter I had suggested that it was no longer possible to have enough knowledge to be in a position to make a synthesis of all the natural sciences, but that he came as near to achieving it as anyone I knew. He replied that he thought one could have enough knowledge to do some synthesis. 'But,' he went on,

one should let the synthesis come 'of itself'. For example my young colleague Mr Dronamraju is observing the visits of various insect species to different colour varieties of the same plant species. Roughly speaking they are voting on whether they like a new variety. This may have been just as important in plant evolution, as was sexual selection in animal evolution (first measured by J. M. Rendel in my laboratory). Now I begin to have some slightly novel thoughts about mind in evolution. Similarly some embryo thoughts first adumbrated in 1932 about the physical nature of mental processes in general are beginning to come to birth. Perhaps the birth will be judged as 'Riduculus Mus', perhaps as one of 'These yelling monsters that with ceaseless cry, Surround me, as thou saw'st, hourly conceived and hourly born.' Yes, I have got a copy of Paradise Lost which I unfortunately do not know by heart, particularly not the author's spelling.
Poscimur. Tea is ready.

When he wrote this letter Haldane had only three more years to live. He was afflicted, as I mentioned earlier, with cancer of the bowel, and returned to England to have an operation, which was temporarily successful, at University College Hospital. During his convalescence he frequently visited us in Conway Street, always bringing a cushion with him, and we returned his calls at a house where he went to live near Golders Green. Characteristically he published a set of light verses about his condition. I remember only the first two lines: 'I wish I had the voice of Homer to sing of rectal carcinoma'. He was a man of whom I sincerely believe that we shall not see his like again.

10 *Return to Oxford*

My election to the Wykeham Professorship earned me a place in the 'Portrait Gallery' of the *Sunday Times*. The text was much briefer than that of my earlier profile in the *Observer* but, if anything, more flattering. Among other things, it referred to me as the Hoad of philosophical discussion, having a powerful service and returning with interest anything that came my way. This provoked from 'Peter Simple' of the *Daily Telegraph* a cartoon of Bertrand Russell leaping, racket outstretched, over a tennis net, with the caption:

> Pancho Gonzales
> Said, flexing his muscle
> 'If Ayer is Hoad
> Then I'm Bertrand Russell.'

If the implication was, as I assumed it to be, that Gonzales in his prime was a better player than Hoad, I think that Peter Simple had hit upon a fair analogy.

Though my election took place in January, I was not scheduled to take office until the new academic year in October, which still left me two terms to keep at UCL. It was soon decided that Stuart Hampshire was to succeed me, returning for this purpose from Oxford where he had replaced Goronwy Rees as Bursar of All Souls. I still had qualms about leaving the department, especially as I had lured Bernard Williams from New College to join it as a lecturer. In fact neither Stuart nor he remained in the department for very long after I left it. I think that Bernard was the first to go, replacing H. B. Acton in the Chair of Philosophy at Bedford College, London, after Acton had exchanged his Chair for one in Edinburgh, partly in protest against

Bedford's decision to admit men as well as women, which he regarded as a violation of its statutes. Bernard did not remain long at Bedford College either, succeeding Braithwaite in the Chair of Moral Philosophy at Cambridge which he later resigned to become Provost of King's. Stuart presided over the department at UCL for a few years longer but was never, or so it seemed to me, entirely at ease in its rather rough and tumble atmosphere and gladly accepted the offer of a Chair at Princeton in the United States. After he was settled in Princeton Renée at last agreed to marry him.

I still possess a document inscribed 'To Professor Ayer from students and colleagues, a gesture of appreciation for all you have given as philosopher and friend' dated 18 June 1959, with seventy-nine signatures. It was given to me at a party in my room at 19 Gordon Square, when I was presented with the original of a famous New Yorker cartoon in which a roguish computer is shown confronting two white-coated technicians one of whom, reading from a tape, reports 'It says "Cogito ergo sum".' The department had also collected money for me to have my portrait painted. I asked Robin Campbell, who had joined the Arts Council, to recommend me an up-and-coming painter and he suggested one who accepted the commission. We had several sittings but I did not like the way the picture was developing and he showed less and less inclination for the task. The result was that we simply let it lapse. He kept the advance on which his agent had insisted and I kept the unfinished picture, without ever displaying it, and the remainder of the money. It would have been dealing more honestly with the donors to have bought something with it, but there was not enough left to attract another artist, and I was content with the cartoon as a memento, without being able to think of any other object that I desired as an addition to it.

Leaving Gully in the care of her father, who had been posted to the American Embassy in London and took her on holiday with him, Dee and I spent one summer holiday in Le Castellet where some rooms had been found for us by Bill and Pussy Deakin. The Deakins had bought a house in Le Castellet, a very pretty village in the Var, within fifteen kilometres of the southern coast, where they eventually settled after Bill had resigned the wardenship of St Antony's. They had not room to put us both up but the accommodation which they found for us was very comfortable. We hired a two-horse power Citroën from a garage in Toulon which conveyed us to the beach at

St Cyr and on other excursions, and we were so much taken with the countryside that we formed a vague intention of finding a house there for ourselves.

It was in our rooms in Le Castellet that I composed a lecture on Privacy which I had undertaken to deliver to the British Academy as its Henriette Hertz Lecture for 1959. It could be regarded as a sequel to the essay 'Can there be a Private Language?' which had appeared in the *Supplementary Proceedings of the Aristotelian Society* for 1954 as the first paper in a symposium, taking place at Oxford, in which the other participant was Rush Rhees, a faithful disciple of Wittgenstein's. I was to reprint both pieces in *The Concept of a Person*, a collection of my essays which I published in 1963.

Re-reading them now I think that the earlier paper was the more important. Like much else in his *Philosophical Investigations* the import of Wittgenstein's exclusion of private languages was not entirely clear, but what he was generally understood to be maintaining was that for a sign to have meaning its use must be governed by a rule the observance of which could be publicly checked. Consequently, a man could not significantly refer to his own private thoughts and feelings unless they were associated with outward manifestations which enabled others to monitor his usage. This line of reasoning had been widely accepted and it was grist to the mill of those, like Ryle and Austin, who sought to deny that our perception of physical objects was mediated by private sense-experiences. I countered Wittgenstein's argument by pointing out that all understanding of signs depended in the last resort on what I called acts of primary recognition. If I was checking my usage I had to rely on other observations, whether or not they took the form of interpreting signs made by other people, and here it made no difference whether the sign I was concerned with referred to a public object or to a private sensation: in either case I ended with the simple identification of some sensory item. There has been much discussion of this issue but I have yet to find that my argument has been confuted.

In the same paper I advanced the view that a Robinson Crusoe, abandoned on his island before he had learned to speak, need find no more difficulty in inventing words to describe his sensations than in inventing names for the flora and fauna of his island. I argued that if he failed it would be for empirical and not for logical reasons. Here too I still think that I was right.

My lecture on privacy did not traverse this ground but was devoted to the different ways in which the distinction between what was private and what was public had been drawn by philosophers and the imperfect extent to which these distinctions coincided with what was said to be mental and what was said to be physical. My most contentious claim was that there were thoughts and feelings to which I could fairly be said to have private access in the sense that my authority as to their occurrence could not legitimately be overridden. This would not be so if the physicalists were right in identifying mental states with states of the central nervous system, for then there might be circumstances in which a physiologist's report of my thoughts and feelings could show my own to be mistaken: there would be no mental territory over which I should be sovereign. I should regard this however rather as an argument against physicalism.

1959 was the year in which I again became actively engaged in politics. My duties at UCL, combined with my broadcasting and my active social life, had kept me fully occupied during the time that I spent in England and my engagement in civic affairs had been limited to two appearances in the law courts, once as a juror and once as a character witness. I had appeared as a character witness on behalf of a friend of Jane Ainley's, who was charged with possessing marijuana. The pub in which he had been arrested was known to be one in which drug trafficking occurred but he claimed that the drug had been planted on him. I could say only that I had met the defendant on numerous occasions and had never found any reason to believe that he took drugs. Some other character witnesses gave similar evidence. The judge in his summing-up laid stress on the respectability of the witnesses who had testified to the defendant's character and Jane's friend was acquitted. I think that he profited by the fact that his case was the last of a rapid series in which each of his predecessors had been convicted, so that the jury was disposed to give him the benefit of the doubt. Jane said that it restored her belief in British justice. I considered that it was more a matter of luck.

There was no doubt about the case in which I served as a juror. It took place at the Old Bailey and lasted several days. Its main interest lay in the fact that the defendant was the son of a notorious murderer of the 1930s. The accusation was one of fraud in the management of a private company, and the case took so long because of the instances of fraud were numerous and complex. I was made foreman of the jury and had no difficulty in persuading its members to join me in finding the defendant guilty, except for one juror, who while having no doubt that the defendant had committed the fraud was not convinced that the evidence offered by the prosecution had established the fact beyond reasonable doubt. Since in those days verdicts had to be unanimous, we spent some considerable time in allaying this juror's scruples. Finally I was able to inform the judge that we had all agreed in finding the defendant guilty and he was sentenced to eighteen months' imprisonment. Though I cannot see any rational argument in favour of retributive punishment, I confess that I have never felt any remorse for my part in this affair.

The re-awakening of my active interest in politics was at least partly due to my friendship with most of the leading Labour politicians. I do not remember how I came to meet them all, but there were very few of them that I did not know personally and fewer still that I did not like. I became a member of what was known as the Gaitskell circle. This brought me closer to Roy Jenkins, whom I had known very slightly since he was first elected to Parliament, and also to Tony Crosland to whom I had not been much attracted when he was a *habitué* of the Gargoyle. I still disliked his tendency to rudeness, even though I did not directly suffer from it, but I admired his energy and intelligence. Nevertheless in the tacit rivalry that was to develop between him and Roy Jenkins, I was always on Roy's side. Woodrow Wyatt was also a member of this group, surprising as this may seem to those who read his current journalism. It is not, however, entirely clear whether it is he or the Labour Party that has changed the most. He never made any secret of his enjoyment of worldly goods which I sometimes thought that he carried to excess. I have, however, to admit that my qualms did not move me so far as to make me decline his generous hospitality.

At that time social life cut across political boundaries much more than it seems to now. Hugh Gaitskell had a passion, even greater than my own, for dancing and his favourite dancing partner was Ann Fleming, the wife of Ian Fleming, the creator of James Bond, but formerly married to Lord Rothermere and having no more affection for the Labour Party than went with her saying that if there had to be such a party it was just as well that Hugh should lead it. Like Pamela Berry, later Lady Hartwell, another Conservative hostess whose salon I frequented, Annie Fleming was a friend of Maurice Bowra's and he and other dons from Oxford mingled at her house with people as diverse as Victor Rothschild, Cyril Connolly and Cecil Beaton. There was a streak of hardness in Annie which offended Dee to the point where she disliked the atmosphere at her parties, but I enjoyed them. I was a friend also of Ian and Caroline Gilmour's, partly because Ian shared my interest in professional football, and at their beautiful house at Isleworth we tended to meet Liberals rather than Conservatives, in particular Jo Grimond, whom I had known at Oxford before the war and Mark Bonham Carter who had fitfully attended my lectures after it. I thought very well of both of them as politicians and was sincerely sorry when Mark lost his seat in the House of Commons.

Social strife was more apt to occur within the Labour Party. For instance the only quarrel I ever had with Hugh Gaitskell was caused by my speaking well of Bertrand Russell. Hugh could not forgive Russell for his activity in the Campaign for Nuclear Disarmament. Partly for the same reason, though their political differences went deeper, Hugh and Michael Foot were barely on speaking terms. For my part, I was a good friend of Michael's, originally as a result of our common connection with Wadham. Michael had been an undergraduate there before the war and had remained very loyal to the college, and I was extremely proud of my election to an honorary fellowship there in 1957.

My appearances on the Brains Trust had made me enough of a public figure for the organizers of the Labour Party's campaign in the general election, which took place in the autumn of 1959, to think it advantageous to make some use of me. I appeared on a televised party political broadcast under the direction of Michael Foot's wife, Jill Craigie, and I also wrote a leading article in the *Observer* under the heading 'Why I shall vote Labour'. I confessed that I was still motivated by my hatred of the Conservatives of the 1930s and I admitted that Harold Macmillan was not a Baldwin or a Neville Chamberlain. I did not think that he would set about dismantling the welfare state, for which we had the Attlee government mainly to thank. Nevertheless I thought that the Labour Party were the safer custodians of it. I also argued, perhaps rightly at that date, that the Labour Party would do more to improve the general standard of education. I wrote politely about the Liberals but said that they had lost their identity, the present-day Tory Party being the heirs of the nineteenth-century Whigs and the Labour Party having supplanted the Radicals. I think that was true at the time. It is only recently that the Conservative Party has become populist and the Labour Party surrendered the better part of its radical heritage to the Social Democrats.

I was surprised by the extent of the Conservative victory in 1959, but do not think badly in retrospect of the government which it brought to power. It was surely very much superior to any of its Conservative successors. I do not believe that my judgement is affected by my personal liking for Harold Macmillan, whom I first met as my publisher before the war and again during the war when I came under his jurisdiction in the Middle East. This is not to say that I approved of the way in which he contrived to allow Mr Butler, who should have succeeded him, to be superseded by Lord Home.

While he was still Foreign Secretary I waited upon Lord Home as one of a deputation to ask him to make some protest against the misbehaviour of one of the Fascist powers, possibly some Portuguese mischief in Angola. He received us urbanely but made it quite clear that he would not do what we wanted. I remember the incident only because it seemed to me that when I spoke a flash of enmity passed between us. Nothing of this sort happened on the few occasions that we have since met socially and I do not suppose that he remembers me, any more than his wife is likely to remember the Greek lessons that we shared in her father's study at Eton.

Since the late 1950s I have not joined in many deputations or taken part in many protest marches, but I have been a steady supporter of humanitarian causes in ways that have not been merely confined to putting my name to letters which someone else has drafted, though I have to admit that most of my writing to the newspapers has taken this form. One of my earliest efforts of a more active sort was to accept the chairmanship of a committee against racial discrimination in sport. It was a very weak organization at that time and I cannot claim that we accomplished anything of practical importance. The partly successful attempts in later years to enforce a boycott of South Africa in every form of sport were mounted by organizations in which I held no official post.

In October 1959 I was one of five persons to be admitted to Fellowships at New College. The others were John Cowan, promoted from being a lecturer in German, Peter Dickens, supporting Lionel Staveley as a tutor in chemistry, Gary Bennett, the new Chaplain who was also a historian, and Dr Lumsden, the new organist. As the senior of the five I had to pronounce the Latin oath of allegiance on behalf of us all, undertaking among other things not to accept bribes to secure the election of inferior candidates, and admitting this to be a common practice. It must have been some time since this admission corresponded to the facts but when at some later date I suggested that the oath be emended accordingly, my colleagues' respect for tradition defeated me.

My seniority among the new Fellows gave me first choice of the available rooms in college. Being still officially a bachelor I was entitled to a full set. I chose the set vacated by the previous Chaplain, who had been preferred to a canonry elsewhere. It was one of the best sets in college. Being on the first floor of a staircase abutting on the garden, which was one of the showpieces of Oxford, it consisted of a large sitting room with windows on one side overlooking the garden and on another the eighteenth-century quadrangle, a small triangular-shaped bedroom, a rather larger room which served me as a work room, a library and occasionally as a dining room, and a very large bathroom with a clothes cupboard, an old fashioned lavatory and an old fashioned bath, later to succumb to modernization, unsought on my part, with its successor packed into a corner but itself originally planted in the middle of the room.

The set had fallen slightly into disrepair and the college gave me money to refurbish it. With Dee to advise me, I had the walls of the sitting room painted a light yellow, the bathroom white, my work room grey, and had ivy wallpaper in the bedroom. I had brought with me from Whitehorse Street a picture of a river scene by Julian Trevelyan which I had bought at a show of his in 1950, and now hung over my mantelpiece. On one of the side walls above some book-shelves, nearly always surmounted by a vase of flowers, which I was rather proud of my skill in arranging, I hung a picture by Jocelyn of two young girls standing out against a background of green leaves with two small birds in the foreground, painted in a style strongly influenced by the frescos of Livia's villa which we had seen together in Rome. On the wall overlooking the quad I hung a row of five prints of what looked like cut-outs of French soldiers of the Second Empire, infantry, artillery and Zouaves. They were grouped in such a way that half the number of soldiers, horses and guns in each print were presented upside-down. These prints were a gift from Jo Saxe, who presumably had acquired them in Paris. My best piece of furniture was a very handsome tallboy which had belonged to Renée's father and somehow fell into my keeping when we separated. I had also retained two painted shell-back chairs. There was nothing exceptional about the rest of the furniture, some of which was provided me by the college. The days of coal fires were over but I kept the rooms warm with a convector and a number of electric heaters.

The rooms on my staircase were nearly all occupied by dons. Immediately below me was John Buxton, Sub-Warden in the year of my arrival, an office which rotated annually among the Fellows, consequently presiding in common room and making the speech of welcome to the new Fellows at the Domus dinner, to be construed financially as dinner on the house, which heralded the beginning of the academic year. He made some complimentary remarks about us and we each replied in kind. John Buxton, himself a former undergraduate at New College, was a tutor in English, specializing in Elizabethan literature. He had been captured early in the war, and the years that he had spent as a prisoner had left their mark on him, making him difficult to know. Ultra conservative, he was wary of me at first, but my manners were good enough to reassure him and we quite soon became on very cordial terms.

Across the landing from me was the Wykeham Professor of Ancient History, in fact Greek History, the expansive Tony Andrewes, whom I had known since he was an undergraduate at New College and I at Christ Church. I have already described in *Part of My Life* how he failed to acquire me as a colleague when he was teaching ancient history at Pembroke before the war. A married man, he lived out of college so that I did nôt see so much of him as I could have wished. He came into college to work, and the sound of his typewriter was audible from my bathroom. Term after term I used to hear it spinning out his commentary on Thucydides.

The rooms immediately above mine were occupied by Herbert Nicholas, the tutor in politics who later became the first holder in Oxford of a Chair of American History and Institutions. Quiet and very polite, he had a strong sense of irony which endeared him to me. Sharing his interest in American politics, I drew him out on the subject as often as I could and learned a great deal from him.

A great asset to us all was our scout Ken Jarman, a figure from the past, who might well have been the subject of an illustration by Phiz in one of Dickens' novels. He used to call me every morning at about a quarter to eight, make a reasonable show of cleaning my rooms while I was breakfasting in the Common Room and keep me well supplied with whisky and cigarettes. He used to serve at the occasional luncheon parties I gave in my rooms until he was incapacitated by an accident which left him very lame. He was knocked down by a bus in the early morning while bicycling to work. His injury did not prevent him from resuming his other duties. When he was finally persuaded to retire he had served me devotedly for eighteen years.

Among the other Fellows the one who became my closest friend was the philosopher Tony Quinton. I had met him on several social occasions since the war; he had read a paper to the Philosophical Society at UCL, and I had spent a fair amount of time with him and his wife Marcelle at the congress in Venice, but it was not until I joined the college that I came to know them well. At first they lived with their two children in a village outside Oxford but it was not long before they all moved into a large flat in Mansfield Road where I used frequently to visit them for dinner, followed very often by a game of chess with Marcelle. I flattered myself that I was slightly the stronger player but there was very little in it. Marcelle's family came from Poland but she had been brought up in America. I do not know whether she or Tony had the greater vitality. A large zestful man, a voracious reader with an extraordinarily retentive memory, the possessor of an infectious wit, Tony was as good company as anyone that I have known. Philosophically, he was a more radical materialist than I, but to a very large extent we shared a common approach.

I believe that I first saw Marcelle and Tony together at the wedding of Raymond Carr, another of the Fellows of New College, whom I knew before I went there. I have already written of him as a frequenter of the Gargoyle in earlier years. A thorough-going hedonist, he was also a conscientious history tutor, and worked hard to make himself an expert in Spanish and South American affairs. He had not yet developed the passion for fox-hunting which was to become such a surprising feature of his late middle-age.

The flat immediately above the Quintons' in Mansfield Road was occupied by Merlin Thomas, the tutor in French, of whom I have already written in *Part of My Life* as inducing me to become a director of *Meadow Players*, which controlled the local repertory theatre, the Oxford Playhouse. My attachment to the theatre was never so strong as I allowed Merlin to suppose, but I did share his interest in contemporary French literature including the writings of Céline about whom he eventually published a scholarly book. I have never shared the view that one ought not to talk shop, especially if one is receiving rather than giving instruction, and my success in getting Merlin to talk about his own subject very largely contributed to the pleasure I took in his company.

Probably the best talker among my new colleagues was Lord David Cecil, Professor of English Literature, whom I had known for many years, mainly as a friend of Maurice Bowra's and Isaiah Berlin's. I was a little surprised by the warmth with which he welcomed me to the college, as I was under the impression that he did not greatly care for me. He was a devout Anglican and I had thought that he disliked the brashness of my anti-clericalism. Even so, he may have been pleased to acquire a colleague who at least belonged to the circle of his friends. As he gave us little of his company, I may well be making too much of what was simply a good-natured impulse.

At that time Tony Quinton was the only New College Fellow in philosophy, but he was soon to be joined by David Wiggins, who came there as a lecturer simultaneously with my own arrival, and was quickly promoted to a Fellowship. David had gone into the Civil Service after taking a first in Greats from Brasenose, and was very glad of the opportunity to exchange into academic life. I thought, and still think him very clever, and we embarked almost immediately upon a long-standing friendship. His philosophical austerity, which I have sometimes wished that he would moderate at least to the extent of diminishing the proportion of logical symbols in his writings to straightforward prose, did not extend to his private life. Our tastes were very much in harmony, down to a strong common preference for railways over travelling by road.

Perhaps the most interesting of the Fellows whom I had not previously met was Geoffrey de Ste Croix, the tutor in Ancient History. I did in fact mention him in *Part of My Life* as the winner of a prestigious tennis tournament for which I entered as a boy. A solicitor before the war, he learned his ancient history in early middle-age as a pupil at UCL of A. H. M. Jones, whose Marxism he shared. He approved of my adherence to the Labour party, but found me far too ready to make concessions to the Establishment. Even in the matter of religion, his intransigence exceeded mine. At New College the Sub-Warden presided at dinner in Hall even when the Warden was present, and it was his business to say grace. This consisted of no more than pronouncing the words '*Benedictus benedicat*' before the meal and '*Benedicto benedicatur*' after it, banging with a gavel as a signal for the whole company to rise at the beginning and motioning to one's colleagues to rise at the end. When I was Sub-Warden, I easily reconciled myself to carrying out this harmless ritual, but Geoffrey would not do it. He would bang the gavel and motion to his colleagues but some other Fellow had to pronounce the divine address. So far as I know he was never put in the awkward position of finding nobody to do it.

I think that New College was the only college in Oxford where the Head of the college, whether he bore the title of Warden, Provost, Master, Principal, President, Rector or Dean, did not preside in Hall when he was present. It was an unusual college in other ways, perhaps the most beautiful in Oxford, though not so grand as Christ Church or so historically distinguished. It had nurtured distinguished men but few of the very first rank. That was the reason why there were very few pictures in its splendid Hall. The explanation for this was its being tied to Winchester. From the time of its foundation in 1379 by William of Wykeham, Bishop of Winchester and twice Chancellor of England, who also founded Winchester School, until well into the nineteenth century, only Wykehamists were admitted to New College. If you were precocious enough, or possessed enough family influence to become a scholar of Winchester, say, at the age of twelve, you could proceed without further mental exertion to a fellowship at New College, remaining there without needing to acquire a degree from the University but only to undergo the formality of taking holy orders, until the death or promotion of its Wykehamist incumbent enabled you to step into a vacant college living. The celebrated Dr Spooner, who brought the term 'spoonerism' into the English language, though most of the better known examples like 'Kinquering Congs' were fathered on him, was the first non-Wykehamist to be a scholar, a Fellow or Warden of the college, and he was still Warden in the early 1920s.

Sir William Hayter, of whom I have already written as helping to secure my election, had himself been a Wykehamist and an under-graduate at New College, before entering the Foreign Office. He had been elected Warden the previous year largely at the instigation of Isaiah Berlin who had been a Philosophy Fellow at New College before returning to All Souls in 1957 as Professor of Social and Political

Theory. I liked William and his wife Iris. New College was not and never had been a convivial college. Playing bridge in Common Room almost every night, which had been the custom at Christ Church before the war, would have been out of the question at New College even in the days when the ritual of circulating the port in Common Room after dinner was still kept up. By the time I arrived there, it was only on guest nights, apart from Domus dinners, that there was a formal use of Common Room, and Sundays and Tuesdays were the only guest nights. I was never in Oxford on Sundays but I made a practice of entertaining guests on Tuesdays, and was always happy to put them next to the Warden if he was in to dinner, as he often was on these occasions. I sometimes thought that he might manage the business of the college more decisively, which would have shortened our college meetings, but if they were often rather boring at least they were seldom contumacious. Besides, we had an energetic Bursar, in the person of Jack Butterworth, soon to become Vice Chancellor of the new university of Warwick, and he dealt expeditiously with the major part of our affairs.

It may well have been a relief to some of the senior Fellows to have so mild a Warden as William, since his predecessor A. H. Smith, promoted from being one of the college's philosophy tutors, had been a turbulent factor both in university and college politics. What chiefly set the college by the ears, as often happens in Oxford, was an aesthetic question. The Warden wanted the row of plain windows in the Old Library facing the fourteenth-century quadrangle to be replaced by latticed windows, which would indeed darken the Old Library but viewed from the quadrangle would give it a more suitable appearance of antiquity. The proposal found little favour with the Fellows but Warden Smith was very good at getting his own way and succeeded in transforming two of the dozen or so windows before he died. The effect was incongruous but we voted to allow the two windows to remain as they were in honour of the Warden's memory.

Warden Smith was commemorated also by a bust by Epstein which stood by the High Table in a corner of the Hall. He had been an admirer of Epstein's work and had commissioned a large statue of Lazarus which was housed in the ante-chapel. In itself, it was quite an impressive piece of work but it looked out of place in the rather small ante-chapel, cheek by jowl with the stainless glass windows by Joshua Reynolds. The chapel itself was much admired, mainly because of the medieval carvings behind the altar. One day the Warden received a letter from a stranger, a tourist in Oxford who had never had any connection with the college, saying that he thought that the appearance of the chapel would be improved by a small El Greco painting of an apostle, which he was prepared to give us. We accepted, for once without demur, and found that the appearance of the chapel was indeed improved. The college could not afford to insure the painting but protected it with a burglar alarm. The same man offered King's College, Cambridge, again without having any connection with the college, a large Rubens to embellish its chapel. There too the gift was accepted and the picture installed but, more characteristically, the view of some of the Fellows was that the appearance of the chapel had not been improved.

What were called the New Buildings at New College were neo-Gothic, conforming to the nineteenth-century taste of the time at which they were erected. Except for a nondescript library we had nothing of a later date. Consequently, when a member of the Sacher family of Marks and Spencer, who had been an undergraduate at New College, offered us a large sum of money to enable us to extend the college so as to accommodate the greater number of graduate students whom we were admitting, we decided to do away with some quite pretty houses which we owned in Longwall, a street lying just outside the boundaries of our garden, themselves conterminous with the old city wall, the subject of an annual perambulation by the Warden and members of the Oxford City Council, and fill the gap with a thoroughly modern building. Out-voting a small party led by David Cecil, who pleaded for a building in a neo-Georgian style, we gave the commission to an architect who was said to have done good work in Cambridge. The only condition we made, which was not kept, was that the building should not protrude above the garden wall. Plans were submitted and approved, the fact being that most of the Fellows, including myself, were unable to visualize what they represented. The result was an eyesore, not greatly redeemed by the Warden's purchase of a Barbara Hepworth sculpture which stood in the approach to the building from the garden. It should, however, be added that the building enjoyed central heating, a rarity in Oxford, and the graduates who were lodged there did not complain of discomfort, so that the money, though not spent to the best advantage, was not altogether wasted.

The increase in the number of graduate students was one of the major differences that had occurred in Oxford in the years that I had been away. This was particularly marked in philosophy. Before the war it was rare for aspiring philosophers to work for doctorates. If they had made their mark as undergraduates, and had done reasonably well in their examinations for a bachelor's degree, they were directly appointed to lectureships or even fellowships in an Oxford college, or at the worst to a post in some red-brick university from which they might hope eventually to transfer to an Oxford or Cambridge fellowship. Having a doctorate was nothing to be proud of, rather the reverse, since it implied that you had not been good enough to obtain an appointment on the strength of your first degree.

I do not know how it came about that in the years succeeding the war the supply of would-be teachers of philosophy who made their way to Oxford increasingly outstripped the number of posts that were immediately available. This created a problem, which was handled magisterially by Gilbert Ryle. Taking the view that doctoral theses, at any rate in philosophy, were seldom worth the time and labour expended on them by the candidate and his supervisor, he brought about the institution of a new higher degree, designated the B Phil, for which the candidate was required to submit a dissertation, and to take three examination papers, one on a chosen authority and two selected by him from a list which included, among other things, logic, the theory of knowledge, moral philosophy, and optional periods in the history of science. The work for this course was intended to take two years, the standard required for passing it was quite high and the theory was that the successful candidate would not only have had more time to find himself a teaching post but would also be better equipped to occupy it.

The degree soon became very popular, attracting candidates not only from Oxford but from the other British universities, the dominions and the United States. In England at least it came near to acquiring the status of a passport to enter the philosophical profession. At the outset there was some opposition to its introduction on the part of the college tutors at Oxford who complained that they had so many undergraduates to teach that they could not assume any extra burden, but Ryle overcame it by giving the lordly undertaking that all the supervision of candidates working for higher degrees, which meant principally the B Phil, would be distributed among the three professors, respectively occupying the Chairs of Metaphysics, Logic and Moral Philosophy. Since the statutory obligation of a professor, at the time of my appointment, was only that he devote thirty-six hours a year to giving lectures or classes, he could assume this extra burden with some ease, so long as the number of graduate students was kept within manageable limits. Unfortunately, it was not. When, a few years later, I found that the number of graduates for whom I was responsible had risen to twenty-two, I put it to Ryle that among the sixty odd tutors of philosophy in Oxford there might be several who would be both happy and competent to acquire pupils of a higher standing. He agreed to our approaching them; I proved to be right; and thereafter I undertook the supervision of no more than seven or eight higher degree candidates, coming to me regularly for an hour's instruction once a fortnight during term, whom almost without exception I much enjoyed teaching.

I had done little formal lecturing during the years I spent at UCL. Most of my teaching had consisted in more or less impromptu addresses to a small audience from which I hoped to elicit questions or objections that would lead to a discussion. At Oxford, where I began by lecturing twice a week, one had to speak for fifty minutes without interruption to an audience that might begin by numbering well over a hundred though it always dwindled as the weeks went by. Initially, at least, I did not have the confidence to speak off the cuff and I used to arm myself with very copious notes, almost to the point of writing the lecture out in full. I had enough experience to put on a show of spontaneity, but the effect of my thorough preparation was that I went through my material too fast. This was partly also an effect of self-indulgence. Ideally a bread and butter lecture should contain only a few cardinal points, repetitiously hammered home. I found it boring to repeat myself, or even to slow down my normally high rate of speech, so that I packed too much into each of these performances for the majority of my audience, a mixture of graduates and undergraduates, to keep abreast of my argument. Nevertheless there was a minority that learned something from them. Julian, who was still at Oxford, asked Peter Jay what my lectures were like and received a reassuring answer.

Meeting Austin in Broad Street by accident just before the beginning of term, I was asked by him what the subject of my first course of lectures was to be. 'Propositions and Facts,' I said. He echoed my words just a shade derisively. 'Here,' he said, 'you will find us all talking about speech-acts.' He was, of course, exaggerating the difference between us. Our philosophical concerns overlapped, though we handled them in very different idioms. His idiom did not suit me and I am glad that I had the good sense not to try to imitate it.

Traditionally, it was held to be part of a professor's duty to give what was known as 'informal instruction'. Not every professor adhered to this tradition, but I welcomed it as an authorization for putting on classes, which I regarded as providing the best means of teaching philosophy. I used to hold them at 5.15 pm on Wednesday evenings in a lecture room at New College and continue until about 7 pm. At the beginning of term the audience tended to be too large for a successful class but its size soon diminished and found its level at something between twenty and thirty. My practice was to take a single topic like 'Causality' or 'Time' or more frequently a recently published book, preferably a book of essays, and make it the subject of discussion throughout the term. I would open the discussion at the first meeting and then assign this task to a member of the class at each successive meeting, selecting the questions with which they had to deal. Sometimes, but not too often, I had to exert cajolery to obtain the necessary quota of volunteers. Both graduates and undergraduates were admitted to these classes, but in the early years undergraduates predominated and I could usually rely on drawing my volunteers from their number. In later years the graduates tended to take over, which raised the level of our discussions at the price of making them less animated.

I took great trouble over the preparation of those classes, even when I was not myself to be the principal speaker, and I very much enjoyed giving them, especially in the early years. I believe that those who came to them enjoyed them too. There was indeed no other reason why they should continue to come. In an anonymous article in the undergraduate paper *Isis*, in which a class of mine was reviewed in company with one of Isaiah Berlin's, I was said to give 'uniquely good value'. Not that my learning was equal to Isaiah's. My superiority, if it existed, lay in my greater ability to orchestrate a class. At my best, I was able to get nearly all its members involved, advancing their own opinions, confuting mine, arguing not only with me but with one another. Except in the very rare instances when someone was being merely pretentious, I made a point of never putting anybody down, generally managing to extract even from what might be very confused utterances something to advance the argument. I pursued the same policy in my supervisions and there too I think that it had a beneficial result.

Austin consolidated his authority during the nineteen fifties by holding classes on Saturday mornings, which were attended by philosophy tutors junior to himself. I followed his example to the extent of forming a group which met on Tuesday evenings roughly between five and seven from the second to the seventh week of term. The meetings had a more social flavour than Austin's classes. A different member acted as host to the group each term, usually in his own college rooms, and provided drinks which were served during the discussion of the paper, which one of the group had read. A programme had been drawn up nominating a speaker for each of the six weeks. His paper, which usually lasted for something less than an hour, was on any subject of his choosing. There was never any question of my dominating the group which consisted at the outset, in addition to myself, of Peter Strawson, David Pears, Michael Dummett, Brian McGuinness, Michael Woods, Patrick Gardiner, Tony Quinton, David Wiggins and James Thomson who had not yet forsaken Oxford for the United States. In the course of time we recruited John Mackie, Gareth Evans, John McDowell, Ronnie Dworkin, Philippa Foot, Paul Grice, Geoffrey Warnock, Herbert Hart, Derek Parfit, Charles Taylor, Dana Scott, Dan Isaacson, John Foster and Simon Blackburn. When distinguished philosophers from the United States like W. V. Quine, Nelson Goodman, Hilary Putnam, Donald Davidson and Dan Dennett came to Oxford for a term or more they were also invited to join us and usually persuaded to contribute papers. The membership of the group has not been constant. John Mackie and Gareth Evans have died. Charles Taylor, Paul Grice and Dana Scott have followed James Thomson to America. Tony Quinton, Geoffrey Warnock and Herbert Hart no longer come, and Brian McGuinness very rarely. Nevertheless the group remains active. Although I no longer live in Oxford I make an effort to attend its meetings. Of the original members, Peter Strawson, Michael Dummett, David Pears, when he is in England, and David Wiggins attend them regularly. I am proud to have founded a society which has flourished for twenty-four years.

11 *Marriage among Other Things*

It was entirely my own fault that my first term back at Oxford did not end on a happy note. A regular feature of life at Christ Church is the Censors' dinner which takes place at the end of the Michaelmas term. As I explained in *Part of My Life* the two Censors are the disciplinary officers of the college, serving for a maximum of five years, divided between the Junior and Senior Censorships. The invitations to their annual dinner are in practice automatically extended to the Dean and Canons, the Official and Research Students, as Christ Church persists in calling those who would elsewhere be called Fellows, and the lecturers who are currently serving the college. Whomever else they ask is a matter for the Censors' discretion, but honorary students, former students or lecturers, who have obtained academic posts in Oxford or other universities, former undergraduates who have achieved some distinction, are liable to be invited. I attended the dinners regularly in the 1930s, when I was a lecturer and then a Research Student, and was quite frequently invited during the years that I was away in London. I had always found them pleasant occasions, for the most part enjoying even the after-dinner speeches which often reached quite a high standard.

I have never had much confidence in my powers as an after-dinner speaker and even when my efforts at it have been successful I have never much enjoyed making them, so that when my old friend and pupil Eric Gray was Senior Censor and asked me to be one of the speakers at a time while I was still at UCL, I told him quite frankly that it was not the sort of thing I cared to do. Since he was barely an acquaintance, I should have had no qualms about returning the same answer to the historian Steven Watson who, as Senior Censor, invited me to speak at the Censors' dinner in December 1959, but I thought, irrationally, that the fact of my having returned to Oxford made a difference and I also felt that it would be cowardly to refuse a second time. Accordingly I accepted his invitation and went to some trouble to prepare my speech. I aimed at a display of astringent wit.

I forget who the other speaker, in addition to Watson himself, was originally intended to be, but he was prevented from appearing and was replaced, at short notice, by Kenneth Wheare, the Rector of Exeter College. Kenneth Wheare, an Anglicized Australian, had been a lecturer and a member of the Senior Common Room at Christ Church when I was a Research Student. His subject was politics, especially in relation to the Commonwealth, and he wrote a definitive book on the Statute of Westminster. Not content to be a historian or theorist of politics, he was an active and skilful member of university committees. Later he was to be a worthy President of the British Academy. He had a deceptively spinsterish appearance, and a pawky wit which he displayed to advantage on this occasion. Speaking rapidly without notes he sustained a flow of light-hearted banter which visibly captivated his audience.

In any circumstance this would have been a difficult act to follow, and I was handicapped by the incongruity of the speech which I had prepared. If I had had any sense, I should have renounced my preparation, improvised a few good-natured remarks about the college and its inhabitants, and accomplished my task without glory but without dishonour. As it was, I pursued the course I had laid down for myself and very soon realized that my flashes of astringent wit were overstepping the mark; they were emerging as insults and were being so received. Again, I should have had the sense to cut my losses and bring my speech to a close with a few platitudes, but I did just the opposite. Like a golfer out of form, I started pressing, until I had offended almost everybody present. Finally I got round to proposing the toast of the House, which was ceremoniously drunk, and sat down to restrained applause. Afterwards, Gilbert Ryle, to whom I had actually paid a compliment, thanked me for doing so, and one or two people like Alasdair Clayre said that I had amused them, but the general attitude towards me was chilly.

My speech had not, in fact, been venomous, only in bad taste, and I could reasonably have hoped that the memory of it would not linger.

Unfortunately at the next Censors' dinner, to which I was not invited, my friend Ernest Stahl, the retiring Professor of German, fell into much the same trap as I had. In the course of proposing the health of the House he described the Students in a way that was intended to be fanciful but was taken to be offensive. If I had been lucky, this would have turned to my advantage. His misadventure would have obliterated mine. In fact, it worked just the other way. The two occasions were conflated in people's memories, his infelicities were added to mine and the whole attributed to me, so that my performance became a legend and I was credited with a contempt for my old college that was almost totally factitious and a hostility that the authorities felt obliged to reciprocate. Twenty years later, after I had confounded expectations by writing indulgently in *Part of My Life* of the House, as I knew it before the war, I was elected to an honorary studentship but I have never yet been invited to another Censors' dinner.

I had better fortune with my inaugural lecture which I waited a year to deliver, had published as a pamphlet by the Oxford University Press and then gave to Macmillan for inclusion in the set of essays which made up my book, *The Concept of a Person*. I entitled the lecture 'Philosophy and Language' and, after paying a sincere tribute to my predecessor Henry Price, I set about showing what a variety of different enterprises the expression 'Linguistic Philosophy' had been used to cover. I wrote mainly about the work of Ryle and Wittgenstein, and argued that neither of them was primarily interested in language as such. I suggested that their main object was to induce us to take a different view of the facts which we were using language to describe; facts which just because of our habitual way of describing them we had been prevented from seeing clearly. I attributed, to Ryle especially, an employment of the verification principle. For him, I said, 'The question is, given that we do make statements of such and such a sort, what are the circumstances that would make them true?' This could be made to appear to be a question about our verbal habits, but the appearance would be delusive. 'The emphasis,' I said, 'is not on our verbal habits themselves, but on the situations to which they are adapted. It is true that an account of the facts which verify a given statement will also be an account of the way in which the words that describe those facts are used; but it still makes a difference where the emphasis falls. The difference is between starting with the words and then looking for the facts to which to fit them, and starting with an identification of the facts and then seeing how they can best be described.'

I still think that the point I was trying to make in this passage is important, but I have to admit that I did not succeed in making it clearly. For one thing I failed to explain what 'looking at the facts' consists in. Perhaps I failed to see that it comes down to there being reasons for preferring one form of description to another, and that this leaves us with the problem of saying what these reasons are. I think that this may have been clearer to Wittgenstein than it was to Ryle, but it is a question that would take me into deeper waters than I can enter into here.

Though I did not explicitly refer to Austin in my lecture, I can see that one of my purposes was to drive a wedge between his approach to philosophy and that of either Ryle or Wittgenstein, and there are passages in which, without mentioning any name, I cast doubts upon the philosophical value of the minute examination of ordinary usage. So far as I know, Austin expressed no opinion of my lecture. He was already ill and he died before the year was out. Though I have said that one of my motives for returning to Oxford was to combat his influence, I am not at all sure that we should have engaged, at least at all overtly, in a struggle for power. I think it unlikely that he would have continued to give his course of lectures, 'Sense and Sensibilia', in which he ridiculed the theory of perception that I had put forward twenty years before in my book *The Foundations of Empirical Knowledge*. Surely he would not have published them in the harsh version which Geoffrey Warnock issued after his death, and in that case I should have had no occasion to embark on the point-by-point rebuttal of his arguments which I published in the review *Synthese* in 1967 under the title 'Has Austin Refuted the Sense-datum Theory?', and reprinted in my collection of essays *Metaphysics and Common Sense*. I believe that he would not have bothered any longer with the theory of knowledge, but would have developed the theses of what I consider to be much his best work, the William James Lectures which he gave at Harvard, edited and published after Austin's death by J. O. Urmson under the title *How to do things with Words*. There was indeed a rumour that he was thinking of moving to the United States.

Austin was a very clever man who had trained himself to capture the nuances of ordinary English usage. The best of his published papers like 'Pretending' or 'A Plea for Excuses' are fresh and imaginative. How much they contribute to the solution of the problems that trouble philosophers is disputable. I believe that Austin thought that they made a substantial contribution, but also that this was not a matter that he greatly cared about, so long as his observations about language were correct. His celebrated dictum 'Importance is not important; truth is' was sincerely meant.

Austin wanted to have disciples, and seemed to have succeeded. It was almost entirely the pursuit of his interests and his methods that constituted what was known in the 1950s as Oxford Philosophy. Yet it is remarkable how evanescent his influence turned out to be. Already before his death, two of the leading Oxford philosophers, Peter Strawson in his book *Individuals*, and Stuart Hampshire in his book *Thought and Action*, had strayed into other fields, and after his death practically nobody tried to follow the example he had set. Geoffrey Warnock and Jim Urmson were scrupulous in editing his literary remains. They praised his ability and character but did not attempt to build on any foundations that he had laid. A symposium on Austin's work appeared in 1967, edited by one K. T. Fann, but it was more critical than expository and displayed no advance on any of Austin's theories. My own riposte to Austin's Sense and Sensibilia was reproduced barbarously by the editor as 'Has Austin refuted Sense-data?', eliciting a rejoinder by Professor L. W. Forguson, otherwise unknown to me, to whom I replied in turn. The contribution made by the American philosopher John Searle to this particular symposium is on the critical side, but he has done as much as anybody to keep Austin's memory alive and is, so far as I know, the only philosopher to obtain any mileage out of the concept of speech-acts. He teaches at Berkeley in California and may well have his own disciples. Where the 'Oxford Philosophy' of the 1950s has long ceased to flourish is in Oxford itself.

At the end of my first academic year back in Oxford, Dee and I decided to get married. We invited three couples to lunch with us at the Ritz, took them with us as witnesses to the ceremony which occurred at the Registry Office in St Pancras Town Hall, and gave a large party in the evening at 13 Conway Street. Our three couples were Margie and Goronwy Rees, Sue and Basil Boothby, and Sonia and Michael Pitt-Rivers. I had known Sonia as Sonia Brownell during the period when she was helping Cyril Connolly edit *Horizon*, before her marriage to the dying George Orwell. Her marriage to Michael Pitt-Rivers did not last very long, but while they were still on good terms with one another, Dee and I had stayed with them once or twice at Michael's enchanting old house and opulent estate at Tollard Royal in Wiltshire. Michael had been in the Welsh Guards during the war but I think that it was only some time after the war that I met him, probably through my acquaintance with his younger brother Julian, the anthropologist. Both brothers, but especially Michael as the elder, were embroiled with their father, a raving Mosleyite, and subsequently with their acquisitive step-mother. Michael at least contrived to remain rich. Sonia obtained a good settlement from him when they were divorced but chose to call herself Sonia Orwell, rather than retain his name or revert to Sonia Brownell. Dee and I still stayed occasionally with Michael but no longer saw Sonia, with whom my own relations, at least, had always been chequered. What finally divided us was my lack of sufficient enthusiasm for the philosophy of Maurice Merleau-Ponty, with whom she had fallen in love. In fact he figures in *Part of My Life* as one of my personal friends and as a philosopher of whom I thought well enough to arrange for his *Phénoménologie de la perception* to be translated into English. Nevertheless, the fact that I disagreed with him on many points and that I was mainly opposed to the movement which he represented was enough to set Sonia against me.

I remember nothing of the party which followed our wedding except that there were a great many guests and that Bill Coldstream was one of them. I had got to know him when he became head of the Slade School of Art, which is attached to University College, respected him as a painter, and appreciated his slightly sardonic outlook upon life. I owe it to him, I think, that I became a member of the Cranium Club, an offshoot of the old Bloomsbury circle, which used to meet regularly once a month for dinner at the Reform Club and has since shifted its headquarters to a restaurant in Soho. At the dinners I have attended throughout the years there have usually been about fifteen persons present, mainly writers, painters, or dons from Oxford or Cambridge, as well as the Stracheys, Bells, Garnetts or Keynes of my own or the succeeding generation, for the most part themselves no longer young.

For our honeymoon Dee and I went first to Venice, which I again found enchanting in spite of the prevalence of German tourists, and from Venice took the Orient Express to Ljubljana, where I drew out the remainder of my stock of dinars. We stopped in Spoleto, now renamed Split, where we visited Diocletian's palace and from there went by sea to Dubrovnik where we settled in a moderately luxurious hotel outside the town.

A circumstance which added to our pleasure was that Hugh and Dora Gaitskell with their younger daughter Cressida were spending their summer holiday in Dubrovnik in a very luxurious villa which the Yugoslav Ambassador in London had arranged for them to occupy. They were treated with great respect by the Yugoslavs and we, as their friends, enjoyed our share of favour. For instance, we accompanied them aboard a well-appointed yacht belonging to the President of Croatia, and sailed down the coast of Montenegro as far as the Albanian frontier and back. One of our companions was the head of the Yugoslavian trade unions. Such men owed their places to their having been Tito's comrades in the resistance to the German and Italian occupation during the war. By now the Russian attempt to treat Yugoslavia as a satellite had ceased to pose a serious threat, which is not to say that Yugoslavia had ceased to be a Communist Society. The fact that he had been one of the heroes of the Resistance had not saved Milovan Djilas from imprisonment, when he criticized the regime on the score of its rigidity. Hugh Gaitskell pleaded for his release but could obtain no firmer assurance than that it would happen some time in the future, as it eventually did.

Among the attractions that Dubrovnik offered was a performance of *Hamlet* staged at the castle. The voice of the ghost emerging from the battlements was particularly impressive. Not understanding Serbo-Croat, I could not tell whether the text had been altered, or how much it had been cut, but it was obvious from the actor's demeanour that Hamlet was being portrayed as a partisan hero, biding his time for the best opportunity of killing Claudius and seizing the throne. He had no need to complain that 'the native hue of resolution is sicklied o'er with the pale cast of thought'. Any show of hesitation that he might give, and he gave next to none, was designed to lull his enemy's suspicions. I have never seen the part of Hamlet played in this way before or since, but the performance, though far from being faithful to the text, provided an effective spectacle.

The Wollheims were also in Dubrovnik together with Vanessa Jebb, who was not yet married to Hugh Thomas. They were staying at a hotel on the other side of the town from ours. Their hotel had direct access to the sea and at high tide the waters lapped against its terrace. We paid them a visit on our last day in Dubrovnik and although the sea was rough and I am not a good swimmer, I succumbed to the temptation, which Dee sensibly resisted, of joining the others in a bathe. There was no difficulty in plunging into the water and for a short time I quite enjoyed being buffeted by the waves. The difficulty was in getting out again. You had somehow to ride the crest of a wave and let it deposit you on the hotel terrace. I attempted this twice and failed each time, letting the wave engulf me as it reached the terrace and fill my lungs with sea water. Then someone reached over from the terrace and pulled me up to safety. At first I felt no worse than a little shaken but after a while I became slightly feverish. By this time we had checked out of our hotel and were staying at the Gaitskells' villa. No sooner was he aware of my condition than Hugh ordered me to bed. The only objection to this was that it interfered with our travel arrangements. We had to leave almost immediately for Ljubljana if we were to make the connection for Venice. Dee fairly easily persuaded me that I was well enough to travel and I began to dress. Hugh came in to the room while I was dressing and in almost no time at all he had me back in bed. When Dee explained about our travel arrangements, he arranged with the Yugoslav authorities for a special aeroplane to take us to Ljubljana, after I had had enough time to recover, and also obtained an assurance that the Orient Express would be held up, if necessary, to await our arrival. In fact the train was late and we did not need to delay it further. I was very much impressed by this glimpse of Hugh Gaitskell in action. Dee is an exceptionally strong-minded woman but her will was no match for his.

Now that I was married, I had formally lost the right to occupy my opulent set of rooms in New College. I was uneasily aware that the unmarried Chaplain, who complained of the noise which he had to endure in his rooms in the New Buildings, was casting a covetous eye upon mine. I was not a member of the committee by which such questions were decided, but I contrived to let it be known that my marriage would make no difference to my presence in college: I should be making just as much use of my rooms as I had before. I never learned what arguments were used on one side or the other, but only that when a vote was taken the outcome was in my favour. For the whole of the nineteen years that I remained in New College I occupied the same set of rooms. The Chaplain continued to suffer for a few more years until he was able to take possession of the rooms above mine which Herbert Nicholas vacated when he decided to set up house in Oxford with his sisters.

Apart from my inaugural lecture, my chief philosophical publication in 1960 took the form of a sharp attack on the argument of a book, *Dreaming*, which Professor Norman Malcolm had recently brought out. My article appeared in the American *Journal of Philosophy* vol. LVII No. 16 and was republished nine years later in my *Metaphysics and Common Sense*. Professor Malcolm made his way from the United States to Cambridge before the war and there became a friend and most devoted disciple of Ludwig Wittgenstein's. The short account of his relations with Wittgenstein, which he published in 1958, is most illuminating in its straightforward simplicity. Adhering unswervingly to Wittgenstein's dictum that 'an inner process stands in need of outward criteria', Professor Malcolm had argued that dreams were not experiences: they were to be explained in terms of our disposition on waking to tell fictitious stories. I had little difficulty in exposing the weakness of this position and in discrediting the reasoning with which he had attempted to support it. Malcolm was offended by my article and his comments on it and my rejoinder to them were published in the *Journal of Philosophy* vol. LVIII No. 11, appearing in 1961. I still think that I had the better of the argument, though I now find it regrettable that I wrote with such acerbity. Whether there is nothing more illuminating to be said about dreams than that they are mainly hallucinations which one undergoes while asleep is another question.

The International Library of Psychology, Philosophy and Scientific Method which C. K. Ogden had edited for the firm of Kegan Paul, Trench, Tubner & Co. had ceased publication, having brought out among others such important books as G. E. Moore's *Philosophical Studies*, Bertrand Russell's *The Analysis of Matter*, and Wittgenstein's *Tractatus*, and a decision was taken in 1960 by the succeeding firm of Routledge and Kegan Paul to renew the series under the same title, with the omission of Psychology, and to appoint me as editor. The first four books that I commissioned included a new translation of the *Tractatus* by David Pears and Brian McGuinness. There was trouble over this, because C. K. Ogden's brother regarded it as an insult to his brother's memory that a new translation should be thought to be required and he tried unsuccessfully to find some legal means of preventing us from reproducing Russell's original introduction. Russell himself was only too pleased to discover that, unlike other followers of Wittgenstein, the new translators believed his introduction to be worth reprinting.

After a few years I delegated some of the work to Bernard Williams who became assistant editor in 1963 and succeeded me as editor in 1965, remaining as advisory editor when Ted Honderich took over the editorship in 1966. In addition to Ian Crombie's two-volume work on Plato, which I have already mentioned, and the translation from the Danish of Peter Zinkernagel's *Conditions for Description*, twenty-six books appeared under my auspices, including translations of works by Goldmann, Perelman, and Merleau-Ponty, two books by G. H. von Wright, written from Finland in English, books by the American philosophers Abraham Edel, Wilfrid Sellars and Moriss Lazerowitz, important contributions from Australia by D. M. Armstrong and J. J. C. Smart, the *Explanation of Behaviour* by the Canadian Charles Taylor, and a wide range of books by English philosophers, including C. D. Broad's *Lectures on Psychical Research*. I received a percentage of the royalties which was no more than a fair return for the work involved. In all I think that I made good the assurance which I gave on the flyleaf of the earliest volume that 'the editorial policy is to publish work of merit irrespective of the school of philosophy to which it belongs'.

I have already written of my interest in professional football and my fidelity to Tottenham Hotspur. The season of 1960–1 was the most successful that they had ever had. They won both the League Championship and the Football Association Cup. This feat had been accomplished twice in the nineteenth century when there was much less competition, by Preston North End in 1889 and Aston Villa in 1897, never before that year in the twentieth century, and only once since, by Arsenal in 1971. In company with Julian I watched the Cup Final of 1961 at Wembley, when the Spurs defeated Leicester City by two goals to none, and wrote an article about it for the *New Statesman*, criticizing Tottenham's performance, which had fallen rather below the best of which the team had shown itself to be capable, assessing the merits of the various players, and guardedly predicting that it would do well in the following season in the European Cup, for which it had qualified by winning the League Championship. I was right in so far as it reached the semi-final and was only narrowly beaten by the Portuguese club, Benfica. It was some consolation that the team again won the FA Cup in 1962 and the European Cup-Winners' Cup in 1963.

More of My Life

The only one of the players whom I came to know personally was Danny Blanchflower. A Northern Irishman, he had been an aircraftsman during the war and was afterwards offered a place at the University of St Andrews which he renounced in order to become a professional footballer. He first attracted attention when playing for the Irish club Glentoran, and had played first for Barnsley and then for Aston Villa in the English League before being transferred to Tottenham in the mid-1950s. In those days players were known as backs, half backs and forwards rather than as defenders, mid-field players and strikers, as they are now, and Danny played at right half-back, a position from which he was able to control the game, which he did most intelligently. He was twice chosen footballer of the year, in the season of 1957–8 and again in 1960–1. He had a good understanding with the manager, Bill Nicholson, himself a former right half-back in Arthur Rowe's push and run team, who took office two years after Danny's arrival at Tottenham and restored Danny to the captaincy to which he had been appointed very early in his Tottenham career but had forfeited in a contest of power with the previous manager Jimmy Anderson. As early as 1949 Danny had been chosen to play for Northern Ireland in international football and he became one of his country's most successful captains.

We first met in 1958 when we appeared together on a television book programme. I was reviewing some popular book on philosophy and he was reviewing a book to do with football. When he discovered that I had some knowledge of the game he was very ready to expound his own theories, which applied not only to the different methods of play but even more to the popular appeal which the game exercised. Besides having this common interest, we took a mutual liking to one another and Dee and I entertained him several times at 13 Conway Street. He could talk well on other subjects besides football, though they did not extend to politics, where he advanced the view that Field Marshal Montgomery should be put in charge of the country. Even if he was thinking only of Northern Ireland the suggestion was bizarre. We lost touch with each other after he retired from active play and became a sports journalist, but were as friendly as ever when we met again a few years ago in Belfast, once more on a television programme, on this occasion both discussing the autobiography of a professional footballer.

I saw less of the Spurs in their triumphant season of 1960–1 than I could have wished because I spent so much of it abroad. In the early part of September I attended a conference of the IIP at Oberhofen in Switzerland. It was a pleasant experience, even though the level of the discussions did not match the beauty of the setting. Then after Christmas Dee and I went to stay with Somerset Maugham at his villa at Cap Ferrat in the South of France. Willie, as he liked his friends to call him, had sought my acquaintance some years before because he was interested in philosophy. Like T. S. Eliot he had been attracted, as a young man, by F. H. Bradley's writings, though unlike Eliot he had not succumbed to Bradley's idealism. I have kept a letter from him in which he attributes to me the view that statements like 'Lying is wrong' are meaningless and understandably takes exception to it. No doubt I did my best in reply to explain my reasons for holding that purely normative statements had emotive but not cognitive meaning. I think that I was flattered by his attentions, not only because he was famous but because I esteemed him as a writer. Among his novels perhaps only *Of Human Bondage* withstands the test of time but I think that many of his short stories like 'Rain' or 'The Letter' deserve to be remembered.

Maugham was eighty-six years old at the time of our visit and the treatment which he had undergone in order to rejuvenate himself had made him look older. He gave the impression of having a quick temper though his manner to us was uniformly courteous. His stammer was noticeable but not embarrassing. His mind was alert and he did some work while we were there, standing at his writing desk. The house was extremely well run, thanks no doubt to Alan Searle whom Maugham described in a letter to me as his 'friend and companion'. The food was unobtrusively good, meals were always punctual and ritually preceded by a round of martinis. Apart from its extensive garden, the house was chiefly notable for the Impressionist and Post-Impressionist pictures which Maugham had collected. They extended even to our bedroom which had its comfort enhanced by a charming set of works by Marie Laurencin.

There were no other guests, but Lord Beaverbrook was staying with his friend and companion Lady Dunn at a neighbouring villa and the four of us went to dine there. The villa itself was unexpectedly ugly and the food not up to Maugham's standard. I had never met Beaverbrook before but Dee had met him several times while she was writing for the *Sunday Express* and had obtained his approval. So much so indeed that he was visibly put out by her telling him that she had left his employ to work for the *Daily Herald*. This may indeed have been due less to his regret at losing her services, though no doubt this was genuine, as to his annoyance at his having been kept in ignorance of her defection. In any case, his show of displeasure was only momentary. He was in particularly high spirits that evening because he believed that he had obtained some pieces of silver for much less than market value from some old ladies who kept an antique shop nearby. He had his butler fetch his acquisitions to the table and we all duly admired them. We left soon after dinner and on the way home Alan Searle asked me if one ought always to tell the truth. 'No,' I said, 'not in all cases.' 'I am glad then,' said Alan, 'that I did not tell Beaverbrook that the old ladies had swindled him. All those pieces of silver which I joined you in commending were fakes.'

I saw Beaverbrook once again when he came by himself to call on Maugham. He was only five years younger than Maugham so that he also had a fairly short expectation of life. They were both concerned with the possibility of survival after death and appeared to think that I, as a philosopher, should be in a position to speak on the subject with some expertise. Ignoring the point about the scope of philosophy, I simply said that I saw no good reason to believe that there would be an after-life, at which moment Maugham showed that this was the answer for which he had hoped. There was no way in which I could honestly reassure Beaverbrook, who wanted to think that he would survive, but I did add that although I could not discover any good reason to accept any form of theism, I thought that if one were to be a Christian it would be most logical to embrace Calvinism, the doctrine that one was predestined to be saved or damned. At the time this went some way towards appeasing Beaverbrook since he was not in any doubt that he was one of those chosen to be saved. Later, however, I learned from his granddaughter Jean Campbell, whom Dee knew as a fellow journalist, that he had resented my avowal of atheism.

Apart from a piece of shameful conduct in first accepting an invitation to speak at the Old Collegers' annual dinner and then taking fright and backing out at very short notice, I had had nothing to do with Eton since Julian left. Early in the new year, however, I found myself most unexpectedly obliged to try to interfere in the affairs of my old school. Dee and I were both slightly acquainted with June Osborn, the widow of Franz Osborn, the pianist. She was later to marry Jeremy Hutchinson. She had a clever son who, according to the headmaster of his preparatory school, was intellectually capable of winning a scholarship to Eton but was debarred from entry because of the Etonian statute which required that the fathers of Collegers should be of British nationality by birth. June had spoken of this to Dee at some party and Dee had relayed the story to me. My reaction was that the information June had been given must be false. After all I had been in College and neither of my parents had been British by birth. My father had been naturalized but he was originally Swiss. Nevertheless the headmaster, whom I accused of being mistaken, stuck to his guns. He was quite sure that the Osborn boy was not eligible for an Eton scholarship.

Learning of this I wrote to the current headmaster of Eton, Robert Birley, who had been an assistant master there in my time and one whom I liked and respected. He sent me a civil but short reply, simply referring me to the Provost. I had never met the Provost, Sir Claude Elliot, and knew nothing about him except that he had once been a don at Cambridge. I wrote to him, apologizing for bothering him, but saying that as a former member of College I was concerned by the report that children whose fathers were not British born were being denied the opportunity to obtain scholarships and that I should be relieved to hear from him that the report was not true. He replied saying that he appreciated my concern, but that the report was true. No such statute had existed when I was in College but it had recently come into force. I wrote back saying that the only motive I could see for the action of the Provost and Fellows in introducing such a measure was their concern at the increased proportion of Collegers whose fathers were Jewish refugees from Europe, that this would only be a passing phase, that even if it were not it was unworthy of Eton to indulge in anti-Semitism and that I proposed to ventilate the issue in a letter to *The Times*. By return of post I was asked not to engage in any publicity until the Provost and I had talked the matter over, and I agreed to this request, at the same time accepting an invitation to meet Sir Claude at the Travellers' Club.

The atmosphere at our meeting was friendly, if not cordial. My first object was to get him to admit the motive for the introduction of the new statute, and this he eventually did. 'But why?' I said. 'What have you against these boys?' 'They are too clever,' he said. I laughed. 'That is an odd reason for keeping them out of College.' 'They are not clever in the right way.' 'I don't understand you,' I said. 'Well, for instance,' he said, 'you couldn't expect them to play the Wall Game.' This induced me to make an unfair move. 'Your statute would have kept me out in any case,' I said, 'because my father was born a Swiss, but my mother was Jewish and I was in the College Wall eleven for two years.' 'Oh,' he said, 'you can't regard yourself as a typical case.' Clearly this conversation was not going to get us any further. I admitted that the only weapon that I had was publicity and said that I would resort to it. He begged me not to do this, saying that the statute had been queried at the Privy Council, that he and the Fellows had only recently managed to get it passed, and that they would look foolish if they now rescinded it. Finally we came to an agreement. He promised to bring the question up for review in a year's time at a Fellows' meeting, and I promised not to say anything to the newspapers in the meantime, while reserving myself the right to lobby Fellows individually.

The results of my efforts were disappointing. Noel Annan, who was a Fellow of Eton by virtue of being Provost of King's, had not known that the statute was new. My old Christ Church pupil, Lord John Hope, was sympathetic but would not commit himself. I thought that I must at least be able to count on the support of Lord Cohen, but far from it. He had actually voted for the measure. He wrote to me that when he received my letter he had made a special journey to Eton to ask the Provost whether he had lent his name to anti-Semitism and had been reassured. It looked as if I had made a very bad bargain.

Then, one day when travelling by train from Oxford to London, I happened to get into the same carriage as Edward Boyle, one of the few members of the government, apart from Macmillan himself, with whom I had more than a nodding acquaintance. We had the carriage to ourselves. 'You were at Eton, weren't you, Edward?' I said. 'Yes,' he said. 'Why?' 'Well,' I said, 'you may be interested in hearing what I have been up to,' and I told him the whole story. He found it incredible but I swore that it was true and said that while he would have to take my word for the episode at the Travellers' Club, the correspondence I had collected should be sufficient evidence. He asked me to send it to him and before long had a letter from him saying that but for the evidence I had given him he never would have believed it and that he was going to get the Prime Minister, himself an Old Colleger, to take action. Weeks passed and I heard nothing further. I was beginning to despair when I received a letter from Eddie saying that he had had some difficulty in getting hold of Macmillan, but that I might now expect something to happen. Sure enough, within a fortnight, there was an announcement in the press saying that it was the view of the Provost and Fellows of Eton that the rule requiring the fathers of entrants to College to be British born was out of date and that they were consequently asking the Privy Council for permission to rescind it. The change came in time for the young Osborn to win a scholarship to Eton. I never learned whether he was happy there.

While this intrigue was in process, I paid a short visit to Morocco. My old friend Charles Whitney-Smith was our consul there, and I was very happy to stay with him and his French wife Micheline in their comfortable house at Rabat. As I remarked in *Part of My Life*, I had spent a few days in Rabat during the war, in transit from Algiers to London, and had thought the French colonial city, with its gleaming white buildings, a great improvement on its old Moroccan neighbour. My second visit strengthened this opinion. Charles had arranged for me to lecture in Rabat and in the sacred city of Fès. I spoke in French on both occasions, giving the same lecture on the subject of political philosophy. I think that it may have been an earlier version of the Eleanor Rathbone Memorial Lecture 'Philosophy and Politics' which I delivered at Bristol University in 1965 and republished in *Metaphysics and Common Sense*. If so, it consisted in a criticism of the received accounts of the grounds of political obligation, and a run of the mill defence of liberal values. In Rabat I lectured at the University but I was not allowed to do so in Fès, because I was not a Moslem, and had to perform in a cinema instead. I was told that the professors at the University of Fès were so orthodox that they did not allow there to be more numbers than there were verses in the Koran, but I was given no opportunity to question them on this point. The professors and writers whom I did meet in Rabat were heavily marked by contemporary French culture. This was a continuing effect of French, as opposed to British, colonial policy and seemed to me a point in favour of the French.

Besides arranging for me to lecture, Charles took me on a short tour of the country. Seeking out Roman remains, we visited Meknès and stayed for a while at Marrakesh. Altogether I very much enjoyed my time in Morocco, my only disappointment being the Arab food. I lack a sweet tooth and do not care for rice in any form; nor did I contrive to consider sheep's eyes as a delicacy.

Back in Oxford for the summer term, I was called upon by the Indian journalist Ved Mehta. The fuss that there had been over Ernest Gellner's book had given him the idea of conducting a series of interviews with British philosophers and turning them into articles for the *New Yorker*. The articles aroused considerable interest and were collected by Ved Mehta into a successful book. Later he followed the same procedure with British historians and it also brought him success.

If one is to understand Ved Mehta and his work it is necessary to know that he has been blind almost from infancy, and that both his behaviour and his writing are largely designed to obliterate this handicap. The person who brought him to my rooms stayed only for a few minutes and Mehta and I remained in each other's company for several hours, travelling back to London in the train together after our interview was officially concluded. During all that time I scarcely needed to guide his footsteps. Not only that but his article was full of visual descriptions. The arrangement of the furniture in the room, my own physical appearance, even the way in which I was dressed were all vividly portrayed. The same was true of his interviews with other philosophers. No doubt he relied to a considerable extent on what he was told by persons who could see, but it seemed to me that he made visual judgements on the basis of his estimates of people's characters, the tone of their voices, his sense of the way they moved. Of course he made mistakes, but a surprising number of these judgements were true or came near to being so.

Mehta did not take notes of our conversation nor did he make use of a tape recorder. He had a good memory, but it did not extend to every detail of what was said, or every shade of meaning, and it was in his professional interest to ginger up the remarks that were made to him, especially when they took the form of one philosopher's criticizing another. The result was that when the articles appeared many of their subjects complained that they had been misquoted. This was particularly true of Ernest Gellner who was provoked to the point of considering bringing a libel action, a course which he sensibly did not pursue. My own complaint was rather that advantage had been taken of my naïveté. When we left my rooms I assumed that we had finished with the interview for the *New Yorker*, and having taken a liking to Mehta and also having had a fair amount to drink I gossiped freely with him on the journey back to London, not taking thought to spare my colleagues. By a piece of good fortune I was able to see the proof of the article in which I figured before it went to press and was horrified to discover that my part in it consisted almost entirely of the indiscretions into which I had been drawn after I believed that the interview was over, with my gossip sharpened into malice. Rather to my surprise, the *New Yorker* agreed to suppress the more offensive passages and though I still did not care for the tone of the article in its revised form, I was at least freed from the show of directing crude insults at persons with whom I had no serious quarrel.

One of the remarks which remained in the article might have been taken to refer adversely to Bertrand Russell and I wrote to assure him that I had not intended to attack him. Gellner, provided by Mehta with more to disclaim, had written to Russell in the same sense. In his reply to Gellner, of which he sent me a copy, Russell revealed that he himself had written to Mehta to complain of being misquoted. For the most part his letter to Gellner was simply consolatory. It included the passage 'It does seem to me . . . that a useful criterion of the extent to which one has broken new ground, is the hostility incurred from the established, the intellectually smug, and the moral eunuchs of our day.' This was a little hard on Mehta who was only out for a journalistic scoop, but very characteristic of Russell. It represented his attitude to the 'Oxford Philosophy' of the 1950s and still more to contemporary politics.

12 *American and Russian Interludes*

A reason why I was able to intercept Ved Mehta's article was that I was living in New York at the time that it went into proof. This was the result of my accepting an invitation from City College to become a Visiting Professor of Philosophy there for the semester of 1961–2. Having spent six terms in the Chair of Logic at Oxford I had been granted a term's sabbatical leave. The post was one for which Bertrand Russell had been judicially pronounced unfit twenty years before. Had the college been responsible for this outrage, I should not have accepted it, but the college had been the helpless defendant in an action brought against the city authorities under ecclesiastical pressure. In fact the philosophers regarded their invitation to me as a modest reparation for the injustice that Russell had suffered.

The infamous Senator McCarthy had been dead for four years, but some of the evil that he did lived after him, and, having already sworn, in order to obtain a visa, that I had never been a Communist and that I had no intention of subverting the government of the United States, I was required as a condition of my appointment to a post at a municipal college to take an additional oath of loyalty. I rather balked at this but was persuaded by Professor Wiener, the Chairman of the department, and an energetic historian of philosophy, to comply with what he called a mere formality, since no underground Communist would have the slightest hesitation in taking the oath. I allowed my qualms to be lulled by this argument though I could hardly have failed to realize that it did not meet the point of principle, that even if the admission of the oath served no practical purpose, it was an unwarrantable intrusion on academic freedom. It occurs to me, however, that if

I was going to take such a high moral line, I should not, in consistency, have consented to make the declarations which were required for my being permitted to enter the United States at all.

I had in fact made my entry a month or so earlier in order to attend a meeting of the International Institute of Philosophy which took place at the University of Santa Barbara. It was my first visit to the west coast. On my way to Santa Barbara, I stayed overnight at Los Angeles which did not at all attract me. It seemed to me a city with no discoverable centre and one that amounted to little more than a mass of motor cars. Neither did I much care for Santa Barbara itself. Part of the reason for this was that I was stranded for the best part of a week on a dry campus, with no reliable means of transport to carry me into the town. The only excursion that I remember being organized for us was a day-long visit to an exceedingly well-funded institute, presided over by the Dr Hutchins who had come into prominence as a youthful President of the University of Chicago, collaborating with Mortimer Adler in the promotion of the Hundred Great Books. They were now aiming at a consensus regarding the nature of key philosophical concepts, but while I did not disapprove of this as an end, I doubted if they would go very far towards achieving it by their method of issuing questionnaires. When it comes to social research, it is often an embarrassment for an institute to be abundantly endowed.

From Santa Barbara I went north to spend a weekend in San Francisco, to which I took an immediate liking as I had to New York on my first visit there before the war. I stayed very comfortably in the hotel which has the famous revolving bar at the top, enjoyed travelling on the trams that imitated switchbacks, discovered excellent French and Chinese restaurants. There may have been smog but not enough to spoil my admiration of the bay. Term had not yet begun at Berkeley, and anyhow I had not been asked to lecture there, but I had friends who showed me over it. I was glad to have seen it, but did not feel tempted to angle for an invitation.

Dee and Gully had made their way independently to the United States to visit members of Dee's family and I flew across the continent to join them in Boston. We remained there only a short time and all that I clearly remember of our visit is my buying a bright red tie, which I still possess, in Filene's Bargain Basement. We then settled down in New York in an apartment on 75th Street near Lexington Avenue, which we rented from the art critic John Richardson and his

friend Robert Rushmore. The rent was seven hundred and fifty
dollars a month which was expensive for those days, but we received
good value for our money. The apartment occupied the two lower
floors of a brownstone house, with a garden attached. It was handsomely furnished, its chief glory being an original Holman Hunt and
several drawings by Picasso. Dee embellished it further by buying a
couple of sea-horses together with a tank for them to live in and the
special food required to nurture them. They lived on the ground floor
with the Picassos and the three of us had two bedrooms as well as a
sitting room on the floor above. Gully, however, shortly had to leave
us to return to school in England. Her father, who had not yet re-
married, came to stay with her in 13 Conway Street.

City College was situated far uptown at Convent Avenue and 138th
Street but I found a convenient bus which took me there and back.
I greatly enjoyed teaching there. I had been warned that my pupils
might be difficult to manage, but I had no difficulty at all. They were
a little wary at first but once they discovered that I was doing my best
for them, they were wonderfully responsive. The atmosphere was as
exhilarating as at the best of my Oxford seminars. I gave two courses,
one for graduates and one for undergraduates, each meeting twice a
week. My method with the undergraduates was to talk throughout
the first meeting in the week and devote the second meeting to a discussion of what I had said at the first. With the graduates it was more
along the lines of an ordinary seminar. My discussions with the graduates were centred on the philosophy of logic and strayed into the
philosophy of science. In my undergraduate course I followed the line
of my book *The Problem of Knowledge*. My audience was constant in its
attendance: about twenty coming to the graduate course and forty or
more to the undergraduate. There were many more men than women,
mostly Jewish boys whose parents were not rich enough to send them
to Columbia. They cared a great deal about their education, as the
following incident shows.

A girl who was enrolled in my undergraduate class brought her
boyfriend to the second of one of our pair of weekly meetings. He
had not been to the class before and in particular had not attended the
lecture which we were supposed to be discussing. This did not prevent
him from taking a major part in the discussion. He wanted to impress
his girl and so he argued with me brusquely about some different
topic; it may well have been existentialism. I thought him a nuisance

but answered him seriously. At the end of the session, the young man disappeared but two or three others came up to me to apologize for his behaviour. 'No other professor,' they said, 'would have been so patient with him.' I disclaimed any special virtue and said that the man had not succeeded in upsetting me. 'You may not have minded him,' replied their spokesman, 'but we do. These classes are important to us and we cannot afford to have our time wasted. We'll make sure that he doesn't come again.' I made a vague liberal protest, but I never did see the man again.

Not only did I get on with my pupils but I was on friendly terms with my colleagues in the department of philosophy. As a visiting professor, I had a lighter schedule than they and received more money, but this did not seem to cause them any resentment. One whom I had met before was Abraham Edel, who had been to New College, though I had got to know him on my previous visit to New York rather than in Oxford. He was a specialist in ethics and in ancient philosophy. I have already mentioned his book on Aristotle and the part that it played in my breach with Penguin Publications, when they refused to honour my invitation to him to adapt it for publication series. Another colleague whom I greatly liked and admired was an Indian, Professor Irani. He had failed to be accorded the status that he deserved, because he had never bothered to obtain a doctorate, but he was an inspiring teacher and an excellent philosopher of science.

I received a good many invitations to lecture at other universities, most of which I accepted. They included a set of invitations, procured for me by the Lazerowitzes to lecture not only at Smith College, where they themselves were teaching, but at the neighbouring College of Amherst and the University of Massachusetts. Dee's younger brother had found a second-hand Cadillac for us, which we could afford to buy with the prospect of selling it again when we left the United States, and Dee drove me in it up to northern Massachusetts. I had visited New England in the summer when I had been to stay with the Cummings at their house near Silver Lake in New Hampshire, but never yet in the autumn and I was overwhelmed by the beauty of its russet forests. It stayed vividly in my memory throughout the twenty-one years that passed before I had the opportunity to experience it again.

I particularly remember my performance at Amherst, because it was the first time that I had been paid as much as $1,000 for a lecture.

We were given dinner at the college beforehand and the envelope containing the cheque was put discreetly beside my plate. The lecture I delivered was the one, 'Metaphysics and Common Sense', which gave its title to a book which I have mentioned several times already. Before it was reprinted in my book it was published in 1966 in an anthology entitled *Metaphysics* which was edited by Morris Lazerowitz in conjunction with Amherst's Professor Kennick. In this lecture I was very much more lenient to metaphysicians than I had been in *Language, Truth and Logic*. I argued that even in the cases where their conclusions were ridiculous, as when McTaggart denied the reality of time and Zeno the reality of motion, it might be profitable not simply to dismiss them but to look at the arguments which were taken to support them, and then one might find, as I have already indicated in an earlier reference to Zeno, that one's attention has been drawn to points of logical importance. I conceded even that one should not automatically rule out the possibility of a radical revision of our current conceptual scheme. A proposal to carry out such a change would need to be somehow linked to our present categories, otherwise it would not be intelligible. Consequently the metaphysician cannot leave common sense too far behind him. 'This does not mean, however,' I concluded, 'that he must tie himself strictly to its apron strings. The insistence that ordinary language is perfectly in order has been a very useful corrective to the wilder flights of metaphysical speculation but, if taken too literally, it can lead to our letting things go by which might profitably be questioned and mobilizing in defence of what does not need defending. It is indeed better to tabulate the milestones along the highway of ordinary usage than to rhapsodize about Nothingness or the Essence of Man; but it would be a mistake to forego the more imaginative kinds of conceptual exploration, merely because of the greater risk of getting lost. In philosophy, nothing should be absolutely sacrosanct: not even common sense.'

One of the invitations which I accepted was to deliver a lecture at the University of Maryland, which is in the neighbourhood of Washington, and I took the opportunity of calling on my old friend Felix Frankfurter, now a Justice of the Supreme Court, and introducing him to Dee. Marion Frankfurter had become an invalid and did not feel well enough to see us, but Felix welcomed us most cordially. A former member of Franklin Roosevelt's Brains Trust, he tended to take a more conservative line in the Court than many people expected, but I do not believe that this was due to a shift to the right in his politics so much as to his taking a narrower legalistic view than some of his colleagues and critics of the constitutional powers of the American judiciary.

Valerie was still living in Rochester with her husband Jack Wright, who held an appointment at the University. They paid us a short visit in New York in the course of which a sneak-thief broke into our apartment in the daytime when we had gone out to lunch and stole Valerie's jewellery. There was never any hope of its being recovered. Though they did not display much mutual affection, I did not perceive that anything was seriously amiss between her and Mr Wright. In fact they were almost on the point of divorce. I have already written of her remarriage and the sadness of her early death.

News reached us that the experiment of leaving Gully in the care of her father at 13 Conway Street was not proving a success and some time before Christmas Dee decided to return to England, leaving me with about a month of my engagement at City College still to complete. When she embarked on the aeroplane she took the sea-horses with her in their tank. They survived the journey but Dee was unable to find enough of the right food for them, even at the London Zoo, and had to resign herself to their loss. She was consoled by the resilience of her dachshund, Monster, who held a privileged position in our household, though old and increasingly incontinent.

Soon after Dee left, I accepted an invitation to speak at what was described as an Arts Festival at the University of Winnipeg in the province of Manitoba in Canada. When I arrived I found that the Festival consisted of my lecture and two or three performances by a not very distinguished ballet company. I was given a frosty reception by the philosophy department but that was nothing compared with the chill of the city itself. It had been so designed that the icy winds from the Canadian prairies cut one in half at every street corner. When I lectured, on some moral topic, I discovered that a remarkably high proportion of my audience appeared to be fundamentalists. I was very happy to escape to the shelter of New York.

Dee's younger sister, Priscilla Chapman, known in the family as Begoonie, was in New York and took me to a party on the evening of my return. At the party I met Marguerite Lamkin who later intro-duced me to Christopher Isherwood. She had known him in California and for some reason which I forget had coached him in her southern way of speaking. At first Christopher refused to meet me, because his predilection for Vedanta had made him intolerant of my philosophical views, but when he was persuaded to try the experiment we soon became very good friends. We found plenty to say to one another without arguing about philosophy. He was then fifty-seven but looked very much younger and his quiet demeanour only superficially belied his remarkable strength of character. I came also very much to like and admire Christopher's friend Don Bachardy, himself a very gifted artist. He did a drawing of me at the time, which I greatly treasure. It was to him that I turned sixteen years later when New College commissioned a drawing of me on my retirement from my professorial fellowship.

It was through Marguerite that I met Henry Geldzahler, who was on the way to becoming Director of the New York Museum of Modern Art, and through Henry that I was again brought into touch with Di Antonio whom I had known long before as a friend of Tony Bower's and his sister's. Di had distinguished himself by making a film of the hearings of Senator McCarthy's charges against the army at which McCarthy's power was broken. He introduced me to Andy Warhol whom I found pleasant but not in any way remarkable. I do not think that he had yet begun his exploitation of pop art, or if he had it had escaped my notice. I attended at least one 'happening' with Marguerite but found it disappointing as a spectacle.

As a means, perhaps, of strengthening the image of Camelot, President Kennedy had instituted a series of seminars which members of his cabinet were expected to attend together with their wives. The intention was, I think, that these seminars should range over the social sciences. At the end of the second meeting, someone persuaded the company that better progress would be made if they had more knowledge of philosophy. It was therefore agreed that a philosopher be invited to address them. The historian Arthur Schlesinger Junior, with whom I had a slight acquaintance, knowing me to be in the country suggested that I be approached. I was surprised by the invitation, but also flattered, and so accepted it without demur. The meeting was fixed for 3 January 1962 and the arrangement was that I should dine and spend the night at Schlesinger's house in Washington, and having dined should deliver an hour's lecture in their drawing room, after which there would be a discussion. My subject was simply to be the nature of philosophy.

The President and his wife were not able to be present and the proceedings were conducted by his brother Robert Kennedy, the Attor-
ney-General. The guests at dinner included the British Ambassador,
later Lord Harlech, but then still called Sir David Ormsby-Gore, and
his wife, and Evangeline Bruce, wife of the American diplomat David
Bruce who was their Ambassador in Paris before coming to London.
I had met Evangeline Bruce once or twice and did not suppose that
either she or the Ormsby-Gores were greatly interested in philosophy.
I thought it civil of them, therefore, to lend me their support.

The company in the drawing room numbered about thirty. Not
clearly seeing how I was to encompass the whole of philosophy in an
hour, I took the course of summarizing my own views, representing
them as an offshoot of an analytic tradition that could be traced back
to Socrates. I was listened to in silence, except that at one point I over-
heard the President's sister, Eunice Shriver, seated in the front row
of my audience, whisper to her neighbour, 'Is it possible that this
man does not believe in God?' After I had finished Robert Kennedy
opened the discussion with some questions about free will to which
I failed to give any conclusive answer. Then Walt Rostow attacked
me sharply for rejecting the Platonic notion of the ideal state, and I
replied in kind, enlisting the support of the economist David Bell.
Next Ethel Kennedy asked me why I had said nothing about Thomas
Aquinas. I confessed that I knew very little about Aquinas, at which
point she clapped her hands. I then went on to say that I doubted
whether she had read much of Aquinas's own writing but that she
had probably studied such neo-Thomists as Jacques Maritain, about
whom I did know something. We then proceeded to argue about
Maritain and Ethel Kennedy became confused, at which point Robert's
voice came quietly but distinctly from the back of the room, saying
'Drop it, Ethel.' She obeyed at once. The discussion then became
general and low-keyed. Robert Kennedy brought the proceedings to
an end by making me a very slightly ironical speech of thanks. I was
not sure that I altogether liked him but I thought him formidable.

I returned to England very soon afterwards and published an
article in the *Daily Herald* under the title 'America doesn't want war'.
I said that my encounter with the members of President Kennedy's
cabinet had left me 'with the very strong impression that here was a
group of men who were earnest, intelligent, high-minded and keenly
aware of their responsibilities' and I argued that this outweighed the

disquieting build-up of American armaments and the influence of fanatical anti-Communists such as the members of the John Birch Society. I think that this assessment was justified by Kennedy's handling of the Cuban crisis in the following autumn, though some of the credit must go to Khrushchev.

Awaiting my return was an invitation from the editors of the Soviet journal *Voprossi Filosofii* (Problems of Philosophy) to write them an article on any subject that I chose. I believe that this was the first time that such an invitation had been extended to a philosopher known to be unsympathetic to Marxism. I accepted it without delay and sent them an essay entitled 'Philosophy and Science'. They translated it into Russian and published it in their next number with a rejoinder by one of their leading philosophers, Professor Kuznetsov. It appeared in its original English version in *Ratio* vol. V No. 2 in 1963 and was one of the essays reprinted in *Metaphysics and Common Sense*. Its main argument was that philosophy differed from any of the natural and social sciences in that its statements were not empirically testable. Their function was to analyze the categorial concepts with which we operate and possibly to suggest ways of improving them. Though I did not make the point explicit, this allowed dialectical materialism to be a philosophical thesis, if it could be presented as a descriptive framework. What I denied was that it was a science, except perhaps in its purely sociological aspect, where the proposition that social changes of a given magnitude were due to class conflict might be considered testable. To sugar the pill, I remarked also that the theological proposition ascribing everything to providence was equally unscientific. In reply, Professor Kuznetsov maintained stoutly, if politely, that dialectical materialism was a science even in its more general form, though the best example he could give was the vague proposition that everything is in a constant state of change. Since I was told that the Russian word by which it is translated is used in a wider sense than the English word 'science' it might well have been that our dispute was mainly terminological.

The publication of these articles was followed by an invitation, which I again promptly accepted, to lecture in Moscow and Leningrad and to bring Dee with me. There was a bureaucratic hitch as a result of which we were still being denied our visas in London on the day on which I was supposed to be giving my first lecture in Moscow, but this was straightened out and only a day or two later we boarded an

Aeroflot aeroplane as first-class passengers. Our principal host was Yuri Melvil, a philosopher of about my own age of Scottish descent, who spoke very good English. The hotel in which we were lodged in Moscow was the Metropole, where we were given a very large, old-fashioned set of rooms. In Leningrad where we spent two of the nine days that we remained in Russia, we stayed at the more attractive but equally old-fashioned Hotel Astoria. By that date the buildings of Leningrad, which had been extensively damaged by German bombardment in the war, had been most painstakingly restored and the city, decked out once again in pink and green and gold, had renewed its claim to be one of the most beautiful in Europe. To our great regret, we had less than a morning to admire the treasures of its picture gallery the Hermitage before we were dragged off to inspect a museum of realistic Russian art, but we did manage to find the rooms where the curators of the Hermitage stowed their Impressionist and Post-Impressionist paintings, a collection almost as fine as that of the Jeu de Paume in Paris. A performance of Tchaikovsky's opera based on Pushkin's famous poem *Eugene Onegin*, which we saw at the Kirov Theatre in Leningrad pleased us less than a Moscow production of Mussorgsky's *Boris Godunov*, displayed not at the Bolshoi Theatre but at a newly built opera house inside the Kremlin with an even vaster stage. The opulence of *Boris Godunov* was very well suited to the Russians' realistic technique.

I was struck once again by the extent to which the young people in Moscow were fascinated by what they took to be American culture. The wearing of jeans was in fashion, though more by boys than by girls, and so was rock and roll. We visited a Russian night-club and were asked to give an exhibition of the Twist, which had recently come to birth in New York. Unfortunately, it is a dance that I have never been able to master, though Dee managed it well. Our combined performance was a disappointment to our audience who had expected something more exotic. In general, the atmosphere seemed little different from what it had been on my previous visit. The shops were still poorly equipped, though we were able to buy two handsome fur hats cheaply. Caviar was still in plentiful supply and the service in the hotel restaurants as slow as ever. We were entertained at the British Embassy by the Ambassador, Sir Frank Roberts, whom I very much liked, and by Yuri Melvil in his small Moscow flat where he lived with his wife, a professor of atheism, his son and his mother-in-law.

They provided us with an excellent dinner, I imagine at no small cost.

In the course of our nine days' stay I delivered five lectures, four of them in Moscow and one in Leningrad. The subjects on which I lectured in Moscow were 'Contemporary British Philosophy', chiefly an exposition of the work of Wittgenstein, Wisdom, Ryle and Austin; 'Pragmatism', pretty well a repetition of the lecture I had given at UCL in which I traced the evolution of pragmatism from Charles Sanders Peirce to the contemporary American philosophers, Nelson Goodman and W. V. Quine; 'The Concept of a Person', an essay which gave its title to my book which I published in the following year and 'Truth', a development of an essay which I had published in No. 25 Fasc. 3 of the Belgian *Revue Internationale de Philosophie* as early as 1953 and was also to reprint in *The Concept of a Person*. In Leningrad I repeated the lecture 'Truth', in which I expounded Tarski's version of the correspondence theory. The logicians in Leningrad, who seemed to me abler than the Moscow philosophers, found my account of truth too realistic: they adhered to the mathematical model which required of a proposition that there be some way of proving it. My critics in Moscow went to the other extreme. On the basis of Lenin's doctrine that consciousness reflects reality, they interpreted the relation of correspondence in an unduly literal fashion.

My essay 'The Concept of a Person' was mainly an attempt to rebut the arguments advanced by Peter Strawson in his book *Individuals* to show that the concept of a person is not susceptible to reductive analysis. Its extension is determined by the fact that the subjects to which we attribute properties implying the presence of consciousness are literally identical to those to which we also attribute certain physical properties. Against this I argued, not altogether successfully as I now think, that persons were indeed identified by their bodies, but that the association of different sets of experiences with different bodies and so with different persons could be explained in causal terms. I was interested to note in the discussion of my lecture that the local materialism went no further than my own. There was no question of the Russians subscribing to the thesis, which has since become fashionable, especially in Australia and the United States, that mental events constitute a sub-class of physical events. They did maintain what is nowadays the generally accepted view that physical objects are not reducible to sense-data, but otherwise they limited themselves to the realist claim that physical objects exist independently of our awareness of them. As for their qualification of this standpoint as 'dialectical', I could not discover what difference it made.

My lectures attracted quite large audiences with a high proportion of students. Since I do not speak Russian, the usual procedure was for me first to deliver the lecture in English and then for a Russian translation of it, made from a copy which I had supplied beforehand, to be read out by one of the local professors or by a professional interpreter. There was then a period in which I replied to questions, which were handed up to me in writing. When the questions came to me from the students they were quite often written in English; in general the students appeared to have a much better command of English than their professors. Except for Melvil, the older professors spoke German if they spoke any foreign language at all.

The questions put to me were designed to elicit further information, rather than to raise objections to anything that I had said. They ranged widely and sometimes had little or nothing to do with the topic of my lecture. Thus, many of them strayed into the field of moral philosophy. I was surprised at the knowledge which they displayed of current English work in this branch of the subject. I deduced that the University Library subscribed at least to the principal foreign journals and that it was not very difficult for students to obtain access to them.

The meetings did not end when my answers to the questions had been translated into Russian. It was then time for one or two or even three of the professors to comment on my lecture. Their remarks were occasionally polemical but always polite, and their tendency was to stress the points of agreement rather than disagreement between us. I was surprised to notice that when their professors were delivering their set speeches the attitude of many of the students was almost openly contemptuous. After these speeches had been translated into English for my benefit, I delivered replies which had to be translated into Russian. Sometimes these replies provoked rejoinders but I, or rather my interpreter, was always given the last word. A result of this cumbersome procedure was that the sessions were very lengthy. In the case of my lecture 'The Concept of a Person' the proceedings lasted for over four hours.

Dee did not attend my lectures and was allotted an English-speaking guide, called Boris, to act as her escort while I was working. An attractive-looking youngish man with a well-groomed moustache, he clearly took pleasure in his assignment, which probably brought him the incidental benefit of raising his standard of living. One afternoon when he had taken Dee up to our suite in the Metropole after a particularly good lunch, he became amorous and started to chase her around the sitting room. After evading him for a while she stopped and said 'I dare say that you have been led to think that American women are on the lookout for lovers, but if so, you must treat me as an exception. I love my husband.' 'I love him too,' said Boris, and resumed his pursuit.

We left Moscow with mutual expressions of goodwill. I undertook to publish in the Routledge and Kegan Paul International Library a translation of whatever book they chose as the best Russian contribution to the recent development of Marxist philosophy and they invited me to remain a contributor to *Voprossi Filosofii*. Unfortunately on my return to London I published an article in the *Observer* to which some sub-editor gave the provocative title of 'Breaching the dialectical curtain'. The tone of my article was friendly but I did express some mild criticism of the entrenched Marxist orthodoxy and remarked that the younger members of my audience seemed more flexible than their elders and more open to new ideas. Most foolishly I ended the article with the sentence: 'The spirit of revisionism has not yet conquered Soviet philosophy; but one can almost hear the beating of its wings.'

What I did not know was that my invitation to lecture in Russia had been the outcome of a liberal victory in a factional struggle which was continually waged, so that the incautious passages in my article, together with the comments which appeared in various English newspapers on my penetration of the Iron Curtain, enabled the conservative faction to regain its ascendancy. An article entitled 'Professor Ayer in London and in Moscow', accusing me of double-dealing, appeared in a Russian journal and I heard privately from Sir Frank Roberts that Yuri Melvil, who had been chiefly responsible for organizing my visit, had called on him in great distress. I wrote to Yuri, expressing my regret for what had happened and received a friendly reply from him, but there was no longer any question of our exchanging ideas in print.

That I was not in deep disgrace was shown by the fact that I was invited four years later to lecture in Budapest where I had a long conversation with György Lukács, whom I have already described as the most influential of neo-Marxists, and that in my capacity as President of the IIP from 1969–72 and subsequently as a Vice President of FISP I frequently had occasion to visit Bulgaria, speak in Sofia and Varna and hold discussions with Bulgarian philosophers in the 1970s. It came to the point when I was invited back to Moscow to attend a congress in 1975 or thereabouts, but this being a time at which the practice of treating dissidents as psychiatric patients appeared to be on the increase in Russia, I declined the invitation. It might be argued that I should have done so on the former occasions, but on such matters I find it difficult to maintain a consistent policy.

After returning from Moscow in the early part of April 1962, we spent the rest of the Easter vacation at a hotel in Le Castellet. Our plan was to follow the example of the Deakins and find a house in the neighbourhood which would serve us for our summer holidays. With the help of a local estate agent we were successful on the second day of our search. The house which we discovered was a three-storeyed late eighteenth-century farmhouse in a hamlet called La Migoua, quite high up in the forest to the south-west of Le Beausset and about twenty kilometres from Toulon. The most convenient beach was at St Cyr, midway between Bandol and La Ciotat. *La Migoua* is Provençal for *Le Moulin* and the hamlet took its name from a disused olive mill. The house already had electricity installed but we had to put in plumbing, redecorate and furnish it. There was a ruin attached to it, which we also bought, as a precaution against having troublesome neighbours. There was also about an acre of ground which we did not put to any practical use. The whole lot cost us the equivalent of about £3000. We were not hampered by currency restrictions because Dee had money in America. We sold the ruin to Jo Saxe who made it habitable and, when he left for America, sold it to Francette Drin. From 1963 until our separation in 1980 we spent part of every summer at La Migoua, though in the latter years not always together. There was a lime tree overlooking a porch at which I used to work and I acquired some skill at playing *pétanque*, the local form of bowls.

Bertrand Russell's ninetieth birthday fell on 18 May 1962 and Rupert Crawshay-Williams and I organized a dinner to mark the occasion. It was held at the Café Royal and about seventy people came to it, personal friends, scientists, philosophers and their wives rather than Russell's political associates. There was a cake with ninety candles, which Russell succeeded in blowing out in two attempts.

Speeches were made by Julian Huxley, E. M. Forster and myself to which Russell replied. In the course of my speech, which was mainly devoted to a eulogy of Russell's philosophy, I told the story of my coming across a bust of Voltaire, at the Hermitage in Leningrad in Melvil's company, and of Melvil's pointing to it and saying 'The Bertrand Russell of the eighteenth century.' Russell seemed to be particularly pleased by this comparison.

When I asked him beforehand whether there was anyone, not already on the list that I showed him, whom he wanted me to invite to the dinner, Russell said that he would like to make it an occasion for meeting the head of his family, the Duke of Bedford. Owing to some longstanding family feud, he had never met the Bedfords or even set foot in Woburn Abbey. I had never met the Bedfords either but when I wrote to the Duke, explaining that Russell had especially asked for him and the Duchess to be invited to the dinner, he accepted at once. They took Dee and me afterwards to a night-club where the Duke, a man of about my own age, proved remarkably adept at dancing the Twist. Not only that but he made a very suitable speech at a concert organized the next day in honour of Russell by his political followers.

One result of their meeting was that Ian Bedford invited Bertrand Russell to spend a weekend at Woburn. When the time came for the visit, Ian took fright and invited me with Dee to help to keep Russell entertained. This was an unnecessary precaution. Russell was enchanted with the house, delighted to come upon pictures or photographs of relatives whom he had known in his youth and a fount of family gossip. It became clear that he could be asked on his own without embarrassment. Independently, we made friends with the Bedfords and visited Woburn quite frequently in the ensuing years. Ian vied with Henry Bath at Longleat in making Woburn a tourist attraction and appeared greatly to enjoy playing the part of a showman. Nicole mixed less freely with the public but took pride in the house and found an outlet for her vitality in giving private parties. I was sorry when the pressure of taxation caused them to resign Woburn to the Tavistocks and make their home abroad.

Emily Boothby, a very attractive girl of about Gully's age, now married to the writer Piers Paul Read, had come to live with us when her father had been appointed Ambassador to Iceland. We visited Basil and Sue in their modest embassy at Reykjavik in the summer of

1962 and toured the island in the company of their eldest son Joe, then still a schoolboy but much later to become a graduate pupil of mine before developing into a successful lawyer. Apart from the verdant seat of assembly of its ancient parliament, the island was chiefly distinguished for the multiplicity of its sulphurous springs, which diffused a fetid odour. Its buildings were small and pretty, like those of a toy farm. There was some local interest in philosophy and I gave an interview to the principal newspaper in Reykjavik. Like other Scandinavians, the Icelanders drank heavily but were extremely formal so long as they were sober.

On 3 September my old friend e.e. cummings died. I reproduce the last letter that I had from him because it is highly characteristic of his style. It was written from Paris on a Monday but I cannot date it more precisely than by saying on internal evidence that it refers to some period after we had moved into 13 Conway Street. It is not included in the published volume of his letters.

'Dear Freddy

Multiple thanks for a very much more than rescue! Its timeliness reminds me only of some earliest shadowdrama; whereby roughriding superspecimens of American manhood (featuring The Stars And Stripes) sow longawaited havoc among bandit-captors of a hamstrung hero & helpless heroine. Here's incidentally hoping that one bread&butter postcard has (however unworthily) acknowledged the quite not-paralelled extremest generosity of a most charming child's delightfulest parent. We miss you all (including Monster) and send you each our love.

—à bientot!

eec'

I had pledged myself to arrange for the annual congress of IIP to take place that month in Oxford. I had been warned that the organization of these congresses, which required not only the devising of several symposia, but also the provision of entertainment for the philosophers and the wives whom some of them brought with them, demanded considerable trouble and expense, but this proved not to be the case. With the help of a small subsidy of £100 from the British Academy, my efficient young secretary Mrs Rosanne Richardson and I managed the whole affair quite easily. The theme of the congress was 'Thinking and Meaning' and its proceedings were published in a special number of the Belgian review *Logique et Analyse*. There was no difficulty in securing speakers, including Gilbert Ryle, who normally fought shy of international congresses. The participants from abroad were housed in New College, in what may have seemed to them rather Spartan conditions, but the attractions of Oxford weighed with them more strongly. In the way of special entertainment we arranged an excursion to Woburn Abbey and dinner at the Bell Inn at Aston Clinton. From the social point of view, at least, I had no doubt that the congress was a success.

The manuscript of my book *The Concept of a Person* was delivered to the publishers Macmillan in October 1962 and published in the following year. It consisted of ten essays, all of which I have already mentioned, with the exception of an essay called 'Names and Descriptions', in which I follow Russell in treating ordinary proper names as doing duty for descriptions and, more dubiously, Quine in suggesting that we can manage without demonstratives; one called 'Fatalism' in which I again stress the symmetry of the past and future and show that the triviality that 'what will be will be' does not imply determinism; a note 'On the Probability of Particular Events' in which I show that the frequency theory of probability faces difficulties analogous to those that I had already discovered in the logical theory, and an essay 'What is a Law of Nature?' in which I argue against the concept of natural necessity. These last two pieces had been previously published in the *Revue Internationale de Philosophie*.

The book was generally well received, was three times reprinted in hardback, and issued in paperback by Macmillan ten years later. It was translated into Italian, Spanish and Flemish. I was most gratified by Bernard Williams' review of it in the *New Statesman*, in which he compared me with Brahms in relation to Wittgenstein as Wagner.

I had accepted an invitation to lecture at the University of Aarhus in Denmark at the beginning of April 1963. Dee was with child but the birth was not expected for another fortnight. In fact, her labour pains began a few hours after I had left her and Margie Rees went with her to the Charing Cross Hospital and stayed with her until the boy was born on 2 April, the birthday of Hans Andersen. I fulfilled my programme of lectures and did not see our son until he was several days old. He was not christened, but Dora Gaitskell and Nicole Bedford agreed to act the part of godmothers. We registered him as Nicholas Hugh Ayer, Hugh in memory of Hugh Gaitskell and

Nicholas because the name appealed to us. I remembered only later that it was the name of my paternal grandfather, the Rector of the Academy of Neuchâtel. My love for this child has been a dominating factor in the remainder of my life.

Index

Index

Index

University College Philosophical Society,
  20–1, 146, 175
Urmson, J. O., 187, 188

Vansittart, Peter, 36
Vaughan, Hilda, 36
Vienna Circle, 29, 41, 98, 113, 132, 156–7
Vranicki, Professor, 160

Walter, Dr Grey, 139
Warhol, Andy, 208
Warner, Rex, 100–1, 106, 111–12
Warnock, Geoffrey, 183, 187, 188
Watling, John, 11, 18–19, 49, 61, 146
Waugh, Evelyn, 35–6
Wedberg, Professor, 77
Weidenfeld, George (Lord), 35
Weldon, Angelica, 44–5, 47–8
Weldon, T. D. (Harry), 60, 157
Wells, Alfred, 126, 167, 204, 207
Wells, Dee (later Ayer), 118, 125–7, 128, 131,
  146, 159, 161, 167–8, 171, 173, 188, 191,
  194, 195–6, 197, 204, 205, 206, 207,
  210–11, 213–14, 215, 216, 218–19
Wells, Gully (Alexandra) (step-daughter),
  126, 159, 167, 203–4, 207, 216,
Wells, H. G., 52, 138
West, Rebecca, 137–8
Wheare, Professor Sir Kenneth, 185
Whitney-Smith, Charles, 199
Whitworth, Robin, 54
Wiener, Professor, 202

Wiggins, David, 176, 183
Williams, Bernard, 61, 87, 166, 167, 193, 218
Williams-Ellis, Sir Clough and Lady (Ama-
  bel), 97
Wilson, Colin, 124
Wilson, Harold (Lord), 76
Winch, Raymond, 21–2
Wisdom, J. O., 91–2
Wisdom, Professor John, 49, 75, 91, 95, 97,
  161, 212
Wittgenstein, Ludwig, 15, 51, 52, 92–4, 95,
  168, 186, 187, 192, 212, 218
Wolfenden, John (Lord), 141–2, 143
Wollheim, Professor Richard, 17–19, 38, 49,
  61, 146, 190–1
Wood, Alan, 131
Woodger, Professor J. H., 49
World Congress of Philosophy, 84–5, 86
Wright, Professor G. H. von, 95, 193
Wright, Jack, 155–6, 207
Wyatt, Woodrow, 170
Wykeham Chair of Logic, Oxford, 160–2,
  166

Yorke, Henry (Henry Green), 20, 78, 79–80
Young, Professor F. G., 49
Young, Professor J. Z., 49, 53, 137

Zea, Professor, 68
Zinkernagel, Peter, 76, 193
Zuckerman, Solly (Lord), 54